ENDORSEMENTS

IN *BEAUTIFUL FEET*, DR SADIRI JOY TIRA HAS WOVEN BEAUTIFULLY
together contributions from multi-disciplinary researchers and missions
practitioners, covering a wide range of contemporary issues—missiological, ecclesiological, generational, gender, global—crucial for the 21st
Century world. The inspiring stories of missionaries used by God to
impact lives are especially compelling to both senior and younger leaders
in the global church and missions.

Loun Ling Lee
Editor, Lausanne Global Analysis
Lausanne Movement

WHILE THIS WORK IN SOME WAYS LOOKS BACK IN ORDER TO
honour a missionary couple, its true orientation is to the future. Featured
articles are meant to fuel Kingdom work. Standard bearers like Patrick
Johnstone contribute while so do more recent newcomers to the stage of
missions. Beyond the generational and topical diversity, the reader will
also find a distinct variety of ethnicities presenting from their particular
world view. In short, this is a rich text that will spur much thought and
hopefully action - just as one would expect under the watchful eye of Dr.
Tira's direction.

Roberto Bolivar
Executive Director of PALM
Former International Worker in China

BEAUTIFUL FEET: FOLLOWING THE CHRISTIAN MISSIONARY Footsteps offers a refreshing take on mission literature by adopting a polycentric lens that transcends geography to encompass generational and demographic diversity. This festschrift delves into the heart of Philippines, providing a nuanced understanding of regional challenges. It skillfully navigates the intricacies of people profiles, cultural dynamics, and global connections. It serves as a valuable case study, guiding readers in effective outreach and encouraging ongoing mission renewal with a call to impactful mass action.

Philip Yan
Director, Centre for Redemptive Entrepreneurship
Tyndale University
Toronto, ON. Canada

BEAUTIFUL FEET, A COLLECTION OF INSIGHTFUL MISSIONAL EXPERIENCES based on inspiring and applicable theology of missiology that exemplifies polycentric mission in all spheres of society. This book is inspiration-filled, my heart kept saying Amen while reading it. Mission clearly is our calling as Jesus followers to live out and transcend cultural and generational differences. Thanks to Dr. Sadiri Joy Tira for making this valuable spiritual legacy accessible.

Amy Cheung
Director, GenesisXD Inc.
Toronto, Ontario Canada

JOY TIRA HAS A GIFT OF MINING THE MOST RELEVANT TOPICS AND writers and bringing them into one place. This is another such place. Here is a true hybridity of experience, culture, ideas, theology and understanding from different parts of the world invited to come together beautifully to explore missiological issues. Enjoy!

Harvey Thiessen
Area Leader
Oceania North America

Beautiful Feet is both unique and timely. Unique in the following senses. First, it brings out what present day missions analysts have in their hearts and minds about the missions movement worldwide. Second, it touches on a variety of relevant themes that need to be brought up together for continuing missions education. Third, it describes missions with a beautiful and thought provoking idea – "feet" – which signifies instrumentality and mobility. Yes, indeed, thank God, there are always "beautiful feet" whether it seems dark and hopeless because the march of beautiful feet that publish glad tidings will never become obsolete until the day of the Lord Jesus Christ.

Met Castillo, M.A., Th. M. D.Miss.
Missiologist, Missionary Trainer and Leader

The Nicholses embrace a life of sacrifice and courage with beautiful feet and generous hand over a marathon run – and continue with heart, voice, and soul during these latter years. In visionary, organizational, or missionary leadership, Doug bears burdens and calls the faithful to urgently and actively respond to theological drift, missional malaise and social needs. I am grateful for this set of essays around varied and relevant dimensions of ongoing obedience to Christ's Final Commission in recognition of an exemplary servant, with applicability to many a ministry context.

Ramesh Richard, PhD, ThD
President, RREACH
Professor, Dallas Seminary
Founder, TOPIC
Convener, GProCommission

BEAUTIFUL FEET
Following Christian Missionary Footsteps

Sadiri Joy Tira, Editor

BEAUTIFUL FEET
Following Christian Missionary Footsteps

Published by Sadiri Joy Tira, Edmonton, Canada

ISBN:
   Paperback   978-1-77354-562-2
     ebook   978-1-77354-563-9

PALM
Ministry
Association

PRAIRIE
COLLEGE

CHRISTIAN
SCHOOLS ...

◆WEA
WORLD EVANGELICAL ALLIANCE

Publication assistance by
PAGEMASTER
PUBLISHING
PageMaster.ca

DEDICATION

This Book is Dedicated to Doug and Margaret Nichols whose feet reached China and the Philippines as missionaries. This Volume is to inspire future Kingdom-Workers to emulate your lives and the ministries you championed.

– Dr. Sadiri Joy Tira

TABLE OF CONTENTS

TRIBUTES TO
DOUG & MARGARET NICHOLS

Doug Nichols, Margaret Nichols - Worldwide Missions Advocate

In 1970, Doug and Margie Nichols arrived as members of Overseas Mission Fellowship in the Philippines. They were fresh graduates from Prairie Bible Institute with a call of God on their hearts to serve the poor and the needy.

A new organization, Christ for Greater Manila (CGM) was being formed to meet the needs of street children in this large city. In 1972 Doug Nichols became the Director of CGM.

This began a career of service for the Lord among the poor and needy that would span decades. A significant development was the incorporation of an organization in the United States called Action International Ministries. In 1975. Today ACTION serves in thirty-nine countries with 390 missionaries.

Doug and Margie have gone on to become Worldwide Missions Advocate. His heart's prayer is for the 75,000 street children of Manila who need the gospel and companionate care. Also, and for older godly missionary men to help encourage and train many of the estimated 51,000 undertrained pastors of the Philippines and around the world.

Wayne Whitbourne
Executive Director
Action International Ministries, Canada

This is an important collection of stories from around the world that reflect the way God has called ordinary people to do the extraordinary work of building the kingdom of God in the far corners of the world. With the call of Gyd on their lives, the Presence of the Almighty in their daily walk, and their courage in the face of many great challenges, they have brought the light and love of God to hungry people and changed the course of history. This is a story that brings glory to God for the work that He can do through people who are dedicated to Him and to doing His will. My prayer is that you will be blessed and challenged as you read this book and walk on this life-giving path.

I was delighted to see Doug and Margi Nichols' story among these rich stories. They graduated from Prairie Bible Institute in 1967 and went on to become career missionaries in the Philippines. In recognition of their lives of service, they were recognized as Distinguished Alumni in 2013 "in recognition of their dedication to compassionate care of the poor and service to the worldwide body of Christ."

I pray that you will be blessed with a burden for the nations of the world as you read this book about people whose "beautiful feet have brought the Good News of the Love of God" to "people who have not yet called on the Name of the Lord!" (Romans 10)

Mr. Mark L. Maxwell
President, Prairie College

Every Christian should engage with godly Christian biographies, as encouraged by the Bible (Hebrews 11). The Scriptures command believers to "remember those who rule over you, who have spoken the word of God to you, whose faith follow, considering the outcome of their conduct" (Hebrews 13:7). Personally I am acquainted with Doug and Margaret, I have closely observed their lives. Their lives and ministries align closely with the inspired commandment in the book of Hebrews. I enthusiastically endorse the valuable content of this book and commend Dr. Joy Tira for publishing it."

Your pilgrim friend always ready to go, willing to stay.

Dr. Elias Medeiros
RTS Professor of Missions Emeritus

The book "Beautiful Feet" is informative, inspiring and motivational. It motivates the reader how to be involved in mission. This book shows different faces of mission work from children to seniors, from the mountains to the urban jungle, from the Philippines to the whole world, from personal and congregational praying to supporting missions, from traditional mission to post pandemic mission strategies and women leadership. I recommend this book not only to mission students or teachers, practitioners and mission organizations but to all Christians who have a heart for God and His work of redemption. Knowing Doug and Margaret since the 70s, their 50 years of faithfulness serving the Master has to be emulated. They did not only reach out to the needy like the orphans and street kids but helping pastors and advocating the servants of the Lord. They regularly pray for Joy and I, encourage us and practically supporting us.

Lourdes (Lulu) Tira
Author, Missionary

ACKNOWLEDGEMENTS

Christian Missions make a difference in this world. This is the reason why this book is created. I am blessed to have a variety of Contributing Writers to fill the pages of this book. Grateful to God for how they shared their time, talents and experiences: Patrick Johnstone, Jason Mandryck, David Lim, Jason Richard Tan, Donna Tan, Narry Santos, Juno Wang, Mark Edward Sudhir, Nativity Petallar, Juliet Uytanlet, Jeff Haanen, Martin Otto, Julie Ma, Jim Whelchel and Katherine Lorance.

My gratitude also goes to Bishop Ef Tendero for writing the Foreword in this book. I also thank the personal and corporate book endorsers who were with me in this book journey: Mark Maxwell, Elias Medeiros, Philip Yan, Met Castillo, Harvey Theissen, Amy Cheung, Loun Ling Lee and my beloved wife Lulu Tira.

God has brought two Filipino diaspora congregations: Friends in Kuwait and Qatar and FLCC and TGCGM in my life and I praise God for them.

I am thankful also to my editorial team: Gerry Baclagon and Damples Dulcero-Baclagon for graphic and book design and Marie Osborne for editing and proofreading.

And lastly my prayer and ministry collaborators who are with me on their knees praying without ceasing.

FOREWORD

There are three compelling reasons to read this Festschrift: the quality of life and ministry of the honorees; the wide range of topics, addressed by an excellent group of contributors; and the unique context of the editor as he organized this project.

Doug and Margaret Nichols came to the Philippines as missionaries in the 1970s. At that time, there was uncertainty about welcoming expatriates. The country had been placed under martial law by strongman Ferdinand Marcos, Sr., and there were calls for nationalizing educational and even religious institutions. Moreover, the opposition, particularly the Communist Party, suspected foreign missionaries of being agents of the U.S. Central Intelligence Agency. And mainstream Protestant leaders had called for a moratorium on foreign missionaries.

But Doug and Margaret tenaciously faced this unfavorable context and established themselves as faithful and fruitful ambassadors for Christ in the Philippines, for three reasons.

First, they exhibited indisputable integrity. They were authentic, down to earth, with no pretense about what they are. They connected with the common people and walked with them. They did not hold back in interacting with and ministering to the slum dwellers of Manila. They mingled with them and demonstrated their genuineness. How they acted on the outside was a reflection of what is inside them.

Second, Doug and Margaret did holistic ministry. They declared the gospel unashamedly and demonstrated it genuinely through their diverse ministry. They established Christ for Greater Manila (CGM, later known as the Christian Growth Ministries) as a multi-faceted ministry. I have insider knowledge of their ministry, as my wife (my fiancÈe at that time) was a CGM ministry worker.

Doug and Margaret led the CGM staff in caring for the poor and needy. They ministered to street kids, fed them, and took them on camping trips for a week of Bible teaching and training in hygiene, self-discipline, decorum, and other social skills .

Then, for those who did not have a home to live in, they established Home for Joy, a halfway house where minors could live until they reached 18 or were accepted into a foster home. Furthermore, they established the Second Mile, a live-in livelihood training program where young men learn trades such as welding, carpentry, and masonry.

With regard to gospel proclamation, they employed various means such as radio counseling, Bible correspondence courses, and organizing a singing group that performed concerts and did street evangelism. They also set up teams to show gospel films and distributed cassette tapes with messages by selected Bible teachers.

Inspired and encouraged by the Nicholses, CGM follow-up workers held Bible studies among informal settlers and even among inmates at the city jails and the National Penitentiary. I was amazed by the courage and boldness of these follow-up workers, who seemed unconcerned by the security risks to which they were exposed. At times I wondered about their safety, but such worries were eclipsed by their genuine concern for the inmates and the joy of seeing many have a true "correctional" experience as they were transformed by the power of the gospel.

Third, Doug and Margaret were passionate about equipping Christian workers. They enabled pastors to become better equipped for ministry by organizing training seminars on preaching, administration, and other ministry skills. Providing resource materials such as commentaries and study Bibles became a long-term advancement program. High-quality books were provided through the Christian Literature for Asians in Ministry (CLAIM) program. Doug persuaded the authors of many books to forego their royalties and then printed them locally for distribution through CLAIM.

To augment their competency training and enhance the character formation of students graduating from various Bible schools, Doug established the Bible School Students' Internship Program (BSSIP).

Participants spent one year as interns, and many then became employees of CGM. My wife joined the CGM staff after completing a BSSIP internship.

Doug also established the Action International Ministry to mentor new expatriate missionaries arriving in the field, in both cultural adjustment and holistic engagement. He provided practical training on how to be effective as missionaries among the urban informal settlers and slum dwellers.

Doug and Margaret had to return to the United States so that Doug could receive medical treatment for cancer. While recovering, they continue to engage in ministry to the Philippines by shipping resources for pastors—books, study Bibles, and summary lessons from Doug's reading of other books. Though past their retirement age, Doug and Margaret are still equipping and encouraging pastors and Christian workers in the Philippines through these resources and by making short-term visits whenever possible.

Their feet cannot stay put where they are. They are driven to move continually, for they have beautiful feet that bring the good news of salvation from sin and eternal life in Christ.

The second attractive feature of this Festschrift is the wide array and in-depth quality of essays from 16 authors spanning three continents of Asia, America and Europe. The wide scope of topics covered reflects the diverse, wide-ranging influence of Doug and Margaret. The contributors include scholars, researchers, counselors, missiologists, and church planters, all of whom undergird their ideas and perspectives with illustrations from real-life experience. They're not speaking from an armchair or an ivory tower; rather, they write from what they have learned, seen, and practiced.

Finally, one more thing that makes this volume a must-read is the circumstances in which the editor produced this volume. Joy Tira is a tenacious person who overcame a great health challenge. He nearly died due to a massive stroke but experienced a miraculous recovery, truly a gift from God. After six months of medical isolation in the hospital, God gave Joy what he asked for, restoring his memories and granting him clarity of thinking that enabled him to complete this project. He laboriously mobilized the contributors, shepherding them and egging them on to finish the task. Like Doug and Margaret, Joy also has feet that cannot rest, even during his times of limited mobility.

I invite missiologists, missionaries, and would-be missionaries to dive in and learn from the contributions and stories of people who have worked with and been inspired by the ministry of Doug, Margaret, and Joy. Their beautiful feet are always on the move. They are great missionaries whose steps are worth following.

Bishop Efraim M. Tendero
Global Ambassador, World Evangelical Alliance
Executive Director, Galilean Movement

Sadiri Joy Tira

PREFACE

How then, can they call on the One they have not believed in? And how can they believe in the One of whom they have not heard? And how can they hear without someone preaching to them? And how can anyone preach unless they are sent? As it is written: "How beautiful are the feet of those who bring good news. Romans 10:14-15 (NIV)

In 2022, I started a book project, a Festschrift: *Tetsunao Yamamori: Missionary Statesman, Strategist, Servant* (Langham Global Library, UK, 2023).

This volume, *Beautiful Feet: Following the Christian Missionary Footsteps* is another Festschrift.

My friend Dr Allen Yeh, a Chinese-American missiologist and currently professor at Biola University (CA, USA), first coined the term "polycentric" to describe missions in the 21st century, i.e., "From Everyone to Everywhere" (2016). In a recent e-conversation, he clarified that this is not simply geographical, but also generational, and encompassing all people -- "everyone"-- regardless of their nationality, ethnicity, gender, or age.

Most of my publications (short articles, blogs, academic presentations, lectures, and books) are about diaspora missions and missiology. In the summer of 2020, I suffered a severe and cruel stroke. This was debilitating, but I did not lose hope. At the height of the COVID-19 pandemic, I was locked down, and for six months I was confined as a "resident" of two hospitals in Edmonton, Alberta. Before I was discharged, when I was slowly regaining my strength, my medical team informed me that I could not go back to my workplace.

I have had a long, new journey. I prayed for God's mercy and restoration of my memory. The Almighty, Compassionate Creator answered my prayers. During those days in seclusion and isolation, I felt like I was living alone inside a cave. Most of the time I prayed, read scriptures, and reflected on my journey. I remembered close friends, family members, and mentors whom God used to shape my life. In particular, I thank the ever-present Jesus Christ, my best friend, for sending other friends to minister in prayer and encouragement, cheering me onward.

In the hospital room, the following Bible verses were engraved in my heart and mind:

"Behold, I have inscribed you on the palms of my hands" Isaiah 49:16 (NASB)

"When I was prosperous, I said, 'Nothing can stop me now!' Your favor, O Lord, made me as secure as a mountain. Then you turned away from me, and I was shattered. ...

What will you gain if I die, if I sink into the grave? Can my dust praise you? Can it tell of your faithfulness?

Hear me, Lord, and have mercy on me. Help me, O Lord.

You have turned my mourning into joyful dancing.

You have taken away my clothes of mourning and clothed me with joy, that I might sing praises to you and not be silent.

O Lord my God, I will give you thanks forever!" Psalms 30: 6-7, 9-12 (NLT)

"[Honor] Remember your leaders who taught you the word of God. Think of all the good that has come from their lives, and follow the example of their faith. Hebrews 13:7 (NLT)

Several men and women mentored and inspired me. After I was discharged from the hospital, I listed the names of these leader-mentors; here is a short part of my list:

George Verwer, the Founder of Operation Mobilization (OM). He was a visionary missionary leader.

Patrick Johnstone, a man of prayer. As we travelled together on board the first OM ship, MV Logos, he launched Operation World, and wherever the ship was docked, he summoned Christians and local churches to pray for world evangelization. I met these two giants of faith during my formative years (1975).

Three other men I must mention:

My biological father, Victorino Tira: His words "Wherever you are, be generous and walk with your head bowed down." are always in my mind.

Two successful elderly businessmen, my great supporters: first, Horatio MacCombs, who would remind me, "Earn as much as you can, save as much as you can, and give as much as you can;" and, "The chicken gave her Master eggs for breakfast, but the pig gave her Master a ham" (this is sacrificial giving not just quantity giving). The other was Jack Klemke, who asked, "Do you believe God loves you; do you believe He will provide for all your needs? Do you believe He is supreme and sovereign? Remember this: God is both the righteous Judge and Accountant...every apple must be accounted for!" Both Horatio and Jack are now in the City of God.

In 1978, I met Doug and Margie Nichols while they were leaders of Christ for Greater Manila. Doug is a compassionate, humble, and generous servant of Jesus Christ. He strongly believes and practices Kingdom ethics and the teaching of the Master: *"For I was hungry, and you fed me. I was thirsty, and you gave me a drink. I was a stranger, and you invited me into your home. I was naked, and you gave me clothing. I was sick, and you cared for me. I was in prison, and you visited me" Matthew 25:35-36 (NLT).*

In addition to these important influences, I must mention Ted Yamamori, Enoch Wan, and Doug Birdsall. They are mentors and friends who taught me that the world is bigger than my circle, along with Wonsuk Ma, Stanley John, Charlie Cook, Raul Santos, Ron

Bachman, Cody and Katharine Lorance, Phil Yan, Amy Cheung, Nigel and Jessie Paul, and Harvey Thiessen. All of them are co-pilgrims, true friends, my "Barnabas" encouragers, prayer partners, and practical ministry supporters. While I was in the hospital, they reached out to me via emails, text messages, and phone calls.

Now in my new journey, however, with my limited capacities, Doug and Margaret Nichols have never ceased to comfort and minister to me and my wife. Doug and Margie, an octogenarian couple, are no longer as active as they were 50 years ago. They are restricted in long-haul travels and administrative leadership roles. But now that God extended my life and healed me, He restored my memory. Having already published the festschrift for Dr. Ted Yamamori, I desire now to honour the Nichols, for they also deserve a festschrift. A "festschrift" is not a biography, but a collection of essays by scholars and like-minded friends or collaborators in Kingdom building.

In the summer of 2023, I assembled a group of researchers and missions practitioners to each contribute a chapter for this new volume. All the topics and issues in this book are missiological and concern the strategies that Doug Nichols has championed, advocated, and supported until today. Hopefully, this book will inform, instruct, and inspire missions practitioners, as well as informing missions historians and professors, particularly the younger generations. Although many of the issues addressed are discussed in the Philippine and Asian context because that was where the Nichols laboured for several decades, the principles, concepts, and strategies can be applied globally by missions agencies, institutions, and denominations or national churches. Therefore, the value extends to a readership beyond the Philippines or Filipinos.

I am thankful to each contributing writer and book endorser. The copy editor and proofreader is Marie Osborne, a retired missionary-educator herself who deserves commendation for her cheerful and thorough job! "Thank you!"

Finally, this book is a renewed call for fervent and persistent prayer for global missions and world evangelism as well as fervent prayer support for missionaries and Kingdom workers of all generations, especially in the midst of our troubled generation and chaotic world, the world God so loved as to redeem and save. (John: 3:16)

Let every Christian and the global church pray, "Oh, God have mercy"; and "Even so, Lord Jesus, come!"

Sadiri Joy Tira
Edmonton, Alberta
January 5, 2024

INTRODUCTION TO BEAUTIFUL FEET

By Sadiri Joy Tira

This volume starts with a Call to Prayer for World Evangelization (Johnstone); in our tumultuous generation, persistent prayer is required (Mandryk);and the book ends by summoning all believers and global missions enterprises to pray for missionaries (Lorance).

Julie Ma's reflection on her missionary life and journey in the hinterlands of the Philippines is inspiring. Julie and her husband Wonsuk are Korean missionaries whose innovative strategies to reach the indigenous tribes proved effective in church planting, discipleship training and mentorship of leaders. They planted seed in a difficult area but now the seed has become a plant bearing fruit. Their calling, character, and spiritual gifts are God-given and fit well in their geographical and cultural context.

The mission field at the beginning of the Third Millennium, particularly during and after the COVID-19 Pandemic, accelerated global migration and diaspora, population explosion, and technological revolution, thus drastically changing the mission landscape. These global changes require special training of future Kingdom Workers. While their calling to make disciples of Jesus Christ (Matthew 28:18-20) will not change, their understanding of national, regional, and global situations must be calibrated with their training and education (Whechel).

To address these ongoing changes in mission fields, the Global Church and local congregations need to adjust their thinking about how they see themselves and how they do missions. Jason Tan and Juno Wang introduce us to the concepts of Polymorphic Ecclesia and Glocal Missions.

There are several case studies in the Philippines, where the Nicholses labored with the agencies and workers they supported. The historical, theological, and missiological issues, as well as the discipleship, strategic church planting, and leadership development models are all transferable to other regional and cultural contexts (Lim, Sundir, Otto, Petallar).

Polycentric Missiology and Generational Missiology as well as holistic diaspora missions are gaining momentum in missiological and institutional circles.

The anthropological issues, e.g., honor-shame and gender equality, discussed by Narry Santos and Donna Castillo-Tan are insightful.

God's mission reaches not simply to different geographical or ethnic groups, but to people of all ages, from children to senior citizens. They too have unique roles in the Kingdom (Petallar, Haanen, Uytanlet, Tira).

This book is written by multi-disciplinary researchers and reflective-ministry practitioners. Hence, it is like many dishes spread out in a buffet" table. This was put together by design because this was how Douglas and Margaret Nichols operated. They championed all the ministries discussed. Indeed, they have "beautiful feet " and their "footprints" remain to be followed by future missionaries.

PRAYER AND WORLD EVANGELIZATION

Patrick Johnstone

If all the desires, requests and goals expressed in Operation World were to be implemented, it would radically change the nations of this world.

Wars would be ended, ethnic hatreds tamed, politicians become honest, ecological restoration begun, global warming and AIDS halted, poverty reduced.

The Church of the Lord Jesus Christ would be provided with godly leaders, it would be renewed, revived, united in vision, mobilized for mission and readied for the return of its Head. Jesus Christ would return with the world evangelized and the Church complete! That is the wish. How much of the earthly and how quickly the eternal agendas would be achieved depends on ONE activity–prayer in the name of Jesus to a loving, sovereign Father.

The ministry of the children of God is not doing but praying, not strategizing but prostrate before God seeking His will, not clever stratagems for manipulating people and events but trusting in God who moves in the hearts of even His most implacable enemies. Through prayer, Nebuchadnezzar and today's dictators get converted, Manassehs and today's persecutors repent, and kingdoms of Babylon and Iron Curtains are torn down. We do not engage in ministry and pray for God's blessing on it; prayer IS the ministry from which all other ministries must flow.

Psalm 2 reveals the Father's Great Commission to His Son and how the destiny of nations is tied in with their rejection of or submission to His Kingly Son. Look at the command and promises of Ps 2:8.

'Ask of Me, and I will make the nations your heritage, and the ends of the earth your possession. You shall break them with a rod of iron, And dash them in pieces like a potter's vessel.'

DARE WE APPLY THIS COMMAND AND THESE PROMISES TO OURSELVES?

God spoke to me from Psalm 2:8 as a young Christian at university in Bristol, England. I heard for the first time of the work of the Dorothea Mission in the urban slums of Southern Africa. I knew that God was speaking to me that this was His will for me, but I asked the Lord for scriptural confirmation, and it was this passage which spoke to me–South Africa was, for me, one of the ends of the earth for which I could ask. I did not realize at the time that this "asking for the nations" would actually define a large part of my ministry for the next 40 years in successive editions of Operation World! Again, this passage leapt to my mind. It was as if God was saying, "I called you to one end of the earth, but now I am giving you all the ends!".

The pages of Operation World give something of the needs and challenges of our needy, sin-sick, doomed world. The nations are there for the asking. God is calling you and me into the ministry of intercession for them. Through these prayers much will happen–above all we could ask or expect. ... Daniel heard God's voice in Daniel 7:27 (RSV):

The kingdom and the dominion and the greatness of the kingdoms under the whole heaven shall be given to the people of the saints of the Most High; Their kingdom shall be an ever-lasting kingdom, and all dominions shall serve and obey them.

The cost is great, for these words were preceded in verses 21-22 by:

As I looked, this horn made war with the saints, and prevailed over them, until the Ancient of Days came, and judgement was given for the saints of the Most High, and the time came when the saints received the kingdom.

We have plenty of opposition in the heavenlies and from human powers and persecutors.

The enemy will seek to frighten us with these and dangle allurements to distract us from the vision of a heavenly, eternal kingdom filled with people from every race, tribe, people and tongue. Yet Jesus offers you a share in his reign. We may look up to Him in agony at times, but see your true position looking down with Him exercising the authority bequeathed to you by Him in the Great Commission He has given to you and every Christian. May you become an intercessor with a world vision that prays Satan-defeating, kingdom-taking, people-reaching, captive-releasing, revival-giving, Christ-glorifying prayers.

Prayer not only changes people, situations and even the course of history, but also those who pray! It is dangerous for the enemy and also 'dangerous' for you.

There is a price to pay to be a person who stands in the gap between fallen man and a righteous God. That price may mean becoming an answer to your own prayers in giving time, finances and even going out as a witness in your Jerusalem (where you now live), your Judea (your own country), your Samaria (the other ethnic groups in your own country) or even to the ends of the earth. Our prayer is that many will give their whole lives for this most noble of causes – to obey Jesus' last command in making disciples of all nations and so ready the Church and the world for the grand climax of His glorious return.

PERSISTENT PRAYER: A GLOBAL CHRISTIAN RESPONSE TO THE CHALLENGES OF OUR TIMES

Jason Mandryk

As we look around our world at the array of disasters, disorders, and disintegration, it is easy to become discouraged. At the time of this writing, conflict in the Holy Land has murderously escalated and much of the Middle East and North Africa region has become a theatre of proxy wars. Russia is accused of over 50,000 war crimes in their invasion of Ukraine. Myanmar keeps bombing its own citizens. A series of coups has rocked the Sahel–a region already traumatized by poverty and Islamist violence. Mexican cartels attempt to outdo one another in horrifying violence. Tens of millions around the world have fled their homes because it was no longer safe to stay there. Hundreds of millions more are likely to have to flee in the decades to come due to severe climate and environment issues. Corruption and systemic dysfunction grotesquely enrich the few while many struggle to endure economic crisis after crisis. Scandals continue to rip apart what we thought were strong and effective Christian ministries, even as droves of people–especially the younger generation–disassociate themselves from the Church. There is no need to add to this sad litany, although it would be painfully easy to do so.

In response to all of the above, we pray and pray and then pray some more. But so often, it feels like our prayers are in vain. Times such as we are experiencing require us to repeat as often as necessary three important reminders.

First is that we must remember that news organizations are mighty engines and that their fuel is conflict and disaster. Reading the news, it is easy to lose sight of the fact that human lifespans are longer than ever in recorded history. Other historic markers? Global health outcomes are better, poverty is less ubiquitous, literacy is higher, and rates of violent crime are lower. All of the woes reported can be 100% true, even while the positive progress that humanity is experiencing goes largely unreported. Bad news sells. Good news? Not so much.

Next is the fact that the best of the good news–the properly Good News–continues to make inroads around the world. Perhaps it is not happening at the rate we would wish, but spread it does. In every country in the world, even those closed to the gospel, there are groups of Jesus-followers gathering together to worship Him. In a surprising number of cases, the places that are most hostile are the very places where those who follow Jesus are multiplying most rapidly.

Third, and perhaps most importantly, the global Church is gaining the understanding that the second factor occurs in response to prayer. And, as a result, Christians are praying at a scale previously unheard of. Some may dispute the claims that prayer is the cause of these missional breakthroughs. But as the widely-quoted and succinct saying of Archbishop William Temple goes, "When I pray, coincidences happen, and when I don't, they don't." Places where Christians are poor and powerless have long known this. Places where the Church is seeing its wealth and influence decline are learning it quickly. Prayer–not military hardware, economic imperialism, nor diplomatic policy, but prevailing, persistent prayer that aligns with the Lord's revealed purposes–is our best answer to every crisis. The secret to understanding how our prayers and God's answers link up is all in the timing.

Occasionally, a servant of the Lord turns up somewhere and immediately ministers in the power of the Spirit such that thousands turn to the Lord, or spiritual strongholds are broken. Every so often, a prayer gathering is held and by morning, the reason for the praying is gloriously resolved. But such wonderful occasions are not the norm. It seems that the economy of God's kingdom works, at least in part, on accrual. The slow, steady accumulation of interest, earned through faithful intercession, acts of Christlikeness, and gospel witness, builds up. It is imperceptible to us—until the breakthrough comes.

Sometimes people live to see the fruit of their own investments in prayer and good works, perhaps after years or even decades. This may be the return of their own prodigal child to their upbringing in the community of faith. It may be the revival in their own community for which they prayed for decades. It may be a missional breakthrough among an unreached people group or the end of an oppressive totalitarian regime.

Yet, often the outcome for which we pray doesn't happen until after we have passed on. And although we don't like to admit it, the hard reality is that sometimes the longed-for breakthrough never comes at all. We do not have a complete explanation of why this is, but it is. God's power and will are seemingly thwarted by those opposed to Jesus' reign. The distraction and disobedience of the saints delays the accomplishment of God's purposes. Why? We still don't fully understand the dynamics of the interactions between our prayers, God's sovereignty, and the free will of both human beings and the powers. We never will fully understand, at least not in this lifetime. But we have assurances from the Maker of the universe that our prayers and our choices do make a difference. They aren't merely shoehorned into the Lord's plan. The plan is in fact dynamically impacted by them.

God is at work, all according to His cosmic intentions. He is not a step ahead of the rest of us. He stands outside of time and space and all the billions of years of the universe are like a speck. But the schedule for this master plan appears to be a flexible one. We read from Scripture, *"The Lord is not slow in keeping his promise, as some understand slowness. Instead, he is patient with you, not wanting anyone to perish, but everyone to come to repentance" (2 Pet 3:9 NIV).* God's flexibility with the timetable is based, not on a lack of resolve, nor a lack of resources, but on the truth that He has chosen to partner with humanity to accomplish these plans and purposes. Peter makes this clear two verses later when he writes, *"Since all these things are thus to be dissolved, what sort of people ought you to be in lives of holiness and godliness, waiting for and hastening the coming of the day of God"* (2 Pet 3:11-12a ESV, emphasis mine). The very notion is staggering—how we as disciples live our lives has an actual impact on when God's plans are fulfilled!

Once we accept that this principle is true, we see that it applies even more broadly. Across the sweep of Scripture, from Genesis to Revelation, we see God waiting for things to reach their fullness before acting.

Anyone involved with global mission will hopefully be familiar with Matthew 24:14: *"And this gospel of the kingdom will be proclaimed throughout the whole world as a testimony to all nations, and then the end will come."* It stands to reason that Part B of this arrangement (the end) will only happen after Part A (world evangelization) is done. God seems almost scandalously willing both to partner with those humans who serve him and also to wait patiently for those who do not to repent.

In Genesis 15:16, God promises that Abram's descendants will emerge from slavery to Egypt and return to the land God was giving to him. But it would only be able to happen generations later, *"for the sin of the Amorites has not yet reached its full measure"* (NIV). In Galatians 4:4, we learn that *"when the set time had fully come, God sent his Son, born of a woman, born under the law, to redeem those under the law, that we might receive adoption to sonship"* (NIV). Paul instructs the faithful in Rome that *"Israel has experienced a hardening in part until the full number of the Gentiles has come in"* (Rom 11:25 NIV). In Revelation 6:10-11, the martyrs cry out to God, asking *"How long, Sovereign Lord, holy and true, until you judge the inhabitants of the earth and avenge our blood?"* What is heaven's response? *"Each of them was given a white robe, and they were told to wait a little longer, until the full number of their fellow servants, their brothers and sisters, were killed just as they had been"* (NIV).

Again and again, we see that God's plan is contingent on human choices. This, I believe, is one major reason why we can be assured that our prayers and our actions actually make a difference. We can accelerate the timeline by our obedience or delay it by our waywardness. We add to the accrual of prayers, even as others around the world add their own contributions. Though it is barely perceptible on a grand scale, our intercession accumulates. And in time, when the full deposit is made, answers come in a way that would seem very sudden if we didn't know any better.

When we at Operation World share about the impact of intercession on global situations, as well as the need for persistent prayer in the face of implacable resistance, we often share a series of three water-based analogies.

The first is that of an iceberg. While the largest icebergs loom over ships like mountains, most of the iceberg's mass is underwater and unseen. So it is with spiritual realities – the invisible realm is far larger than we perceive. The West's secular materialist worldview blinds us to this, but it is evident in Scripture that there is much more going on than what our human eyes can see. On occasion, God pulls back the curtain and allows His servants a clearer picture of the forces in play. Our prayers may often feel like mere words, but the reality is that they can have profound effects in the spiritual world.

The second picture is that of a river flowing through a rocky canyon. What possible effect can a meandering stream of water have against the durability of stone? A few drops will make no mark. Neither will thousands or even millions of litres. But given enough time—as long as the water keeps flowing, even the hardest of rock gives way. We've all seen photos of the Grand Canyon or of Big Bend National Park. The persistence of a river's impact on stone is undeniable. Prayer, as with water, may take time, but with time, it has the power to reshape the world.

The final analogy is drawn from personal experience. On the grounds of our mission base in the UK, there was a particularly magnificent specimen of oak tree. It towered above other trees; it must have been well over 30 metres tall. It looked invincible. But on a rare January night when the temperatures dropped below freezing and a heavy snow fell, the woods resounded with an almighty crash. The morning light revealed that the mighty oak had shattered near the base and toppled, taking a couple of trees with it on the way down and obliterating an unfortunate section of fencing. A brief examination revealed that the core of the trunk was rotten. The change in temperature rendered the dead heart of the tree brittle and weak. The cumulative weight of the snowflakes piling up on bough and branch eventually brought the giant down. How much does a snowflake weigh? Which one of them was it that felled the mighty oak? Our prayers may seem insubstantial, but cumulatively, they have the power to bring down giants.

The promises of Scripture give us the confidence to pray with authority for what seems impossible. And the principles spelled out above help us not to panic or lose heart when we speak to the mountain and nothing happens.

It would seem to me that such notions apply not only to prayer, but to missionary work as well. Those who have been chipping away at the rock face of the Great Commission over the course of a lifetime can attest that this is often the case. Sometimes we labour for years–decades, even–with no evident fruit. Missions history is littered with testimonies of faithful Kingdom workers who felt that they had failed because they saw few or none come to faith in Christ during their long years of service. Whether they were aware or not, the tenet of accrual and the tenet of fullness eventually converge, and, under God's sovereignty, the longed-for change comes.

"Great things are not done by impulse, but by a series of small things brought together."[1] Vincent van Gogh was a deeply philosophical, and at many points of his life, religious man. Troubled though he was, he understood this fundamental principle. In keeping with the spirit of the age, the tempo of our expectations seems to be aligned with the speed that it takes to microwave our food or perhaps order takeaway using whichever app is popular in our region. So, it should come as no surprise that the greatest of all things, the fulfilment of the Great Commission, may require the Lord's own patience. Over a century ago, John P. Jones, in part as a response to the enthusiastic urgency of the Student Volunteer Movement, shared this conviction in The Modern Missionary Challenge: "This enterprise is not only the greatest that the world has ever known; it is also the most difficult of achievement. Let us not fall into the error of thinking that Christianizing the nations and bringing the world to the feet of our Lord is the task of a day or of a generation."[2]

The need for such patient persistence is why I have great admiration for those who have served long in the Lord's harvest fields and prayer closets. Whether the breakthrough has come, or is still to come, through their faithfulness they have made tremendous deposits into accounts that one day will be wonderfully redeemed. Be it a missionary couple who remain on the field for a lifetime, an intercessor who prays without ceasing until they are promoted to glory, an Overseas Filipino Worker who never stops shining the light of Jesus in a dark and difficult situation, the local evangelist who outlasts disinterest and stone-faced rejection every single week, or anyone else who endures until the end, their persistence in taking no rest and giving heaven no rest will be rewarded in due course. Of that we have God's own assurance.

----

1 Vincent van Gogh. *Vincent Van Gogh, The Letters,* Letter 274. The Hague: Van Gogh Museum: Van Gogh Letters Project. https://vangoghletters.org/vg/letters/let274/letter.html

2 Jones, John P. *The Modern Missionary Challenge: A study of the present day world missionary enterprise: its problems and results.* (New York, Revell, 1911), 251.

ASSESSING MISSION PARADIGMS FOR EFFECTIVE HOLISTIC MINISTRIES IN PHILIPPINE MISSIONS

David S. Lim

From the start of this century, the world has shrunk and become flat. We now live in a global village, so it is now proper to claim literally, "The whole world is my parish," and missions is now "from everywhere to everywhere." With just a smart phone, we can minister cross-culturally without regard to national boundaries through social media. Global issues like climate change, drug trafficking, human trafficking, and religious extremism impinge on us all. Vast populations continue to face overwhelming challenges: massive poverty with a growing gap between the poorest and the richest, globalized materialism in "consumer societies," and a resurgence of religious conflicts.

How has Philippine Christianity perceived and performed our holistic mission (HM) in light of these realities in the world since the founding of the Philippine Missions Association (PMA) in 1983? The key founder, Dr. Met Castillo, confirmed to me that Christ for Greater Manila (CGM), led by Doug and Margi Nichols, was one of the active founding members from the very start. This shows that the PMA had a clear understanding of a holistic approach to Christian ministries from the beginning, and that there was a close partnership between nationals and foreign missionaries then.

Through the years, PMA has consistently promoted HM in both the home and overseas fronts. Although her flagship program has emphasized raising the largest and perhaps the most effective Evangelical mission force among the nations since 2001 until now, the holistic ethos of mobilizing lay workers to serve among the poor has prevailed.[1] Her mission mobilization program has tried to equip a million tentmakers–"Overseas Filipino Workers" (OFWs)[2] --by 2020 to catalyze disciple-multiplication movements (DMMs) among the unreached people groups (UPGs), especially in Asia.[3] This follows the CGM model of mobilizing lay volunteers to help in their special ministries among the urban poor, particularly among prisoners, street children, and prostituted women, as well as church planting ventures in the depressed areas of Metro Manila.

PMA will continue to use our present missions strategy to reach Asia, which has the greatest number of unreached peoples living in regions dominated by major religious faiths and political ideologies with almost negligible Christian influence.[4] Can we partner with the Christ-following minorities of Asia to effectively reach our Muslim, Buddhist, Hindu, Communist, and secular neighbors effectively, so that the Great Commission can finally be fulfilled among them?

I have published an article on the various versions of HM, which has popularized the call for the Church to be God's agent of community transformation. It is entitled "Diakonia and Evangelism as Functions of Mission: Theological Reflections," in *Evangelism and Diakonia in Context* edited by Rose Dowsett, et al., (Oxford: Regnum, 2016). Part I of that work shows the global Christian consensus on the missiology of HM, which consists of evangelism and social action and serves as the theological basis for the church's involvement in community (and societal) transformation. I explained its six main descriptors: bifocal, integral, evangelistic, diaconal, liberative and contextual.[5]

Then Part II depicted six mission paradigms (MP) which trans-formation theologians, missiologists, and practitioners are using in the world today, as various churches try to implement their understanding of holistic mission, namely: transformational development, organizational development, liberation movements, Neo-Pentecostal ministries, disciple multiplication, and insider movements.

This chapter will assess the effectiveness of each of these six MPs in fulfilling the Great Commission. What kind of churches will we be planting and growing among the UPGs in Asia and beyond that will be most effective in transforming communities and cultures?

MISSION PARADIGM #1: TRANSFORMATIONAL DEVELOPMENT

The first MP which has been used by Nichols's CGM is the community developmental approach to church development among the poor. This approach, usually called "transformational development," comes from Christian non-governmental organizations, or in short, Christian development organizations (CDOs) and mission agencies with holistic orientation. These are usually lay-initiated and inter-denominational in nature, and work in partnership with church-based CDOs, like Caritas, Church World Service, Mennonite Central Committee, etc. For evangelism, they work towards planting churches among the poor through incarnational workers (usually lay, with community development training) who will eventually pass on the leadership and ownership of the CD project to their church or denomination.

In a world of increasing climatic and systemic challenges, these CDOs have specialized in responding to the perennial attacks of natural evils (like typhoons, floods, earthquakes, and volcanic eruptions) and structural evils (like malnutrition, poverty, corruption, violence, etc), through the participative approach which has been developed in actual mission praxes. By promoting child-based development through child sponsorships, most of the largest CDOs, led by World Vision--which has grown since 1953 to be the biggest NGO in the world today[6]--have been in the forefront of tackling global issues side by side with governments, the United Nations, corporate foundations, and generous individuals.

They welcome partnership with churches and church-based CDOs in empowering people by setting up programs which tackle and overcome their local problems–for God's justice and peace to be established in "caring and sharing communities" contextually in the world around them. The Participatory Learning and Action approach has been used alongside the Bible to mobilize church people to serve and bless their communities contextually.[7] Through the Samaritan Strategy that starts with worldview change, churches can launch "seeds of love" projects that will begin to extend their love for their neighbors.[8]

Most of the global South, especially Africa,[9] has remained poor in spite of billions of dollars in foreign development aid and rich national resources.[10] To alleviate poverty, the poor have been empowered to join the supply chain of the local and even global market. Through micro-enterprise development and micro-credit loans,[11] the poor can grow their own businesses, and even organize savings-for-investment groups which will grow into cooperatives and social enterprises.[12] They can then be linked to the "business as mission" movement, which considers businesspeople as ministers in the marketplace, with four bottom lines: financial, social, spiritual, and ecological.[13] The more progressive ones have joined the global movement for opposing the dominant capitalist market economy and advancing the "social (European) or solidarity (global South) economy," which consists of social entrepreneurship and fair trade.

Micah Global, which is composed of most of the major church-based and inter-denominational CDOs today, is positioned to work with global movements in the United Nations' "2030 Agenda" to achieve the "17 Sustainable Development Goals" along with its 169 targets.[14] But since many of them also resource their operations from the funds of governments and business foundations, their advocacies have been confined only to those that deal with soft power (economic) and not hard power (political) transformation. Nonetheless, this is still a big step forward.

Their partnership with governments and the private sector have also limited their options in including evangelism in their portfolio of programs. Yet almost all of them still include evangelism and church development among their success indicators. Most of the development sector has also accepted this holistic approach, because they have realized that spirituality enhances community development, for societal transformation needs to include moral values formation, especially for long-term sustainability.[15]

Yet this mission paradigm has found two lingering problems which limit its effectiveness: its dependence on foreign resources, and its dualistic two-tiered worldview. The finances of CDOs are mainly sourced from the outside, and even when projects are led by nationals, their human resources tend to be educated urban professionals (World Vision) or the professional pastor of a church inside the community who acts a bridge between the CDO (e.g., Compassion, Tearfund) and the community. Moreover, they also tend to focus on the rational and technical approaches (thus minimizing the affective and spiritual dimensions) to strategic planning with their technical "log frames" and results-based management for achieving their goals.[16]

MISSION PARADIGM #2: ORGANIZATIONAL DEVELOPMENT

The second and most dominant MP among denomination-al churches has been the setting up and maintenance of church structures and their related service agencies. Most of the churches in the post-Christian regions of the Global North are considered nominal (if not lapsed) and secularized; and most of the denominations in the global South also suffer from the lethargy and inertia of maintaining the expensive patterns and structures of the past. Yet many still have good HM models and the potential of making significant contributions as responsible "salt and light" citizens in their societies, with prophetic witness to Christ through advocacies against poverty, injustices, corruption, and other systemic evils.

For most churches, evangelism leads to church growth, meaning increasing church membership and building church-related institutions, like schools, hospitals, orphanages, etc. The basic unit, called the local church, is defined as "a community of baptized believers in which the word of God is preached, the apostolic faith confessed, the sacraments are celebrated, the redemptive work of Christ for the world is witnessed to, and a ministry of *episkopé* exercised by bishops or other ministers in serving the community."[17] The success of their HM programs can be seen in the continuing witness of the schools and hospitals of the historic denominations, the largest of which is the Roman Catholic Church.

Their HM denotes involvement in and support of church-initiated and church-related ministry programs to help the poor, specifically in relief and rehabilitation, community and economic development, and justice advocacy as well. Through the years, some of these programs have become organizations which the churches finance directly through their collected funds, and often indirectly through encouragement of their members to volunteer, participate, and take leadership roles in such ministries.

The RCC has focused on the academic diaconate: Universities are outstanding environments for articulating and developing this evangelizing commitment in an interdisciplinary and integrated way. Catholic schools, which always strive to join their work of education with the explicit proclamation of the gospel, are a most valuable resource for the evangelization of culture, even in those countries and cities where hostile situations challenge us to greater creativity in our search for suitable methods.[18] *The Cape Town Commitment* likewise calls for support of "Christ-centred schools and universities that are committed to academic excellence and biblical truth," and encourages young Christians "to consider a long-term career in the secular university, to teach and develop their discipline from a biblical worldview, thereby to influence their subject field."[19]

Though these institutions are expensive to develop and maintain, and their evangelistic output may be minimal, their projection of the compassionate and servant nature of the church is invaluable. Church buildings project the church's (and God's) presence, but their clergy-centered hierarchical structure as well as their closed doors and high walls with minimal programs for the poor in their neighborhoods may be the biggest challenges for this kind of MP. In this world full of hardened ideological and religious loyalties, the call for the church to model identification with the poor and the powerless in order to manifest the love of God in its witness following the incarnational example of her Lord Jesus may be the most difficult hurdle for this MP, since world Christianity with its colonial past is one of the wealthiest and most powerful institutions on earth today.

MISSION PARADIGM #3: LIBERATION MOVEMENTS

The third MP has been developed among and by the poor, originally from the oppressed contexts of Latin America in the 1950s. Though liberation theology used the Marxist materialistic dialectics as its framework in interpreting Scriptures and social realities, its inter-class conflictive and militant stance has since been tempered by the reconciliatory and non-violent posture of peace/shalom in world Christianity,[20] particularly in the Anabaptist tradition.

Liberationists have led the call for the "preferential option for the poor" and a new ecclesiology where the basic units of the church are the basic Christian communities (BCCs), which have been renamed basic ecclesial communities (BECs) in contexts where they have been linked to Communism and its willingness to use violent means. The parishes are decentralized into small groups of 20 adults maximum, as "the new way of being church."[21] The poor are empowered through prayer and interactive reflection of their situation in light of Scripture to change social relationships and structures that keep the poor poor. Other activities include conscientization seminars, cooperative development, and mass action (hunger strikes, marches, rallies, etc.) by which the disenfranchised use their numbers and determination to act together to realize a better future for their community.

This holistic witness has led in the prophetic struggle for human rights and socio-political change,[22] which have been expounded repeatedly in WCC statements, like: Jesus has told us *"You cannot serve God and mammon"* (Matt. 6:24, KJV). The policy of unlimited growth through the domination of the global free market is an ideology that claims to be without alternative, demanding an endless flow of sacrifices from the poor and from nature. "It makes the false promise that it can save the world through creation of wealth and prosperity, claiming sovereignty over life and demanding total allegiance, which amounts to idolatry." This is a global system of mammon that protects the unlimited growth of wealth of only the rich and powerful through endless exploitation. This tower of greed is threatening the whole household of God. The reign of God is in direct opposition to the empire of mammon.[23]

The perpetuators of such a politico-economic system are the super-rich global multinational corporations and the political elites who accumulate so much wealth and power without regard to their global warming impact on nature, which in turn negatively impacts the poor, as they struggle to subsist in the globalized "consumer society." Similar to Evangelii Gaudium, the WCC concludes:

> *We want to affirm our spiritual connection with creation, yet the reality is that the earth is being polluted and exploited. Consumerism triggers not limitless growth but rather endless exploitation of the earth's resources. Human greed is contributing to global warming and other forms of climate change. If this trend continues and earth is fatally damaged, what can we imagine salvation to be? Humanity cannot be saved alone while the rest of the created world perishes. Eco-justice cannot be separated from salvation, and salvation cannot come without a new humility that respects the needs of all life on earth.[24]*

The national elites took over the norms, values, and customs of their colonial masters, and kept the "elite democracies" in the global South intact for generations.[25] These political dynasties with their military and business cronies have remained entrenched in power through massive graft and corruption.[26] Liberation movements call for aggressive and consistent political action, while also rallying for a return to pre-colonial values, particularly communal property. The poor in their BECs theologize from the underside by reflecting on the vision of a purer, simpler past of their people[27] and of the biblical paradise (Gen. 1-2), as well as the eschatological hope of "a new heavens and a new earth" (Isaiah 65:17-25), where everyone (and not just others) will enjoy the fruit of their labor (vv. 21-22).

In all these liberation movements so far, the ecumenical wing of world Christianity has been the major force to inspire and unite them into a truly global movement, and perhaps has also provided most of its leadership.[28] Furthermore, it has also provided the main bulk of the persecuted and martyrs for the common good in varied contexts.

Yet they bring out a missiological challenge: Is world Christianity really ready to do mission from the periphery and the underside; just as it has aimed to do theology from the bottom up, through grassroots or vernacular theologizing?[29] Is the church willing to identify with the poor and divest herself of her wealth and property, with their big structures of pomp and pageantry, to conform to the way of her Lord who had no pillow to lay his head on, and to the way of the apostles who claimed, "Silver and gold I have none, but in the name of Jesus rise up and walk"? If so, the liberation and the next three MPs have to be taken seriously in future discussions, planning, and priority actions of HM.

MISSION PARADIGM #4: NEO-PENTECOSTAL MINISTRIES

The recent rise of independent (oftentimes of Pentecostal or charismatic bent) churches has produced our fourth MP. Considered the "third wave of Pentecostalism,"[30] they popularized the concept of truly autonomous indigenous churches, with each setting their own policies and owning their own properties – a new way of being church for many denominations. Many denominations which have not transitioned to a more decentralized "association of churches" structure have learned to classify many of their strong churches (most of them are mega-churches), which have become autonomous, as "affiliate churches." Though hardly grabbing headlines since they are made up of the poor,[31] these Neo-Pentecostal churches have sprung a big surprise by operating significant HMs.

For evangelism, Neo-Pentecostals as fresh converts have the excitement and zeal to share their faith effectively with their relatives and friends, and even strangers. Such spontaneous and contagious witness is often combined with power encounters, like healings (physical, emotional, and social) and deliverance from demonic oppression, which result in effective HM. Since they remain lay-led (only a few can effectively aspire to become educated clergymen) in small groups that are extensions of their church, their witness extends to government, business, media, and all sectors of society.

Their experience of "personal identity transformation" helps them to overcome a "marred identity" and "passive fatalism" due to their sense of powerlessness.[32] Such empowerment in defining oneself as a victor and not a victim, and--in God's eyes--a somebody and not a nobody,[33] also results in new moral behaviors which are pro-developmental and which challenge the cultural practices and traditional religion that CDOs usually avoid addressing in order to avoid charges of cultural imperialism.

This often results in restoration of good relationships in families and communities, which in turn create hospitable environments and helpful lifestyles for the common good. Hence, "Neo-Pentecostal churches are embedded institutions that change people and their narratives, alter social behavior and create new meaning, vision and hope for the future."[34]

Such a "realized ideal" of lay mobilization has been called for in Evangelii Gaudium. Even if many are now involved in lay ministries, this involvement is not reflected in a greater penetration of Christian values in the social, political and economic sectors. It often remains tied to tasks within the Church, without a real commitment to applying the gospel to the transformation of society. The formation of the laity and the evangelization of professional and intellectual life represent a significant pastoral challenge.[35]

Through their Pentecostal theology and active laity, these churches have been able to break the sacred-secular dichotomy. The Cape Town Commitment highlights the "falsehood of a sacred-secular divide" which "has permeated the Church's thinking and action," by affirming that "God is Lord of all of life." It labels this dichotomy as "a major obstacle to the mobilization of all God's people in the mission of God, and we call upon Christians worldwide to reject its unbiblical assumptions and resist its damaging effects. We challenge the tendency to see ministry and mission (local and cross-cultural) as being mainly the work of church-paid ministers and missionaries, who are a tiny percentage of the whole body of Christ."[36]

Moreover, unlike CDOs, the Neo-Pentecostal leadership, programs, and finances are indigenous rather than from the outside,[37] often with hardly any need for training in basic HM.[38] Yet they also need to learn from modern science and technology, as well as the social critique of structural issues that sustain poverty and corruption in the world.[39]

The Neo-Pentecostal potential for maximum mobilization for effective HM is also diminished by its retention of clergy-led structures. Its mission practice still consists of sending effective church planters (often clergy-types) to plant churches (often to transplant the sending church's pattern) in other places. Unless combined with great cultural sensitivity and ecclesiastical flexibility, such strategy will have slow and less effective results.

MISSION PARADIGM #5: DISCIPLE MULTIPLICATION

The ideal of total lay mobilization for HM constitutes the fifth MP. The "emerging churches," which also propose "a new way of being church," challenge other churches "to find ways of responding to today's needs and interests in ways which are faithful to what has been received from the beginning."[40] To this day, the diaconic and kenotic stance of self-sacrifice and self-emptying have been repeated in many global ecclesiastical statements on HM. Yet the prevailing model of the church and her mission has been that of conformity to the hierarchical clergy-centric forms of organization, hence it has been properly labeled "Christendom." The churches in the Global South share exactly the same traditions and structures as their counterparts in the Global North.

In contrast, the disciple multiplication MP calls for a decentralized and flat structure of the church, which is often labeled "house (or simple or organic) church movements (HCM)." Those who advocate this church model theologically point to the "priesthood of all believers" as their doctrinal linchpin. Every Christ-follower[41] can be equipped to be a disciple-maker anywhere, and a tentmaker in cross-cultural contexts. Many have learned from the practice of the Navigators, a group founded by Dawson Trotman, who introduced the one-on-one disciple-making model of "spiritual reproduction" (based on 2 Timothy 2:2) in 1933.

Those who found this model strategically learned from the church structure that arose from the experience of "forced divestment" of Christendom in the Maoist persecution of the church in China from 1949 to 1982. The simplicity of house church networks that resulted in spontaneous and rapid expansion of the church in China demonstrated that there is a better way of being church holistically.[42] Globally, most of this MP's practitioners came out of the Neo-Pentecostal renewal, and this- may be labeled the "fourth wave of the Spirit."[43] They call the church to be transformed into networks of small groups and networks in all sectors, especially among the poor.[44]

Every believer can be a local "lay pastor" and/or a cross-cultural "lay missionary." They can lead house-churches (with a maximum of 15 adults) not just in their places of residence, but also in their places of work, study or leisure. The small size makes it simple enough for ordinary people to participate and lead, as well as keeping it flexible and humanly manageable. In many situations, this makes the church persecution-proof and poverty-proof. After all, the full presence of Christ is among them, even if only two or three are gathered in his name (Mt 18:20).

The small size also allows a simple body-life that develops transparency and mutual ministry and accountability in informal face-to-face relationships (cf. 1 Cor 14:26; Heb 10:24). Believers are automatically trained "on the job" to become leaders as they learn to discover and use their spiritual gifts while participating in discussions and ministries, as well as taking turns in leading group activities.

Only discipled believers can reproduce and multiply (evangelize and disciple others). Quality disciples are made only in small groups with "high-touch" relationships. Unlike "cell groups" in megachurches, house-church leaders are released within a couple of weeks (definitely not more than a month) and entrusted with the responsibility and the corresponding authority (in short, *empowered*) to lead their own ministry and "house church network(s)." Consistent with the cruciform of HM, each Christ-follower and HCM chooses to remain "poor" as a nameless, faceless, and powerless witness with a "simple lifestyle" and "sacrificial servanthood" to manifest the power of God and His love with their "neighbors" through almsgiving (cf. Mt 6:1-4).

Each of these groups are autonomous, co-existing with others in a fluid decentralized network structure of interdependent cells, which Pope Francis hints he will promote in the RCC: "a sound decentralization,"[45] which she can easily implement through the BECs that have already been formed in many parishes.[46] This also fulfills The Cape Town Commitment's call for church and mission leaders "to understand the strategic impact of ministry in the workplace and to mobilize, equip and send out their church members as missionaries into the workplace, ... in their own local communities," and "to integrate 'tentmakers' fully into the global missional strategy."[47]

Transformation happens naturally as Christ-followers form cells that serve and bless their colleagues and friends in their neighborhood or their workplace (as businesspeople, managers, teachers, medics, seamen, even domestic helpers).[48] Each just needs to find a partner to evangelize and disciple a few of their converted contacts who will be able to disciple others also. Even as tourists, they can combine their sight-seeing with a disciple-making objective: develop friendship with one or two "persons of peace" (cf. Luke 10:5-7), and share their "life in Christ" with them, sensitively in a servant or learning mode (cf. 1 Peter 3:15).

Missiologically, disciple multiplication through HCMs fulfill all the elements of indigeneity: self-governing, self-supporting, self-propagating, and self-theologizing, as they reflect on the relevance of the Scriptures by themselves (Acts 17:11; 20:32). This is how vernacular theology will be produced and propagated. Moreover, these "lay pastors and missionaries" will be more effective witnesses than clergy types, because they will have greater credibility (not paid to witness for Jesus), better role modeling (2 Thess 3:6-10), and more contextualized witness in society.

Those trained in community development methodology will have the added advantage of having learned to do networking and partnership with other groups, including religious groups, so as to gain friendships with community leaders (including religious leaders) for effective HM.

Though HCMs intend theologically to remain non-legal and even underground, many have sought government and public recognition of their Christian identity, like what happened in China, especially with the urban churches led by educated clergy. Such "backsliding" has been mainly due to the lessening of government restrictions as well as the influx of external Christendom models and resources. The historical trend to return to institutionalization and inertia of Christianity and its mission is being repeated again today. Can this malady ever be overcome?

MISSION PARADIGM #6: INSIDER MOVEMENTS

Yes, there indeed exists a last MP that may be even more effective, especially in crossing religious and ideological boundaries. The "Insider Movement" MP aims to establish Christ-centered communities where all Christ-followers love and serve their neighbors in Jesus' name holistically[49]--without extracting their fruits from their socio-religious identities, thereby transforming their cultures not just from the bottom up but also from the inside out. Religious buildings (like mosques and temples) are transformed into community ministry centers, managed by local networks of house-churches or BECs, each with their own missional projects, and contextually operated (locally and cross-culturally). WCC hints at this "radical contextualization"[50] approach:

> *In doing evangelism, it is important to build relations of respect and trust between people of different faiths. We value each and every human culture and recognize that the gospel is not possessed by any group but is for every people. We understand that our task is not to bring God along but to witness to the God who is already there (Acts 17:23-28). Joining in with the Spirit, we are enabled to cross cultural and religious barriers to work together towards Life.[51]*

This MP lives out and bears witness to the cruciform and kenotic approach of HM to the full. This is most appropriate in contexts where the churches are small and insignificant minorities in relation to their society, one that is dominated by other faiths and ideologies which may even be anti-Christian. Christ-followers just need to appreciate each community's environment, culture, and religion, and implant faith in the form of prayer to God in Jesus' name and meditation on God's word (1 Tim. 4:4-5). Jesus Christ and his kingdom must be fully incarnated anew in each religion and ideology. Converts to Christ should remain in their community and seek to enhance and enrich their socio-religious traditions by prayerfully reflecting on and applying the Scriptures from within (cf. 1 Corinthians 7:17-20). In the language of Frontier Missiology, this is to "liberate Christ from Christianity," for "only Christ saves, not Christianity."[52] Advocates and supporters of this MP are called "alongsiders," for the key actors in this HM are the "insiders."

Different forms of Christ-centered communities have arisen and will arise in people-groups and their cultures that have otherwise been defined by Islam,[53] Hinduism,[54] and other faiths. This aroused a great controversy in the missionary community in the United States, so that *The Cape Town Commitment* addressed this concern, stating:

So called insider movements' are to be found within several religions. These are groups of people who are now following Jesus as their God and Saviour. They meet together in small groups for fellowship, teaching, worship and prayer centred around Jesus and the Bible while continuing to live socially and culturally within their birth communities, including some elements of its religious observance... Some commend such movements. Others warn of the danger of syncretism. Syncretism, however, is a danger found among Christians everywhere as we express our faith within our own cultures. We should avoid the tendency, when we see God at work in unexpected or unfamiliar ways, either (i) hastily to classify it and promote it as a new mission strategy, or (ii) hastily to condemn it without sensitive contextual listening.[55]

To better understand this MP, a most helpful theological contribution to transformation missiology may be that of J. H. Bavinck who introduced the Latin word *possessio*, to take possession:

...the term 'accommodation' is really not appropriate as a description of what actually ought to take place. It points to an adaptation to customs and practices essentially foreign to the gospel.... We would, therefore, prefer to use the term possessio, to take in possession. The Christian life does not accommodate or adapt itself to heathen forms of life, but it takes the latter in possession and thereby makes them new... Within the framework of the non-Christian life, customs and practices serve idolatrous tendencies and drive a person away from God. The Christian life takes them in hand and turns them in an entirely different direction; they acquire an entirely different content. Even though in external form there is much that resembles past practices, in reality everything has become new. The old has in essence passed away and the new has come. Christ takes the life of a people in his hands, he renews and re-establishes the distorted and deteriorated; he fills each thing,

each word, and each practice with a new meaning and gives it a new direction.[56]

God's grace should be permeating and "taking over" each culture, worldview, and religion uniquely. This view contrasts with the past colonial and paternalistic approaches that failed to develop faith that is truly indigenous by the people themselves. HMs must be world-affirming and culture-sensitive so that Christ-centered communities that are truly reflective and transformative of their people's socio-religio-cultural identity may emerge. This has become very important as the world moves towards greater religious and ideological conflicts (especially in Christian-Muslim relations), which some have indicated may even lead to "clash(es) of civilizations."[57]

CONCLUSION

As we face the rest of the 21st century, holistic missiology has not yet made a significant transformational impact in setting up a coherent alternative to the oppressive global market system, nor a significant evangelistic impact among people of other faiths and cultures. Which of the six MPs will be most effective in fulfilling *missio Dei* today that will bear fruit and even much fruit in our postmodern world? Our missional efforts have not been wanting in zeal, dedication, prayer, and even sacrifice. The problem seems to be with the MPs that have been used: which of them can maximize our faithfulness to the HM that has been articulated clearly by world Christianity, even if it may mean breaking with our favored missiology and mission paradigm?

The past four decades since the holistic missiological consensus in 1983 have seen the development of new mission strategies, particularly through Christian NGOs (MP #1) like Nichols' CGM, which emerged alongside the traditional missional programs of many churches (MP#2), the liberation movements (MP #3), as well as the Neo-Pentecostal churches (MP #4). Yet we also have witnessed the emergence of two approaches that have the potential of effective HM through disciple multiplication movements where ordinary

Christ-followers are empowered to be holistic disciple-makers and tentmakers (MP #5), as well as through the radically contextualized mission-through-insider movements (MP #6).

Perhaps world Christianity can focus on using these last two MPs to multiply disciples and incarnate Christ among the nations, humbly learning to implement their best practices. Even if most churches would hesitate to make this paradigm shift themselves, they should at least encourage and support these kinds of holistic ministries. These may be the best ways forward to fulfill the Great Commission effectively and extend the kingdom of God strategically in our postmodern pluralistic world. "Lord Jesus, may the knowledge of Your glory fill the earth as the waters cover the sea." Amen.

----

1 At the Lausanne Forum at Pattaya in September 2004, the Filipino delegation publicly declared their commitment to deploy 200,000 missionaries (mostly OFWs as tentmakers) into the 10/40 Window by 2010 (Christian Esguerra, "200,000 OFWs Seen as Potential Missionaries," *Philippine Daily Inquirer*, March 24, 2005: A4); and in 2009, PMA extended it to 1,000,000 (with 3,000 career missionaries) by 2020, which would constitute 10% of OFWs. Evangelicals and Pentecostals have been 8-10% of the 110 million Philippine population since the start of this century.

2 The International Labor Organization lists 11 million Filipinos living abroad as of March 2022, which is 10% of the population. "Why are OFWs Heroes of the Philippine Economy?" at https://www.bria.com.ph/articles/why-are-ofws-heroes-of-the-philippine-economy/.

3 Some of the best works on HM by Evangelicals are found in Vinay Samuel and C. Sugden, eds., *Mission as Transformation* (Oxford: Regnum, 1999).

4 In February 2022, Joshua Project reported there are still about 7,400 unreached people groups, and the absolute number of non-Christians is increasing; and, "There are more people alive today that do not know Christ than at any other time in history. In https://joshuaproject.net/assets/media/handouts/status-of-world-evangelization.pdf.

5 Some of the best works on HM by Evangelicals are found in Vinay Samuel and C. Sugden, eds., *Mission as Transformation* (Oxford: Regnum, 1999).

6 For its best practices, see Bryant Myers, *Walking with the Poor: Principles and Practices of Transformational Development* (Maryknoll: Orbis, 1999). Cf. T. Yamamori, et al. (ed.), *Serving with the Poor in Asia* (Monrovia: MARC, 1995), and T. Yamamori, et al (ed.), *Serving with the Urban Poor* (Monrovia: MARC, 1998).

7 Nicta Lubaale, "Doing Mission at the Margins of Society: Harnessing Resources of Local Visions," in *Mission Spirituality and Authentic Discipleship*, ed. W. Ma and K. Ross (Oxford: Regnum, 2013), 36-37.

8 Sarah Wambua, "Mission Spirituality and Authentic Discipleship: An African Reflection," in *Mission Spirituality and Authentic Discipleship*, ed. W. Ma and K. Ross (Oxford: Regnum, 2013), 67-71.

9 E.g., William Easterly, *The White Man's Burden: Why the West's Efforts to Aid the Rest Have Done So Much Ill and So Little Good* (New York: Penguin Press, 2006).

10 S. Corbett and B. Fikkert, *When Helping Hurts: How to Alleviate Poverty without Hurting the Poor and Yourself* (Chicago: Moody, 2009).

11 On Christian MED, see David Bussau and R. Mask, *Christian Microenterprise Development: An Introduction* (Oxford: Regnum, 2003).

12 On Christian social entrepreneurship, see S. Rundle and T. Steffen, *Great Commission Companies* (Downers Grove: InterVarsity, 2003).

13 Sarah Wambua, "Mission Spirituality," 71-72. Cf. T. Yamamori, et al. (ed.), *On Kingdom Business: Transforming Missions Through Entrepreneurial Strategies* (Wheaton: Crossway, 2003).

14 Cf. www.unstats.un.org/sdgs/.

15 Dena Freeman concludes, "When it comes to bringing about social and economic change, it seems that approaches that focus on individuals are rather more effective." *Pentecostalism and Development: Churches, NGOs and Social Change in Africa* (Basingstoke: Palgrave Macmillan, 2012), 25.

16 Bryant Myers, "Progressive Pentecostalism, Development and Christian Development NGOs: A Challenge and an Opportunity," *International Bulletin of Missionary Research 39*, no. 3 (2015), 118-119.

17 From the report of the Joint Working Group of the World Council of Churches and the Roman Catholic Church, "The Church: Local and Universal," Sec.15, in Growth in Agreement II, 866, cited in *The Church: Towards a Common Vision (Geneva: World Council of Churches*, 2013), Sec. E, No.31, 17.

18 *Evangelii Gaudium*, Sec. 134, 107.

19 Part IIA. Sec. 7, 39.

20 Most church traditions have historically adhered to the "just war" ethics, with violent struggle for justice as the last option under certain conditions.

21 On BECs, see Leonardo Boff, Ecclesiogenesis (Maryknoll: Orbis, 1986); Pablo Richard, *Death of Christendoms, Birth of the Church* (Maryknoll: Orbis, 1987); Michael Okyerefo, "Spirituality and Historic Mission Christianity in Africa: Ghanaization in Roman Catholicism," in *Mission Spirituality and Authentic Discipleship*, ed. W. Ma and K. Ross (Oxford: Regnum, 2013), 38-46; and Clemens Mendorca, "Mission According to the Catholic Church in Asia: A New Way of Being Church," in *Mission Spirituality and Authentic Discipleship*, ed. W. Ma and K. Ross (Oxford: Regnum, 2013), 127-138.

22 Cf. Leroy Rouner, *Human Rights and the World's Religions* (Notre Dame, IN: University of Notre Dame Press, 1988).

23 "Together Towards Life: Mission and Evangelism in Changing Landscapes." *International Bulletin of Missionary Research 38:2* (April 2014), Sec. 31, 12-13; also Sec. 30, 12; and Sec. 108, 69.

24 Ibid., Sec. 23, 10-11.

25 Cf. D. Johnston and C. Sampson, Religion: *The Missing Dimension of Statecraft* (New York: Oxford University Press, 1994); John De Gruchy, *Christianity and Democracy* (Cambridge: Cambridge University Press, 1995); Paul Gifford (ed.), *The Christian Churches and the Democratization of Africa* (Leiden: E. J. Brill, 1995); Paul Gifford (ed.), *Democracy and Civil Society in the Third World: Politics and New Political Movements* (Cambridge: Polity Press, 1995); and Africa has had the additional problem of various tribes forced to live in political boundaries not of their choice. Cf. Robert Aboagye-Mensah, "Mission and Democracy in Africa: The Problem of Ethnocentrism," *International Bulletin of Missionary Research 17* (1993),

130-133; and Najib Ghadbian, *Democratization and the Islamist Challenge in the Arab World* (Boulder, CO: Westview Press, 1997).

26 Cf. Paul Mattheny, "Ferment at the Margins: Philippine Ecclesiology Under Stress," *International Bulletin of Missionary Research 25:4* (October 2011), 203; and Matthews Ojo, "African Spirituality, Socio-Political Experience and Mission," in W. Ma and K. Ross (eds), *Mission Spirituality and Authentic Discipleship* (Oxford: Regnum, 2013), 47-61.

27 Mattheny, "Ferment," 203.

28 Jackie Smith, Ron Pagnucco, et al. (eds), *Social Movements and Global Politics: Solidarity Beyond the State* (Syracuse: Syracuse University Press, 1997).

29 E.G. Lode Wostyn, *Doing Ecclesiology: Church and Mission Today* (Quezon City: Claretian Publications, 1990), and Simon Chan, *Grassroots Asian Theology: Thinking the Faith from the Ground Up* (Downers Grove: InterVarsity Press, 2014).

30 Pentecostalism's "first wave" developed into Evangelical denominations, while the "second wave" emerged from and remained in the established denominations, quite significantly in the RCC and the Anglican Communion. The leadership and constituency of these two waves belong mainly to the educated middle class.

31 Samuel Escobar, "The Global Scenario at the Turn of the Century." In *Global Missiology for the 21st Century: The Iguassu Dialogue* ed. William Taylor (Grand Rapids: Baker, 2000), 40-42. Cf. Donald Miller and T. Yamamori, *Global Pentecostalism: The New Face of Christian Social Engagement* (Berkeley: University of California Press, 2007).

32 Myers, "Progressive Pentecostalism," 117-118.

33 Freeman, "Pentecostalism," 13, 24-25. Cf. Christian Jayakumar, *God of the Empty-Handed: Poverty, Power and the Kingdom of God*, 2nd ed. (Victoria, Aust.: Acorn Press, 2011).

34 Freeman, "Pentecostalism," 24-25.

35 Evangelii Gaudium, Sec. 102, 81-82.

36 Part IIA, Sec. 3, 35-36.

37 Freeman, "Pentecostalism," 24; and Myers, "Progressive Pentecostalism," 119.

38 On holism in pentecostal theology, see Myers, *Walking*, 61-81; and Al Tizon, *Transformation After Lausanne: Radical Evangelical Mission in Global-Local Perspective* (Eugene, OR: Wipf & Stock, 2008), 92-97, 141-148.

39 Cf. Nimi Wariboko, "Pentecostal Paradigms of National Economic Prosperity in Africa," in *Pentecostalism and Prosperity: The Socioeconomics of the Global Charismatic Movement*, ed. Amos Yong and K. Attanasi (New York: Palgrave Macmillan, 2012), 35-59.

40 *The Church*, Sec. 7, 7.

41 This is the popular substitute term for those who hesitate to use "Christian," due to its historical association with Christendom.

42 Samuel Escobar, "Evangelical Missiology: Peering into the Future at the 21st Century," in *Global Missiology for the 21st Century: The Iguassu Dialogue*, ed. William Taylor (Grand Rapids: Baker, 2000), 115 called for "pre-Constantinian church and mission."

43 David Lim, "Asian Mission Movements in Asia Today," *Asian Missions Advance 41* (October 2013): 29-36; and "Asia's House Church Movements Today," *Asian Missions Advance 52* (July 2016): 7-12. Cf. Lubaale, "Doing Mission," 30-32.

44 Wolfgang Simson, *Houses That Change the World* (Carlisle: Paternoster, 2001), and Radovan Zdero, *The Global House Church Movement* (Pasadena: William Carey Library, 2004). Cf. David Garrison, *Church Planting Movements* (Midlothian, VA: WIGTake Resources, 2004).

45 *Evangelii Gaudium*, Sec. 16, 16.

46 Theologically the BECs were conceived to be fully the church, but in practice they became cells attached to the local/parish church, just like the cells in today's mega-churches. Cf. C. Rene Padilla, "The Future of Christianity in Latin America: Missiological Perspectives and Challenges," *International Bulletin of Missionary Research 23*, no. 3 (July 1999): 105-112.

47 Part IIA, Sec. 3, 36.

48 Escobar, "The Global Scenario," 34. Cf. David Lim, "History and Ministry of Philippine Missions Association: Leading the Global Shift to Tentmaker Missions," Asian Missions Advance 41 (October 2013): 2-6.

49 David Lim, "Catalyzing 'Insider Movements' Among the Unreached," *Journal of Asian Mission 10*, no. 1-2 (March-September 2008): 125-145.

50 Cf. David Lim, "Towards a Radical Contextualization Paradigm in Evangelizing Buddhists," in Sharing Jesus in the Buddhist World, ed. D. Lim and S. Spaulding (Pasadena: William Carey Library, 2003), 71-94; and Charles Kraft, Christianity in Cultures (Maryknoll: Orbis, 1979).

51 "Together," Sec. 110, 70.

52 Cf. Harley Talman and J. J. Travis, ed., *Understanding Insider Movements: Disciples of Jesus within Diverse Religious Communities (*Pasadena: William Carey Library, 2015), and William Dyrness, *Insider Jesus* (Downers Grove: IVP Academic, 2016).

53 David Garrison, *A Wind in the House of Islam* (Monument, CO: WIGTake, 2014).

54 Roger Hedlund, "Previews of Christian Indigeneity in India," *Journal of Asian Mission 3*, no. 2 (2001): 213-230; Herbert Hoefer, *Churchless Christianity* (Pasadena: William Carey Library, 2001); Herbert Richard, *Following Jesus in the Hindu Context* (Pasadena: William Carey Library, 1999); and David Singh, "Sunder Singh and N V Tilak: Lessons for Missiology from the 20thCentury," in *Mission Spirituality and Authentic Discipleship*, ed. W. Ma and K. Ross (Oxford: Regnum, 2013), 139-156.

55 *The Cape Town Commitment,* Part IIC, Sec. 4, 47-48. Entitled "Love respects diversity of discipleship," it concludes with: "In the spirit of Barnabas who, on arrival in Antioch, 'saw the evidence of the grace of God' and 'was glad and encouraged them all to remain true to the Lord' (Acts 11:20-24)," appealing to the "guiding principle [of] the apostolic decision and practice in Acts 15:19," and to "exercise humility, patience and graciousness in recognizing the diversity of viewpoints, and conduct conversations without stridency and mutual condemnation (Romans 14:1-3)."

56 J. H. Bavinck, *An Introduction to the Science of Missions* (Philadelphia: Presbyterian & Reformed, 1960), 178-179, quoted in H. L. Richard, "All Things are Yours," in *Understanding Insider Movements,* ed. H. Talman and J. J. Travis (Pasadena: William Carey Library, 2015), 290.

57 This phrase was introduced and popularized in Samuel Huntington, "The Clash of Civilizations," Foreign Affairs 72, no.3 (1993): 22-49. There is a global program for Islamization since the Medina Conference in 1979, and Saudi Arabia promotes the extremist ideology of Wahhabism through madrassahs (schools).

BIBLIOGRAPHY

Aboagye-Mensah, Robert. "Mission and Democracy in Africa: The Problem of Ethnocentrism." *International Bulletin of Missionary Research 17* (1993): 130-133.

Boff, Leonardo. *Ecclesiogenesis*. Maryknoll: Orbis, 1986.

Bussau, David, and Russell Mask. *Christian Microenterprise Development: An Introduction*. Oxford: Regnum, 2003.

Chan, Simon. *Grassroots Asian Theology: Thinking the Faith from the Ground Up*. Downers Grove: InterVarsity Press, 2014.

Corbett, Steve, and Brian Fikkert. *When Helping Hurts: How to Alleviate Poverty without Hurting the Poor and Yourself*. Chicago: Moody, 2009.

De Gruchy, John. *Christianity and Democracy*. Cambridge: Cambridge University Press, 1995.

Dyrness, William. *Insider Jesus*. Downers Grove: IVP Academic, 2016.

Easterly, William. *The White Man's Burden: Why the West's Efforts to Aid the Rest Have Done So Much Ill and So Little Good*. New York: Penguin Press, 2006.

Escobar, Samuel. "The Global Scenario at the Turn of the Century." In *Global Missiology for the 21st Century: The Iguassu Dialogue*, edited by William Taylor, 25-46. Grand Rapids: Baker, 2000.

___. "Evangelical Missiology: Peering into the Future at the 21st Century." in *Global Missiology for the 21st Century: The Iguassu Dialogue,* edited by William Taylor, 101-122. Grand Rapids: Baker, 2000.

Esguerra, Christian. 2005. "200,000 OFWs Seen as Potential Missionaries." *Philippine Daily Inquirer*, March 24, 2005: A4.

Freeman, Dena, ed. *Pentecostalism and Development: Churches, NGOs and Social Change in Africa*. Basingstoke: Palgrave Macmillan, 2012.

Garrison, David. *Church Planting Movements*. Midlothian, VA: WIGTake Resources, 2004.

___. *A Wind in the House of Islam*. Monument, CO: WIGTake, 2014.

Ghadbian, Najib. *Democratization and the Islamist Challenge in the Arab World*. Boulder, CO: Westview Press, 1997.

Gifford, Paul, ed. *The Christian Churches and the Democratization of Africa*. Leiden: E.J. Brill, 1995.

___, ed. *Democracy and Civil Society in the Third World: Politics and New Political Movements*. Cambridge: Polity Press, 1995.

Hedlund, Roger. "Previews of Christian Indigeneity in India." *Journal of Asian Mission 3*, no. 2 (2001): 213-230.

Hoefer, Herbert. *Churchless Christianity*. Pasadena: William Carey Library, 2001.

Huntington, Samuel. "The Clash of Civilizations." *Foreign Affairs* 72, no. 3 (1993): 22-49.

Jayakumar, Christian. *God of the Empty-Handed: Poverty, Power and the Kingdom of God*, 2nd ed. Victoria, Aust.: Acorn Press, 2011.

Johnston, Douglas, and Cynthia Sampson. *Religion: The Missing Dimension of Statecraft*. New York: Oxford University Press, 1994.

Kraft, Charles. *Christianity in Cultures*. Maryknoll: Orbis, 1979.

Lubaale, Nicta. "Doing Mission at the Margins of Society: Harnessing Resources of Local   Visions." in *Mission Spirituality and Authentic Discipleship,* edited by Wonsuk Ma and K. Ross, 28-37. Oxford: Regnum, 2013.

Lim, David. "Towards a Radical Contextualization Paradigm in Evangelizing Buddhists." in *Sharing Jesus in the Buddhist World*, edited by D. Lim and S. Spaulding, 71-94. Pasadena: William Carey Library, 2003.

___. "Catalyzing 'Insider Movements' Among the Unreached." *Journal of Asian Mission 10*, no. 1-2 (March-September 2008): 125-145.

___. "History and Ministry of Philippine Missions Association: Leading the Global Shift to Tentmaker Missions." *Asian Missions Advance 41* (October 2013): 2-6.

___. "Asian Mission Movements in Asia Today." *Asian Missions Advance 41* (October 2013): 29-36.

___. "Asia's House Church Movements Today." *Asian Missions Advance 52* (July 2016): 7- 12.

Mattheny, Paul. "Ferment at the Margins: Philippine Ecclesiology Under Stress." *International Bulletin of Missionary Research 25*, no. 4 (October 2011): 202-207.

Mendorca, Clemens. "Mission According to the Catholic Church in Asia: A New Way of Being Church." in *Mission Spirituality and Authentic Discipleship,* edited by W. Ma and R. Ross, 127-138. Oxford: Regnum, 2013.

Miller, Donald, and T. Yamamori. *Global Pentecostalism: The New Face of Christian Social Engagement*. Berkeley: University of California Press, 2007.

Myers, Bryant. "Progressive Pentecostalism, Development and Christian Development NGOs: A Challenge and an Opportunity." *International Bulletin of Missionary Research 39*, no. 3 (2015): 115-120.

___. *Walking with the Poor: Principles and Practices of Transformational Development*. Maryknoll: Orbis, 1999.

Ojo, Matthews. "African Spirituality, Socio-Political Experience and Mission." In *Mission Spirituality and Authentic Discipleship,* edited by W. Ma and R. Ross, 47-61. Oxford: Regnum, 2013.

Okyerefo, Michael Perry Kweku. "Spirituality and Historic Mission Christianity in Africa: Ghanaization in Roman Catholicism." In *Mission Spirituality and Authentic Discipleship.* edited by W. Ma and R. Ross, 38-46. Oxford: Regnum, 2013.

Padilla, C. Rene. "The Future of Christianity in Latin America: Missiological Perspectives and Challenges," *International Bulletin of Missionary Research 23*, no. 3 (July 1999): 105-112.

Pope Francis. *Evangelii Gaudium*. Vatican, 2014. http://w2.vatican.va/content/ francesco/en/apost_exhortations/documents/papafrance   sco_esortazi- one-ap_20131124_evangelii-gaudium.html.

Richard, H. L. "All Things are Yours." In *Understanding Insider Movements*, edited by H. Talman and J. J. Travis, 289-292. Pasadena: William Carey Library, 2015.

Richard, Herbert. *Following Jesus in the Hindu Context.* Pasadena: Wm. Carey Library, 1999.

Richard, Pablo. *Death of Christendoms, Birth of the Church.* Maryknoll: Orbis, 1987.

Rouner, Leroy. *Human Rights and the World's Religions.* Notre Dame, IN: University of Notre   Dame Press, 1988.

Rundle, Steve, and Tom Steffen. *Great Commission Companies.* Downers Grove: InterVarsity, 2003.

Samuel, Vinay, and C. Sugden, ed. *Mission as Transformation.* Oxford: Regnum, 1999.

Simson, Wolfgang. *Houses That Change the World.* Carlisle: Paternoster, 2001.

Singh, David Emmanuel. "Sunder Singh and N V Tilak: Lessons for Missiology from the 20th Century." In *Mission Spirituality and Authentic Discipleship,* edited by W. Ma and R.Ross, 139-156. Oxford: Regnum, 2013.

Smith, Jackie, Ron Pagnucco, et al, ed. *Social Movements and Global Politics: Solidarity Beyond the State.* Syracuse: Syracuse University Press.

Talman, Harley, and J. J. Travis, ed. *Understanding Insider Movements: Disciples of Jesus Within Diverse Religious Communities.* Pasadena: William Carey Library, 2015.

Taylor, William D., ed. *Global Missiology for the 21st Century.* Grand Rapids: Baker, 2000. *The Cape Town Commitment.* Peabody, Mass.: Hendrickson, 2011. http://www.lausanne.org/content/ctc/ctcommitment.

The Church: Towards a Common Vision. Geneva: World Council of Churches, 2013. https://www.oikoumene.org/en/resources/documents/commissions/faith-and-order/iunity-the-church-and-its-mission/the-church-towards-a-common-vision.

Tizon, Al. *Transformation after Lausanne: Radical Evangelical Mission in Global-Local Perspective.* Eugene, OR: Wipf & Stock, 2008.

"Together Towards Life: Mission and Evangelism in Changing Landscapes." *International Bulletin of Missionary Research* 38, no. 2 (April 2014): 68-70. https://www.oikoumene.org/en/resources/publications/together-towards-life-mission- and-evangelism-in-changing-landscapes.

Wambua, Sarah. "Mission Spirituality and Authentic Discipleship: An African Reflection." *In Mission Spirituality and Authentic Discipleship.* edited by W. Ma and R. Ross, 62-73. Oxford: Regnum, 2013.

Wariboko, Nimi. "Pentecostal Paradigms of National Economic Prosperity in Africa." In *Pentecostalism and Prosperity: The Socioeconomics of the Global Charismatic Movement,* edited by Amos Yong and K. Attanasi, 35-59. New York: Palgrave Macmillan, 2012.

Wostyn, Lode. *Doing Ecclesiology: Church and Mission Today.* Quezon City: Claretian Publications, 1990.

Yamamori, T., B. Myers and D. Conner, ed. *Serving with the Poor in Asia.* Monrovia: MARC,1995.

Yamamori, T., B. Myers and K. Luscombe, ed. *Serving with the Urban Poor.* Monrovia: MARC,   1998.

Yamamori, T., B. Myers and Kenneth Eldred, ed. On Kingdom Business: Transforming Missions Through Entrepreneurial Strategies. Wheaton: Crossway, 2003.

Zdero, Rad. *The Global House Church Movement.* Pasadena: William Carey Library, 2004.

CULTIVATING A POLYMORPHIC *EKKLESIA*: LESSONS FROM HOUSE CHURCHES IN THE PHILIPPINES

Jason Richard Tan

INTRODUCTION

The COVID-19 pandemic painfully forced the global church to rethink its current expression of doing church. The ubiquitous *corporate church model* that requires a place for gathering, paid ministers and staff, and a board of elders to oversee the ministry has proven to be vulnerable to outside threats.

For the first time in a century, millions of churches around the world were forced to close their worship hall because of a health hazard. This government-imposed disruption did not just last for a few weeks; surprisingly, it lasted for two years and, for some, even more. The closure caused many churches in Metro Manila to lose up to 30% of their members; a few even closed the church permanently. In our denomination, a noticeable number of pastoral leaders left the city and went back to their hometowns.

This event should serve as a warning to the global church that if a pandemic could cause churches to stop meeting together, there is no reason why future threats couldn't have the same impact on our ministry. Therefore, in order to survive potential risks such as war, famine, economic collapse, or another pandemic, the global church should not only be aware of different types of church models but must also be ready to seamlessly incorporate or transition to a new one when needed.

This paper calls for churches to cultivate a *polymorphic* mindset to doing church, that is, whatever church model a faith community adopts, it must be ready and willing to "un-adopt" it and take on a new model as demanded by their changing context. In biology, polymorphism occurs when an animal, like a bird, has more than one possible variation in their gene that allows diverse feather pigmentation. In a sense, polymorphic churches must readily adopt different forms or types of church models as their context requires in order to preserve the faith community and continue its ministry and mission.

How can we cultivate a polymorphic mindset? We start by recovering the true nature of the word 'church' or *ekklesia* and explore how context has influenced the various models of ministry that we have today.

THE EVOLUTION OF EKKLESIA TO BASILICA

Over the centuries, our definition of the word "church" has evolved and shifted from "a gathering of believers" to a "building" or place of worship (e.g., a cathedral). Common English dictionaries define the word "church" as a place of worship or building. Sometimes, it refers to the organizational structure or what the church considers a ministry or activity.

Our love for tradition has kept the forms of our churches from evolving or changing. Church buildings and church models often become part of the tradition and, worse, dogma. Replacing the piano with an electronic keyboard often results in no small feud in churches, and how much more changing its ecclesiastical model. Yet, as we shall see, every ecclesiastical model is a product of context rather than of theological reflection or Scripture.

The word *ekklesia* in Koine Greek and the first-century Greco-Roman environment refers to an 'assembly of people' gathered for any particular purpose, be it political, social, or religious. However, in the New Testament, it is specifically nuanced to mean the "assembly of the people of God" (1 Peter 2:10). In Scripture, the word *ekklesia* is never used to refer to a building or a place but to the community of believers, even when this faith community requires a place as a meeting point.

In the NT, the *ekklesia* (faith community) often met in its leaders' homes (or oikos). The following passages show that the oikos are often differentiated from the *ekklesia*.

> *Greet also the church that meets at their house. Greet my dear friend Epenetus, who was the first convert to Christ in the province of Asia. (Romans 16:5, NIV)*

> *Give my greetings to the brothers at Laodicea, and to Nympha and the church in her house. (Colossians 4:15, NIV)*

> *... to Apphia our sister, to Archippus our fellow soldier and to the church that meets in your home (Philemon 1:2, NIV)*

Paul was careful to distinguish the place of meeting (oikos) from the church (*ekklesia*) and even takes a step further by saying,

> *The churches in the province of Asia send you greetings. Aquila and Priscilla greet you warmly in the Lord, and so does the church that meets at their house. (1 Corinthians 16:19, NIV)*

"The churches (plural - *ekklesia*i) of Asia greet you," and not "the oikos in Asia greet you." For Paul, the *ekklesia* is the church and not the oikos. Yet, prior to using the oikos (house, home, or household) as a gathering place, the church (*ekklesia*) often met at the Temple courts or in synagogues. However, when believers became the object of hostilities by Jewish authorities, they were prevented from meeting at these places, and the church (*ekklesia*) was forced to meet in their private homes (*oikos*). Therefore, using the home as a place of worship was born out of necessity since early church believers who needed a place of prayer and worship were not always welcome in synagogues.[1]

However, when persecution became severe, the believers decided to use other places for worship. Some believers in Rome met in catacombs. As distinguished New Testament scholar Everett Ferguson writes,

> *In some parts of the Empire this persecution of 258-259 was the bloodiest the church endured. On August 6 Pope Sixtus II was discovered conducting a service in the Catacomb of Praetextatus and was martyred, as were all seven of his deacons.[2] Emerson Manaloto, citing other scholars in his recent book, Let the Church Meet in Your House illustrated how the oikos developed over the first three centuries.[3]*

In places where religious gathering is allowed, believers renovated their private homes to accommodate more people. These *oikos* became what is known as domus ecclesiae, or private homes that were made bigger.

Then, as the context and situation changed, the *ekklesia* began to use public buildings for their regular meetings as a home could no longer accommodate the growing number of members. These public places of worship are known as *aula ecclesiae*. Then, at the start of the 4th century, as the Roman Empire converted to Christianity, the *ekklesia* was given their own place of worship, which is known as a *basilica*, a state-funded building meant for religious public assembly; this is perhaps the closest example of a modern-day megachurch.

The history of architecture of places of worship illustrates that the evolution of church buildings in the first three centuries resulted from context rather than theology or Scripture. The faith community or *ekklesia* found expressions in various forms as their situation allowed them.

At times, the faith community met in private homes (oikos) or extended private buildings (*domus ecclesiae*); at other times, they met in a public building (*aura ecclesiae*), which may have been rented or built as a place for public worship. Then, basilicas or cathedrals were erected as the Roman Empire changed its allegiance to Christ.

Yet, in all these expressions, the *ekklesia* remained the community of Christ; this is the true substance of what it means to be a church. The believing community is the *ekklesia* of Christ, not the form or structure that houses it.

The faith community (*ekklesia*) is the kernel or substance, while the church model or type of organized ministry is the husk or form that embodies the believing community. The husk may be in the form of a *house church, megachurch, corporate church, institutional church* (e.g., Anglicans or Catholics), churches in the marketplace or schools, or even in a virtual space. Each church model is a product of context and serves as a host of the faith communities (*ekklesia*) that best suits their situation or context.[4]

No church model is more divinely inspired or theologically correct than the other; there is no such thing as a normative church model or type. Church models are influenced by context and serve only to provide an organizational structure for the *ekklesia*. On the other hand, any of these forms may stagnate the *ekklesia* when the form becomes more important than the substance, which is the faith community itself. When tradition becomes the driving force of the community rather than love and careful theological reflection, the faith community suffers.

We must bear in mind that each church model (e.g., megachurch or house church) offers a venue for the *ekklesia* to express itself in all its fullness as Christ's community, depending on its context, de-mographical composition, and leadership structure. Yet, we must resist the temptation to think that our model of church ministry is the standard model for others to follow. As Paul Hiebert and Eloise Hiebert Meneses remark,

> *One thing is clear. There will be no one form of church that serves as the model for all the others. There will be house*

churches, store-fronts, local congregations, and megachurches; ethnic churches and integrated churches; churches that stress high ritual order and those that emphasize informality. No one of them can serve the spiritual needs of all people. And each of them has its own temptations and faults.[5]

Churches can no longer afford to stick to one model if they are to survive future threats to their existence. The believing community that we have come to know as the *ekklesia* must not only be ready to embrace different forms of doing church, but must also intentionally cultivate and explore other forms of church models, thus exhibiting a polymorphic mindset. Knowing these different models may even open new models for the church to consider as it grapples with existential threats.

LESSONS FROM THE HUMBLE HOUSE CHURCH MODEL

Given the various church models we know from history, one model has stood the test of time and context: the *house church model*. House churches have been growing steadily and silently for many decades, particularly in restricted countries hostile to Christianity. The actual number of house churches cannot be documented, but estimates show that it is between 4.8 - 22.6 million, with members ranging from 77 to 300 million, depending on how they are counted.[6]

The house church model is by far the most resilient church model Christianity has ever given birth to. It thrives in the most inhospitable places, defying political, religious, and ethnic persecutions. It flourishes even among the impoverished, marginalized, nomadic, and illiterate peoples despite no outside funding, elaborate programs, or access to the internet.

While many churches stopped meeting due to the COVID-19 pandemic, house churches saw little to no disruption in their day-to-day ministry. One network in the Philippines grew from 6 pastoral leaders to 180 house churches, with over 600 people attending their weekly worship in just 24 months. Moreover, 80% of those attending are new believers, and all its lay leaders are self-supported.[7] Amazingly, this story is not unique to them.

The house church model has been around since the birth of Christianity. Joel Comisky says, "The house-based ministry was so common that throughout the book of Acts, every mention of a local church or church meeting, whether for worship or fellowship, is a reference to a church meeting in a home."[8]

The house church model has proven over the centuries that it can survive and even thrive in any situation, including persecution, war, and famine. This is surely the case in many restrictive countries. Since believers are not allowed to gather in a physical church, the vast majority of churches meet in their homes, and strong networks of house churches are responsible for the explosive growth of Christianity in China and the Middle East.

The house church model is resilient because of the following traits that differentiate it from denomination-oriented church-planting programs. These attributes contribute to maintaining a movement's momentum and keeping any church resilient. Conversely, when these traits are altered due to changes in the church structure or model of ministry, the movement slows down.

1. SHARED LEADERSHIP

The quickest way to stop a movement is to implement control over what needs to be done and who gets to approve it or do it. Creativity and initiative are quickly stifled when those in power insist on controlling decisions. The New Testament Church survived severe persecution because it did not have a centralized power structure. Each leader felt empowered to gather the church in his home and, when possible, start a church in a new area without having to ask permission from their superiors.

In Acts 11, Luke writes that the church in Antioch was started by unknown men from Cyprus and Cyrene who didn't need the approval of the church in Jerusalem. The only thing left for the leaders of Jerusalem to do was to support the new initiative by sending Barnabas to them. Luke records,

> Now those who had been scattered by the persecution in connection with Stephen traveled as far as Phoenicia, Cyprus and Antioch, telling the message only to Jews. Some of them, however, men from Cyprus and Cyrene, went to Antioch and began to speak to Greeks also, telling them the good news about the Lord Jesus. The Lord's hand was with them, and a great number of people believed and turned to the Lord. News of this reached the ears of the church at Jerusalem, and they sent Barnabas to Antioch. (Acts 11:19-22, NIV)

New Testament churches were not dependent on a centralized governing body to do ministry but were free to act as the Spirit enabled them, and as a result, a robust ministry to the Gentiles was established. Although the Apostles were seen as sources of apostolic teachings, new initiatives in ministry rose apart from their oversight. The same can be said of the church in Rome, which unknown believers started.

A centralized, hierarchical church structure tends to respond more slowly to outside threats and new opportunities, often stifling innovation and creativity. Polymorphic churches must learn to decentralize power and share the leadership platform by making their organizational structure broader whenever there are new contextual challenges to consider.[9]

2. SHARED CORE VALUES AND IDENTITY

When governments forced churches to stop congregating, many churches didn't know how to respond to the situation because there was a lack of shared values. Church members of highly structured churches were used to just following instructions from their church leaders. In comparison, the early church understood what it meant to be a faith community. They knew enough about the basic teachings of Jesus and of the Apostles to lead, disciple, evangelize, plant new churches, and even discern false teachers (Revelations 2).

Furthermore, the early faith community strongly observed practical ministries such as prayer, worship, breaking of bread, hospitality, proclamation of the Gospel, and care for the sick. These ministries were part of their core values and corporate mission. It naturally and organically came out of their identity as God's assembly. We do not see any evidence of artificially created activities to enhance fellowship in the church. There were no seminars on hospitality or bridge events. Their ministries were identity-oriented, and they developed naturally, as did their relationships.

The shared mission and values of the house churches became their shared identity, which in turn created a network of house churches. Believers knew they could trust and depend on each other, yet they functioned independently when it came to day-to-day operations.

3. SHARED INFORMATION

The early church tested those who claimed to be apostles and examined the Scriptures to determine whether they taught the truth or not (Revelations 2:2). Even the Apostle Paul was placed under scrutiny, which shows that they are not easily impressed by popularity, position, or power: "Now the Bereans were of more noble character than the Thessalonians, for they received the message with great eagerness and examined the Scriptures every day to see if what Paul said was true" (Acts 17:11).

Their ability to engage in theological reflection stemmed from their extensive exposure to biblical teachings. But how was this achievable at a time when access to written Scripture was limited? Ancient civilizations heavily depended on the transmission of knowledge through oral traditions, which played a profound role in shaping the faith community's worldview. The narratives and parables found within the Scriptures served as the fundamental pillars of individuals' core values and their biblical perspectives, forming the basis for theological contemplation. One remarkable aspect of stories is their remarkable capacity for transmission and dissemination; thus, everyone had access to information.

On the other hand, when we control information, we stifle the growth of a church. I know a pastor who became upset with a teenager who started her own Bible study group after taking a short seminar on Discovery Bible Study (DBS). This format teaches leaders to facilitate a study of God's word and is used extensively among Disciple Making Movements (DMM). Instead of encouraging the child, the pastor made her stop and said, "You must finish the discipleship training program before you can start your own group." It is this kind of control of information that prevents churches from growing rapidly or even when responding to threats.

4. SHARED ACCOUNTABILITY

The early church was known for its generosity, especially to those in need, and their acts of kindness were rooted in their unwavering principle of holding each other socially accountable. The responsibility to care for those in need was paramount to the early church, and the leadership took it seriously by appointing deacons to make sure that Grecian widows were cared for properly as much as Jewish widows. This is recorded by Luke in the Book of Acts:

> *In those days when the number of disciples was increasing, the Grecian Jews among them complained against the Hebraic Jews because their widows were being overlooked in the daily distribution of food. So the Twelve gathered all the disciples together and said, "It would not be right for us to neglect the ministry of the word of God in order to wait on tables. Brothers, choose seven men from among you who are known to be full of the Spirit and wisdom. We will turn this responsibility over to them" (Acts 6:1-3, NIV).*

Due to the close-knit community of house churches in the Philippines, it is common for people to leave the care of their children to their neighbors and fellow believers. Some even feed and care for the pastor's kids until the parents arrive home from visitation. This sense of social accountability builds deeper bonds within the faith community.

5. SHAREABLE MODEL

The house church model is a simple shareable model. Any faith community may easily adapt to this model with little financial support or paid or professional staff. Adaptability to context is key to a resilient church community. Churches can transition from house church to corporate to house church or to megachurch, depending on their context and capacity. Gary Comer argues,

> Contrary to Christ's example, we have come to define 'disciple' by such criteria as knowledge, behavior, and fellowship, whereas Jesus saw discipleship as the embodiment of his heart, actions, skills, and fruit...Because of this misappropriation, we now have a pandemic of isolated Christians feverishly studying their Bibles but neither living what their Bibles are calling them toward nor seeing Scripture from a lens that distinguishes Jesus' methods in a transferable way.[10]

A POLYMORPHIC CHURCH MODEL

When the Philippine government restricted public gatherings, many small churches were forced to terminate their pastor or close the church. Small corporate-type churches rely heavily on physical gatherings to collect tithes and offerings for their weekly income, which is divided between the pastor's weekly stipend and rent. The physical restriction was a financial death sentence for these churches whose members belong to the lower socioeconomic group.

The situation forced many small and economically poor churches to rethink the way they do church. The majority tried to use an online platform for their weekly worship, but their lack of "IT know-how" and limited internet access was restrictive for their members, so these churches lost connections with their members, and the situation became a source of frustration for numerous pastors. A few, however, evolved and adapted the house church model. Six pastors in our network decided to pursue this option, and in just a few weeks, they saw a great change in their ministry. These six churches grew to a total of 180 small groups in just two years. They later called their group the *Simbahay House Church Network*.[11]

Switching to the house church model not only saved them money on rent and utilities but also proved to be a saving grace for the ministry. It allowed them to allocate their limited resources to support their pastor. Additionally, since pastors were relieved of the weekly responsibilities of sermon preparation and managing Sunday events, they had more time to visit families regularly. During these visits, families willingly contributed their tithes and offerings.

After two years, circumstances changed. With the easing of the pandemic, some of these churches chose to reconvene in rented spaces, while others opted to construct better church facilities. What sets them apart is that they have built a stronger faith community during their transition back to a corporate church model. This serves as a prime example of a polymorphic church community.

Nevertheless, transitioning from one church model to another entails more than just deciding to change one approach for another; it necessitates a shift in the ministry paradigm. The most challenging aspect of this transition is changing the mindset. So, how did these churches transition from one church form to another?

1. THEY TRANSITIONED FROM PREACHING TO FACILITATING LEARNING

The *Simbahay* house church pastors began empowering and teaching their small group leaders how to facilitate reflection from the Scriptures. Instead of preaching a sermon, leaders were taught to read from God's word, usually a story, and they involved everyone in reflecting and sharing their thoughts about the passage, including children. This approach not only made the reading of Scripture understandable, but it also enabled them to develop an organic approach to theological reflection.

Since house leaders are not expected to teach or preach, many of them are ready, willing, and happy to facilitate discussion. This made the difference. The group was not dependent on the pastor to provide theological reflection. Instead, they were empowered to do their own reflection.

2. THEY TRANSITIONED FROM TEACHING MEMBERS TO MENTORING LEADERS.

As they transitioned to a House Church Model, pastors were freed from preparing their weekly sermons, discipleship classes, or coordinating the weekly Sunday worship event. This gave the pastors more time to coach and mentor new leaders.

Since the house church leaders were forced to oversee their families, nearby church members, and neighbors for their weekly worship, this meant more leaders needed guidance. And as new leaders were formed, the faith community began to grow exponentially.

3. THEY TRANSITIONED FROM CHURCH ACTIVITIES TO SPIRITUAL AND SOCIAL ACCOUNTABILITY

Too often, corporate churches tend to create artificial social gatherings to justify coming together, such as men's fellowship, young couple's fellowship, or youth fellowship. As a result, most of our relationships are also artificial.

However, because of the pandemic, many people had real-world needs and struggles. As the faith community began to meet these basic needs for food, baby's milk, medicine, or transportation, the faith community began to develop deeper social connections. Some of these pastors even began visiting prisons and hospitals during the pandemic just so they could extend prayer and emotional support to people in their community.

The church began to have practical relevance in a time of need. And as the church walked with the people in their suffering, there was a reason for the community to rejoice with the church after the pandemic.

4. THEY TRANSITIONED FROM A PAID WORKER TO A BI-VO-CATIONAL MISSIONARY

Few things are more disheartening and demoralizing than losing one's livelihood. This is aggravated when you find your skills irrelevant and opportunities scarce. Millions of Filipinos lost their income as a result of the lockdown, and pastors are no exception. The vast majority of Filipino pastors and church planters can be likened to daily wage earners since they receive their pay or stipend weekly. This income mainly comes from the tithes and offerings of their church members.

Since the lockdown prohibited church gatherings, many pastors were left without financial aid or support for several weeks. As of this writing, the Philippine Council of Evangelical Churches (PCEC) is raising funds to help 40,000 pastors who are struggling to support their own families. The vast majority of these pastors come from a corporate church model where they are dependent on church salaries for their daily needs.

As for the house church pastors, they began to look for a livelihood in order to provide for their families so that they could keep ministering to their churches as bi-vocational ministers.

CONCLUSION

Our ministry paradigm must change because our reality has changed. Churches must be willing to adapt, or they will risk becoming irrelevant, or, even worse, cease to exist. In the book *The Great Dechurching*, Jim Davis and Michael Graham paint a grim reality of what is happening in America,

> *What we have witnessed in the last twenty-five years is a religious shift about 1.25 times larger but going in the opposite direction. In that time, about 40 million people have stopped attending church. More people have left the church in the last twenty-five years than all the new people who became Christians from the First Great Awakening, Second Great Awakening, and Billy Graham crusades combined. Adding to the alarm is the fact that this phenomenon has rapidly increased since the mid-1990s.[12]*

As our world becomes more hostile to Christianity and Christians become ever more polarized, the Church cannot sit idle and hope that all these changes will blow away. It needs to be adaptive and become a polymorphic church, intentionally "adopting" and "un-adopting" church models and ministry approaches without compromising the essence of Christ's teachings.

Like an emergency drill, churches should teach their faith community to transition to different models of doing ministry to keep the church resilient from any threat, even from itself. At worst, this approach to doing church might disrupt the current church program or the men's fellowship next year, but this may teach us to survive whatever threat comes our way.

Global instability is getting worse with each passing year, and the global church cannot afford to be idle and watch from the sidelines. It must be agile, discerning, and able to adjust quickly to any context. Yet, it seems that the greatest threat to the church does not come from the outside but from the inside. The greatest hindrance to the Kingdom of God is the institutionalized church that insists on spreading an institutionalized faith.

Paul Hiebert proposed "a fourth self" within the traditional "Three-Selfs Church," namely, the concept of self-theologizing.[13] In light of the current existential challenges facing the Church, there may be a need for the emergence of a another new self – one that can be described as "Self-Evolving."

Jesus proclaimed, "…and on this rock I will build my church, and the gates of Hades will not prevail against it" (Matthew 16:18); it is challenging to envision that He intended to establish an institutional, rigid, and unchanging organization rather than a dynamic, fluid movement. After all, only a dynamic and adaptable movement can effectively fulfill the command to "go and make disciples of all nations" (Matthew 28:19).

Occasionally, the Church requires what Leonard Boff refers to as "ecclesiogenesis" or the process of reinventing itself. Perhaps now is the opportune moment to contemplate the idea of a polymorphic church.

----

1 Met Q. Castillo, *The Church in Thy House* (Manila: Alliance Publishers and OMF, 1982), 48; Seipp, Derek Seipp, "Poised for Growth: First Century Methods Fueled the Early Church Movement," *Evangelical Missions Quarterly* 57-2 (2021): 38-40.

2 Everett Ferguson, "Persecution in the Early Church: Did You Know?," *Christianity Today* (1990) https://www.christianitytoday.com/history/issues/issue-27/persecution-in-early-church-did-you-know.html.

3 Emerson T. Manaloto, *Let the Church Meet in Your House* (Carlisle, UK: Langham Global Library, 2019), 33-37.

4 This paragraph is part of a paper presented during the 35th PCEC National Assembly, July 11-13, 2023, Marriott Hotel, Clark, Pampanga, titled *PCEC Healthy Church Framework: Magandang Samahan ng Mga Kinatawan ni Hesu-Cristo*, prepared and edited by Jason Richard Tan.

5 Paul Hiebert and Eloise Hiebert Meneses, *Incarnational Ministry: Planting Churches in Band, Tribal, Peasant, and Urban Societies* (Grand Rapids, MI: Baker Books, 1985), 328.

6 According to Justin Long, Director of Global Research for *Beyond* ministry, there are at least 77 million believers in 4.8 million house churches today (2020, 39). On the other hand, Wolfgang Simson's *Global Status Report on House Churches* (July 2021) estimates that there are "at least 22.6 million house churches worldwide with a total of around 300 million members." No one knows for sure how many churches there are in existence today. This is due to the difficulty in tracking movements and restrictions in many countries hostile to Christianity. Wolfgang Simson is the co-author (with George Barna) of *The House Church Book: Rediscover the Dynamic, Organic, Relational, Viral Community Jesus Started*, 2009.

7 The *Simbahay House Church Network* in the Philippines started during the pandemic.

8 Joel Comisky, "What Was the New Testament Church like?" *Christianity Today* SmallGroups. com March 9, 2015. https://www.smallgroups.com/articles/2015/what-was-new-testament-church-like.html. Accessed October 1, 2021; Castillo 1982.

9 See *Polycentric Mission Leadership* by Joseph Handley.

10 Gary S. Comer, *ReMission: Rethinking How Church Leaders Create Movement* (New Kensington, PA: Whitaker House, 2018), 64.

11 *Simbahay* is a Filipino play on words. *Simba* means "to worship" or "go to church," and *Bahay* means house or home.

12 Jim Davis and Michael Graham, *The Great Dechurching: Who's Leaving, Why Are They Going, and What Will It Take to Bring Them Back?* (Grand Rapids, MI: Zondervan, 2023), 5.

13 Paul G. Hiebert, *Anthropological Insights for Missionaries* (Grand Rapids, MI: Baker Book House, 1985), 195-224.

BIBLIOGRAPHY

Bonem, Mike. "Measuring What Matters: Despite the barriers, churches are finding effective metrics of soul transformation." *Christianity Today / Leadership Journal* (2012).

Bosch, David J. *Transforming Mission: Paradigm Shifts in Theology of Mission.* New York: Orbis Books, 1991.

Brafman, Ori and Rod A. Beckstrom. 2006. *The Starfish and the Spider: The Unstoppable Power of Leaderless Organizations.* New York: Penguin Group, 2006.

Castillo, Met Q. *The Church in Thy House*, 2nd Printing. Manila: Alliance Publishers, Inc, 1993.

Castillo, Met Q. *Let's Plant Viable Churches: A Manual for Church Planting in the Philippines.* Metro Manila: Wingspread Publishing House, 2021.

Castillo, Met Q. *The Church in Thy House.* Manila: Alliance Publishers and OMF, 1982

Coleman, Robert E. 1971. *The Master Plan of Evangelism* (Tenth printing). Classic.

Comer, Gary. *ReMission: Rethinking How Church Leaders Create Movement.* New Kensington, PA: Whitaker House, 2018.

Comisky, Joel. "What was the New Testament Church like?" *Christianity Today* SmallGroups.com March 9, 2015 added https://www.smallgroups.com/

articles/2015/what-was-new-testament-church-like.html. Accessed October 1, 2021

Davis, Jim and Michael Graham. *The Great Dechurching: Who's Leaving, Why Are They Going, and What Will It Take to Bring Them Back?* Grand Rapids, MI: Zondervan, 2023.

Ferguson, Everett. "Persecution in the Early Church: Did You Know?" *Christianity Today* (1990) https://www.christianitytoday.com/history/issues/issue-27/persecution-in-early-church-did-you-know.html

Handley, Joseph W. Jr. *Polycentric Mission Leadership: Toward a New Theoretical Model for Global Leadership.* Oxford: Regnum Books International, 2022.

Hiebert, Paul G. *Anthropological Insights for Missionaries.* Grand Rapids, MI: Baker Book House, 1985.

Hiebert, Paul and Eloise Hiebert Meneses. *Incarnational Ministry: Planting Churches in Band, Tribal, Peasant, and Urban Societies.* Grand Rapids, MI: Baker Books, 1985.

Lim, David (2017). "God's Kingdom as Oikos Church Networks: A Biblical Theology" *International Journal of Frontier Mission* 34:1-4: 25-35, https://www.ijfm.org/PDFs_IJFM/34_1-4_PDFs/IJFM_34_1-4-Lim.pdf (accessed January 21, 2022).

Manaloto, Emerson T. *Let the Church Meet in Your House.* Carlisle, UK: Langham Global Library, 2019.

McGavran, Donald A. 2009. "A Church in Every People: Plain Talk About a Difficult Subject." In *Perspectives on the World Christian Movement: A Reader.* 4th edition. Edited by Ralph D. Winter and Steven C. Hawthorne, 627-632. California: William Carey Library.

Seipp, Derek. "Poised for Growth: First Century Methods Fueled the Early Church Movement." *Evangelical Missions Quarterly* 57-2(2021), 38-40.

Smethurst, Matt. (2020) The Church Irreplaceable: Why God's People Must Gather. *Desiring God.* https://www.desiringgod.org/articles/the-church-irreplaceable?fbclid=IwAR0QvpqJ5gFbp59jsWjB8pmImUIJT04rhSpsHRNHKJR0ZUQ9AMF1KxFc9zk Accessed July 21, 2020.

Tan, Jason Richard. 2023. *Teach the Church to Make Disciples.* Paranaque City, Metro Manila: Church Strengthening Ministry.

_____2020. *Leading the Church in Turbulent Times.* Paranaque City, Metro Manila: Church Strengthening Ministry.

_____2019. "Matrices for Understanding Pastoral Leadership and Implications for the Global Landscape of Theological Education." *Insights Journal for Global Theological Education* 5, no. 1: 33-47. Accessed April 29, 2020. https://insightsjournal.org/matrices-for-understanding-pastoral-leadership-and-implications-for-the-global-landscape-of-theological-education/

White, James Emery. "A Metric that Matters: Why we've stopped counting members and started tracking "active attenders." *Christianity Today / Leadership Journal* (2014).

Yeh, Allen. (2016) *Polycentric Missiology: Twenty-First Century Mission from Everyone to Everywhere.* Downers Grove, IL: InterVarsity Press.

GENDER EQUALITY AND WOMEN LEADERSHIP

Donna Castillo-Tan

"I do not wish them [women] to have power over men, but over themselves."

> — *Mary Wollstonecraft,*
> *A Vindication of the Rights of Woman*
> *(1792)*

Gender equality is an enduring issue that spans generations. It is crucial to recognize the equal worth of women and treat them with respect and dignity. Various forms of gender inequality exist, some more overt than others. Addressing all these forms is essential. We must build a society and culture where women are valued and provided equal opportunities as men. Remember, women and girls comprise nearly half of the world's population[1] and hold significant potential.

The United Nations (UN) affirms that gender equality is a fundamental human right and is essential to achieving peaceful societies that promote full human potential and sustainable development.[2] Moreover, it has been presented and often stated that empowering women spurs productivity and economic growth.[3] Yet despite how important women's role is for the betterment of society and what empowering them can do to the world, nothing much is being done to give her the opportunities to participate. Women worldwide are generally not given equal opportunities and are subject to violence and abuse to this day. When there is improvement, it is extremely and painfully slow. According to the Global Gender Gap Report (or GGGR) 2023, it will take 131 years to close the gap and reach full parity.[4]

I. THE ISSUES AND CHALLENGES

"The indignities inflicted on women around the globe, intentionally or otherwise, is a moral burden we all must bear."[5]

The issue of gender equality, specifically women's rights, can be traced back to 1792 with its first advocate, Mary Wollstonecraft.[6] Since then, there has been notable progress in improving gender equality, but not at the pace we would like it to go. In the 2021 GGGR report, where the number of years to close was 135.6,[7] it stated that "closing the global gender gap [in 2021] has increased by a generation from 99.5 years to 135.6 years." This implies that "[A] nother generation of women will have to wait for gender parity."[8] This is if gender parity continues at the current rate. But what if it drastically slows down again due to another global pandemic, famine or war?

We simply cannot ignore the issues of gender inequality. It is embedded in almost every global issue the world faces.[9] This shows just how widespread the global issue of unequal treatment and/or mistreatment of women is.

We still have countries like Afghanistan, Syria, Yemen, Pakistan, Iraq, South Sudan, Sudan, Sierra Leone, Chad, and DR Congo that are listed as "Worst Countries to be a Woman in 2021"[10] The women in these countries, including South Asia and Sub-Saharan Africa, suffer abuse and violence in and outside their homes.[11] In sub-Saharan Africa, "the lifetime risk of dying in childbirth is 1 in 22 (compared to 1 in 4,800 in the United States); in China 39,000 baby girls die every year because they do not receive the same medical care that boys receive; ... a new bride is ritually burned to death in India approximately every two hours."[12] While poverty is an independent, and significant global issue, it does affect women and children more than it affects men. "Women living in poverty are at an increased risk of experiencing gender-based violence, lack of access to sexual and reproductive health care, and millions of girls are currently out of school."[13]

Even in a developed country like the United States, where there is vocal advocacy for gender and racial equality, gender inequality remains a persistent issue in the headlines. The challenge becomes more complex when considering the inclusion of non-binary and LGBTQ+ identities to the gender equality and women's rights table. What's even more puzzling is the irony that, while the U.S. supports women in their pursuit of equal rights, it allows a trans woman (formerly male) to compete in women's national swimming competitions and win, creating a controversial situation![14]

The news got worse during the COVID-19 pandemic. Women faced disproportionately high job losses, disruptions in education, and increased unpaid care responsibilities. Women's health services, already underfunded, suffered significant disruptions, affecting their sexual and reproductive health. Despite playing a central role in responding to COVID-19, including frontline healthcare work, women continue to be overlooked for the leadership positions they rightfully deserve.[15]

More than equal rights, women worldwide simply desire equal access to the opportunities that men get. "Women see hard work and equal opportunities as the most important aspects (88 percent and 85 percent respectively) to getting ahead in life".[16]

II. IMPLICATIONS TO SOCIETY

Gender Bias with Women in the Workplace

While the global issue of gender equality and women's rights affects all sectors of society,[17] one area to highlight is how the better and equal treatment of women has an ongoing effect on the economic development of the country. Kristoff and WuDunn, in their book Half the Sky report that both the UN and the World Bank openly recognized the "potential resource that women and girls represent,"[18] with the World Bank particularly stating that "Investment in girls' education may well be the highest-return investment available in the developing world."[19] Furthermore, the World Bank's 2001 study, Engendering Development Through Gender Equality in Rights, Resources, and Voice, stated "that promoting gender equality is crucial to combat global poverty"[20] with UNICEF concurring this in its major report arguing that "gender equality yields a 'double dividend' by elevating not only women but also their children and communities."[21]

Clearly, women empowerment is believed to accelerate the economic development of a country and, in effect, globally. The United Nations Development Programme (UNDP) further summed up all research in this way: "Women's empowerment helps raise economic productivity and reduce infant mortality. It contributes to improved health and nutrition. It increases the chances of education for the next generation."[22]

Yet sadly, these reports still need to have an impact in society. E. Bayeh in a study on the correlation[23] of gender equality to the economic development of Ethiopia, shares that,

> ...the role of women across different dimensions of sustainable development is less reflected in the country. The use of a women's labour force in the economic development of the country is minimal. The political sphere of the country is, by and large, reserved for men alone. The place of women in society is also relegated to contributing minimally to the social development of the country. In addition, women's rights are not properly being protected in order for women to participate in various the issues of their country but are subjected to abysmal violations.

In South Asia, fewer than one in four women hold a paying job, which is less than half of the global average.[24] In the United States, it is reported, "Overall, women who were full-time, year-round employees made 83 cents for every dollar men made in 2020, based on median earning data from the Census Current Population Survey. That means women are paid about 17% less than men." We also need to factor in how culture may dictate that certain jobs are better suited for men and certain jobs better suited for women. For example, nurses and babysitters are expected to be women, and firemen and construction workers are expected to be men.

In the past two years of the Global Pandemic alone, women suffered steeper job losses than men, with the number of women in the workforce down by 54 million in 2020 and a total of 45 million women who left the labor market altogether.[25] A survey done in the Philippines showed that "22 percent of female professionals agree that they have fewer career advancement opportunities, and 14 percent claim they are paid less than men in their profession...[while] half of working women in the Philippines have experienced that their being a woman played a role in missing out on opportunities, promotion, and pay."[26] Furthermore, due to the global lockdown, "88 percent of Filipinos have started working from home"[27] and among them are many working women, but they face more barriers than usual. Most of the respondents named the lack of time as the top barrier for women in achieving opportunities, and this is likely due to having to juggle remote work and family responsibilities.[28] "Close to half of the working mother respondents (47 percent) said they are struggling to balance their work and household responsibilities, with 42 percent saying their duties at home are getting in the way of their career development."[29] Thus, the reality is women are still at a disadvantage in the workforce. One reason is that opportunities are still limited and, in some cases, even scarce; another reason is the need to be full-time on the domestic front and the challenge to balance both. "Women are still disadvantaged by their greater domestic labor commitments and impaired access to well-paid jobs; and, in extreme cases, denied the right to live."[30]

GENDER BIAS WITH WOMEN AND THE JUSTICE SYSTEM

Gender inequality is a significant predictor of poverty and injustice in our world today.[31] Justice involves fair, equal treatment in all aspects of life, regardless of one's background. Women often experience marginalization and are frequently victims of discrimination, persecution, abuse, and violence.

Violence has such a strong connection to women that when one thinks of a victim of violence, most would assume it is a woman. Violence against women and girls not only devastates their lives but, even more, undermines the building of strong democracies and just societies.[32]

Gender Bias with Women and the Dilution of the Issue

Despite societal progress through various eras and cultural shifts, women still bear the burden of devaluation, albeit in different forms. The fight for women's equality remains a profound struggle in many countries. However, today, the focus on women's rights and gender equality seems to be overshadowed by the ideologies of the postmodern and even posthuman generation. Gender bias is no longer solely about women; it now includes trans-women, trans-men, gay, lesbian, bisexual, asexual, queer, and fluid identities. Multiple advocacies have joined the conversation, extending beyond women's issues.

Real women may never reach the end of their quest for equal rights, fair treatment, and appropriate value due to the additional issues and baggage now being added to their struggle.

III.   THE PHILIPPINE SETTING

The Philippines has a history of strong women warriors and leaders like Urduja, Gabriela Silang, and Melchora Aquino (Tandang Sora). It has also had two women presidents: Corazon Aquino and Gloria Arroyo, and women senators as early as 1947 (Geronima Josefa Tecson).[33] The Philippines could indeed be a leader in gender equality. After all, it has been said,

> *At the core, Philippine society is a matriarchal society...women directly and indirectly run the family, businesses, and institutions. Women also, most [sic] often than not, by default, become the family's treasurer... The underlying power and strength of*

Pinays is rooted in pre-colonial indigenous Philippine society where equal importance was given to women and men. Women were traditionally entitled to property, to engage in trade, and, in the absence of a male heir, hold the position of village chieftain. Women were also powerful and esteemed high priestesses and healers known as babaylans or catalonans. Such was the power of women in pre-colonial Philippine society that they also had the right to divorce their husbands if they chose to do so.[34]

It is on a high note that the country can boast of its ranking 16th in the Global Gender Gap Index 2023, with a gender gap score of 0.791 and an improvement of +3 points since 2022.[35] The Philippines is the lone Asian country on the top 20 list!

According to research, women's status in the Philippines can be seen as highly advanced compared to women in other nations, particularly regarding education, professional opportunities, political representation, and legislative involvement.[36] Even within the country, a consensus exists among people regarding this perception, with 51% of Filipinos believing that gender equality has improved in the country and is not as significant an issue as it was during their parents' time.[37] This represents a significant achievement, as Ryanne Co of Tatler Asia points out. Co attributes the Philippines' strong position in terms of gender parity or equality to its matriarchal system, which has elevated it above the United Kingdom, Canada, and Australia in this regard—an institution rooted in the pre-colonial era.[38] Moreover, the Philippine Constitution recognizes the vital role of women in the country's well-being and ensures their equal treatment.[39]

Rank	Country	Score		Score change	Rank change
		Score	0–1	2022	2022
1	Iceland	0.912		+0.004	·
2	Norway	0.879		+0.034	+1
3	Finland	0.863		+0.003	-1
4	New Zealand	0.856		+0.014	·
5	Sweden	0.815		-0.007	·
6	Germany	0.815		+0.014	+4
7	Nicaragua	0.811		+0.001	·
8	Namibia	0.802		-0.005	·
9	Lithuania	0.800		+0.001	+2
10	Belgium	0.796		+0.003	+4
11	Ireland	0.795		-0.010	-2
12	Rwanda	0.794		-0.017	-6
13	Latvia	0.794		+0.023	+13
14	Costa Rica	0.793		-0.003	-2
15	United Kingdom	0.792		+0.012	+7
16	Philippines	0.791		+0.009	+3
17	Albania	0.791		+0.004	+1
18	Spain	0.791		+0.002	-1
19	Moldova, Republic of	0.788		-0.001	-3
20	South Africa	0.787		+0.005	·
21	Switzerland	0.783		-0.012	-8

Figure 1: Screenshot of TABLE 1. The Global Gender Gap Index 2023 rankings, page 11 of the Global Gender Gap Report 2023 (Source: https://www3.weforum.org/docs/WEF_GGGR_2023.pdf)

However, some sectors have concerns about the current state of gender equality and women's rights in the Philippines.[40] There are disparities on the ground, with women experiencing domestic violence, sexual abuse, economic disadvantages, workplace discrimination, exploitation as migrant workers, prostitution, and displacement due to conflict.[41] A 2022 report states that "One in four Filipino women experienced gender-based violence, and 41% of victims did not seek help."[42] One would think that such would be unheard of in these postmodern times!

In the early months of the onset of the COVID-19 pandemic in the country, a local birthing center reported an alarming spike in pregnancies and the shocking reality that four of ten women who came to the clinic for prenatal checkups were between thirteen and eighteen years old.[43] This would be the reality that barely verifies the studies. There is a strong disparity between what is reported and what is real.

Meanwhile, the survey respondents who acknowledged improvement in gender equality also recognize the persistence of gender bias in the workplace, with about 31% who believe gender equality is challenging to achieve.[44] Despite the country's high rank in gender equality, the road to full parity seems to be long from seeing fulfillment. However, research indicates that this perspective may arise from broader societal views on gender. According to the same survey, 74% consider gender equality an important value for a fair society; however, more than half of the respondents believe that it has already made satisfactory progress.[45] This mindset may lead to complacency, even though the Philippines is leading in this area, in Asia and globally. Such a prevailing mindset could significantly delay women's quest for equal opportunities and fair treatment, rendering them voiceless and helpless.

I recall the 2019 incident involving Gretchen Custodio Diez, a transgender woman denied access to the women's restroom by a janitress.[46] Her experience gained significant attention on social media, and unfortunately, the janitress faced much criticism while people rallied to defend Diez. I wondered where the defenders for the janitress were. It seemed like no one, including women's rights groups, stood up for her. Everyone seemed to prioritize Gretchen's "rights" over the rights of the janitress who was simply doing her job. It was political correctness that overshadowed the injustice, with society seemingly more willing to criticize a woman just doing her job than a man insisting on using the ladies restroom.

Meanwhile, signs of inequality continue to persist in the form of devaluation, racy jokes, stereotypical portrayals in movies, and the way women present themselves to others. These factors continue to show that women and men are not treated and valued equally.

No Longer a Matriarchal or Patriarchal Society, but a Gender Equal Society.

Addressing this disparity might involve acknowledging and discussing both "matriarchal" and "patriarchal" perspectives in our conversations. These discussions often perpetuate the divide. As mentioned earlier, many historians and sociologists believe that "The Philippines has indigenous roots in matriarchal systems"[47] dating back to the pre-colonial period. The shift from equality between men and women to a patriarchal culture occurred with the arrival of colonizers. The long history of colonialism subjected women, teaching them to be subordinate to men and limiting their roles to homemaking.[48] However, remnants of our heritage of gender equality still surface in the current society. Consequently, there continue ongoing debates and arguments about gender equality, with representatives from both sides asserting and defending their due positions in society. Further, there may be no need to use "matriarchal" and "patriarchal" terms because that has to do with kinship lineage, which is another topic.

After all, numbers don't lie. The Philippines ranks 16th on the Global Gender Gap Parity report, surpassing countries like Switzerland (21st) and the United States (43rd), highlighting the country's treatment of both men and women. Despite personal observations suggesting otherwise, Filipino women face few or no restrictions in pursuing their ambitions or careers. The police force, for instance, has seen an increase in the number of women applicants, and there is a noticeable increase in women CEOs, CFOs, and business owners. Women have taken on prominent roles in government, including the Senate, Congress, and positions such as governors, mayors, and even the presidency. Women holding leadership positions is not uncommon in the Philippines.[49]

IV.   MISSIONAL IMPLICATIONS AND CHURCH APPLICATION

The Lord announces the word, and the women who proclaim it are a mighty throng: Psalm 68:11

In Genesis 1:27, God created both man and woman in His own image, emphasizing equality from the beginning. They were intentionally made equal in God's eyes, possessing equal value ("And God saw all [including man and woman] He had made, and behold, it was very good." Genesis 1:31 NASB), equal tasks ("God blessed them, and said to them..." Gen 1:28), and equal benefits (both had the same freedom and restrictions in the garden of Eden, Gen 1:29-30). Neither was created as having more (or less) value than the other.

The creation of Adam before Eve does not imply positional status before God. It is evident that even if Adam was created first and Eve second, she was not a second thought. Eve was created as an intentional act. God saw that Adam would not be able to do the work alone, and therefore he needed a "suitable helper," a *kenegdo ezer*. The word *kenegdo* implies someone who completes the other half; thus, creating Eve was meant to complement Adam.[50] It also implies someone who stands in front, to protect Adam, and not just alongside as an assistant nor at the back as a subordinate.

Conversely, the term *"Ezer,"* which means "help," takes on a different connotation when considering its other usages outside of the two instances in Genesis 2:18 and 20 that specifically refer to the woman God created. In these other references, *"Ezer"* is a reliable warrior or dependable defender. These instances include God acting as Israel's ally in war and other nations coming to Israel's aid.[51]

When God created man and woman, He established distinct roles for them, but their intrinsic value remained equal in His eyes. The subordination of women in other Bible stories stems from cultural influences of the people, not from God's intentions. This is why God often made deliberate efforts to emphasize the importance of women, such as when He revealed Himself as "El Roi" to Hagar, a woman and a slave. (Genesis 16). God highlighted women like Rahab in the Hall of the Faithful (Hebrews 11:31), enabled Deborah to serve as a Judge in Israel despite societal norms (Judges 4), revealed His identity as the Messiah to the Samaritan woman at the well (John 4:5-30), and first appeared as the risen Lord to Mary Magdalene (John 20:14-16).

We also encounter significant examples of influential women in the early church, such as Junia, acknowledged as an outstanding apostle (Romans 16:7). Additionally, we see the husband-wife duo of Pricilla and Aquila (Romans 16:3), with Pricilla being mentioned ahead of her husband, suggesting a more prominent leadership role. Dorcas was also noted as a disciple of Jesus in Acts. These women's names underscore their importance and leadership positions in early church history. In his letters, Paul demonstrates respect for women, recognizing their roles as ministry partners and their contributions to the church. He honors notable women like Lydia, Phoebe, Junia, Priscilla, Euodia, and Syntyche. It is essential to understand that the passages where Paul seems to address women's roles "are not general statements about women in the church. Paul actually loved and valued women, and they were among his ministry partners."[52]

As women hold half the sky, so also do they make up half the church. In her book, *Half the Church: Recapturing God's Global Vision for Women*, Carolyn Custis James shows us how as a church, we are guilty of discriminating women. We delegate to her the menial jobs like kitchen work, and back-office work; while the "more important" matters of the church, like evangelism, outreach and leadership are tasks often given to the men.[53] The men go out to the streets to evangelize while the women should only be tasked to meal preparation for the men when they return. And yet, women compose half of the church! And so, if this is the case, then the church is wasting away more than half of its important resources (women) by not releasing them to exercise their gifts and capacities!

On Women in Church Leadership Roles in the Philippines

The pressing question that demands an answer is: why does the treatment of women as equals change in the church setting? If, based on the evidence presented earlier, the Filipino woman is not only capable but often exceeds expectations in various areas of society, why are women confined to very specific roles, responsibilities, and tasks when it comes to church ministry?

One colleague shared that she is a trained military officer in the Armed Forces of her country, possessing leadership experience, but when it came to her church situation, she was not allowed leadership roles. Instead, she was suggested only to certain roles that women are expected to fill.

Tira and Wan, in their paper on a Filipino case study of diaspora, say, "Filipino women have a vital role in fulfilling the Great Commission [with particular reference to]...the thousands of household maids deployed in high places in the Buddhist, Jewish, and Islamic world."[54] These women are strategically placed inside homes of people of influence in these cultures, with great opportunities to influence the lives of their employers and their children with the gospel, something for which "Western conventional missionaries do not have the privilege."[55] While at first we might not think too highly of these women since they are, after all, "just maids," in God's kingdom building what they do for God is of utmost honor! Tira and Wan even liken the influence and position these Filipino women are in to the likes of Jochebed, who raised Moses, though her own child biologically, but officially belonging to the Pharoah's daughter, to become an important figure in both Egypt and Israel.[56]

It would be detrimental for the church to underestimate women and restrict their contributions to advancing God's Kingdom. For example, in preaching and teaching, the church often receives only wisdom from male educators and preachers, resulting in a one-sided perspective. The church is at a disadvantage when it fails to recognize and utilize the gifts and capabilities of all individuals, including women, in spreading the gospel. God Himself confirms the significant potential of women as bearers of the Good News when the Psalmist declared, "The Lord gives the command; The women who proclaim the good news are a great army" (Psalm 68:11 NASB).

God created women with a purpose, and when the church restricts their participation and voices, it falls short of fulfilling God's intended purpose. Even more concerning, it could be interpreted as questioning God's design of women. When we doubt a woman's capabilities, skills, and worth, we doubt God's plan in creating her. Are we implying that God made an error when He created women? Are we suggesting that they do not play a vital role in advancing the gospel or building up the church? However, it is evident that God did not create Eve, whom He declared to be made in His image, as an inferior being.

Further, it is even ironic that Philippine missions recognize the "trend in Philippine feminization in missions continues,"[57] meaning that most Filipino missionaries, whether as full time career missionaries or tentmaking missionaries or OFW kingdom workers, are women. There is no problem with women being missionaries. In fact, there is excitement. But the tide shifts for her in the church setting. It simply does not make sense.

If Filipinos readily acknowledge women in leadership positions in areas outside of the church, such as government, business, and companies, then the same recognition should extend to their leadership roles within the church. When a woman serves as the CEO of a business or a lady mayor, her stature and leadership abilities grant her a platform. However, this recognition often does not carry over to the church setting. While such prominent figures may be invited to give special lectures, serve as guest speakers at women's events, and occupy prominent seats in the church, they are rarely granted the privilege to stand on the same platform as the pastor and deliver the Word of God.

My point here is not primarily about granting women grand titles or the highest positions but rather about enabling women to minister in the same capacities as men, giving them the space and freedom to exercise their spiritual gifts within the safe confines of the Body of Christ. Gender should not be a factor when it comes to utilizing spiritual gifts for the benefit of the church. Imagine telling someone they cannot exercise their gift of hospitality, giving, or mercy based on gender. When did spiritual gifting become gender-based? It's not about gender; it's about the appointment of the Holy Spirit.

Gender equality and women's rights are deeply ingrained issues not only in society but sadly, also within the church, where it should not be an issue. However, the responsibility for advocating for the equal treatment of not just women but of all people falls heavily on the church itself, which proclaims believers to be "one in Christ" and to be free in Christ Accordingly, we must act on what we proclaim when we say "there is no longer Jew or Greek, slave or free, male or female. For you all are one in Christ Jesus." (Galatians 3:28, NLT).

Let Woman be the Image Bearer She was Created and Designed to be.

Amidst the chaos and confusion from discussions on gender equality, many women have found themselves lost, afraid, and uncertain about their identity and potential. Where can women discover a safe space to be themselves and fulfill their God-given purpose? Where can they speak without judgment, act without criticism, laugh without misunderstanding, and love without fear of hurt? The answer lies at the feet of Jesus.

At Jesus' feet, there is always a reserved place for women, as Mary of Bethany confirmed. Even if taking our place at His feet might lead to trouble, where people may judge, ridicule, criticize, or attempt to confine us to certain roles, at Jesus' feet, women will find safety, acceptance, and the assurance of being His beloved daughters. Therefore, we who also sit at Jesus' feet should welcome her as equal. We, who also sit at Jesus' feet should make sure her place there is safe, affirming, loving and empowering.

And until the day comes when the world fully recognizes women's roles and contributions, those who understand the importance of women's voices in the church and society must serve as their willing advocates. We must be their voice, tirelessly advocating for their worth, visibility, and full acceptance as equally valuable heirs to the kingdom of God. We must fight for them to be heard and listened to as equally valuable spokespersons for Jesus Christ and proclaimers of the Good News (Psalm 68:11).

We must see more and more women confidently stepping into what God has called them and designed them to do in all areas, not just teaching or preaching, but in whatever good work God has created them for (Ephesians 2:10). And let us not forget that for the global church to effectively and significantly move forward, it is increasingly important that Christians, men **and** women, brothers **and** sisters, work together.

----

1 As of October 4, 2023, World population live reported 4.98 billion males in the world (50.5% of the world population) and 4.02 females (49.5%). https://countrymeters.info/en/World, October 4, 2023. This would be an estimated gender ratio of 101 males per 100 females.

2 "Gender Equality," *United Nations*, https://www.un.org/en/global-issues/gender-equality, accessed April 14, 2022.

3 "Gender Equality," *United Nations*.

4 The Global Gender Gap Report 2023, June 2023, *World Economic Forum*, p. 5, https://www3.weforum.org/docs/WEF_GGGR_2023.pdf.

5 Regina Mahone, "Half the Sky: Turning Oppression into Opportunities for Women Worldwide," review of *Half the Sky*, by Nicholas Kristof and Sheryl WuDunn. *Philanthropy News Digest*, April 15, 2016, https://philanthropynewsdigest.org/features/book-reviews/half-the-sky.

6 University of Exeter, "A brief history on gender (in)equality," *Future Learn*, https://www.future-learn.com/info/courses/understanding-gender-inequality/0/steps/66837, accessed April 14, 2022.

7 https://www.weforum.org/reports/global-gender-gap-report-2021.

8 Gender equality and women's rights are embedded in the global issues of poverty, hunger, good health and well-being, quality education, gender equality, clean water and sanitation, affordable energy, decent work, and economic growth; industry, innovation and infrastructure, reduced inequalities, sustainable cities and communities, sustainable consumption and production including climate action, and peace, justice, and strong institutions. In "What does gender equality look like today?" UN Women, October 6, 2021, https://www.unwomen.org/en/news/stories/2021/10/feature-what-does-gender-equality-look-like-today

9 Gender equality and women's rights are embedded in the global issues of poverty, hunger, good health and well-being, quality education, gender equality, clean water and sanitation, affordable energy, decent work, and economic growth; industry, innovation and infrastructure, reduced inequalities, sustainable cities and communities, sustainable consumption and production including climate action, and peace, justice, and strong institutions. In "What does gender equality look like today?" UN Women, October 6, 2021, https://www.unwomen.org/en/news/stories/2021/10/feature-what-does-gender-equality-look-like-today

10 Leah Rodriguez, "The 10 Best and Worst Countries to be a Woman in 2021," *Global Citizen*, October 22, 2021, https://www.globalcitizen.org/en/content/best-worst-countries-for-women-gender-equality/

11 Rodriguez, "The 10 Best and Worst."

12 Mahone. "Half the Sky."

13 Rodriguez, "The 10 Best and Worst."

14 https://www.usatoday.com/story/sports/college/2022/03/18/lia-thomas-trans-woman-win-ncaa-swimming-championship/7088548001/

15 "What does gender equality look like today?" UN Women, October 6, 2021, https://www.unwomen.org/en/news/stories/2021/10/feature-what-does-gender-equality-look-like-today

16 Limos, "Remote Work."

17 The GGGR measures gender equality in four areas: political empowerment, economic participation and opportunity, educational attainment, and health and survival, with the gender gap on political empowerment as still the largest of the four gaps tracked, with only 22.1% closed to date and health and survival being the closest to parity at 96%. Of the 146 countries covered by the 2023 index, the Health and Survival gender gap has closed by 96%, Educational Attainment by 95.2%, Economic Participation and Opportunity by 60.1% and Political Empowerment by 22.1%. In https://www3.weforum.org/docs/WEF_GGGR_2023.pdf, p. 9-12

18 Nicholas D. Kristoff and Sheryll WuDunn, *Half the Sky: Turning Oppression into Opportunities for Women Worldwide* (New York: Vintage Books, 2009), p. xx.

19 Lawrence Summers in Kristoff and WuDunn, p. xx.

20 Kristoff and WuDunn, p. xx.

21 Kristoff and WuDunn, p. xx.

22 Kristoff and WuDunn, p. xx.

23 Endalcachew Bayeh, "The role of empowering women and achieving gender equality to the sustainable development of Ethiopia," *Pacific Science Review B: Humanities and Social Sciences*, Volume 2, Issue 1, 2016, Pages 37-42, https://doi.org/10.1016/j.psrb.2016.09.013.

24 Rodriguez, "The 10 Best and Worst."

25 "What does gender equality look like today?" UN Women, October 6, 2021, https://www.unwomen.org/en/news/stories/2021/10/feature-what-does-gender-equality-look-like-today

26 Mario Alvaro Limos, "Remote Work Is a Heavier Burden on Filipino Women Than Men, According to Study," *Esquire*, March 3, 2021,https://www.esquiremag.ph/life/women/filipino-women-work-opportunities-linkedin-a00293-20210303-lfrm?utm_source=Facebook-EsquireMoney&utm_medium=Siteshare&utm_campaign=20220414-fbnp-life-filipino-wom-en-work-opportunities-linkedin-a00293-20210303-lfrm-fbold&fbclid=IwAR1z-rpKrnCks-vhGmSkTeFY63YaZvrVdh0FQG1u2awwk-PjMXw6n079B3sE

27 Limos, "Remote."

28 Limos, "Remote."

29 Limos, "Remote."

30 Dilli, Carmichael, and Rijpma, "Introducing the Historical Gender."

31 "Women's Rights and Gender Justice," *Oxfam*, https://www.oxfamamerica.org/explore/issues/womens-rights-and-gender-justice/, accessed April 22, 2022.

32 "Women's Rights," Oxfam.

33 Nigel Tan, "Filipinas who were first in Philippine History," Rappler, March 21, 2014, https://www.rappler.com/newsbreak/iq/53470-filipinas-first-ph-history/

34 Wilfred Gacula, "The Power of Pinays – A Short Essay," *SOMA Pilipinas,* accessed October 4, 2023 at https://www.somapilipinas.org/community-1/powerofpinays#:~:text=At%20its%20core%2C%20Philippine%20society,default%2C%20become%20the%20family%27s%20treasurer

35 https://www3.weforum.org/docs/WEF_GGGR_2023.pdf, p.11

36 Gender Profile of the Philippines https://www.jica.go.jp/activities/issues/gender/reports/ku57pq00002hdv3w-att/phi_2008_summary_en.pdf

37 Limos, "Remote Work."

38 Ryanne Co, "Gender Parity In the Philippines: Is the Country Truly As Progressive As It Seems?" Tatler Asia, August 7, 2021, https://www.tatlerasia.com/power-purpose/ideas-education/gender-parity-in-the-philippines.

39 The 1987 Constitution states two prominent provisions. The first is in the Declaration of Principles Article II Section 14 which asserts , *"The State recognizes the role of women in nation-building and shall ensure the fundamental equality before the law of women and men."* Additionally, according to the Article XIII-Labor: Section 14, *"The state shall protect working women by providing safe and healthful working conditions taking into account their maternal functions, and such facilities and opportunities that will enhance their welfare and enable them to realize their full potential in the service of the nation"* from Carlos Antonio Anonuevo, "An Overview of the Gender Situation in the Philippines," Friedrich-Ebert-Stiftung Philippine Office, September 2020, accessed October 4, 2023 from https://library.fes.de/pdf-files/bueros/philippinen/50069.pdf.

40 Co, 2021.

41 Gender Profile of the Philippines https://www.jica.go.jp/activities/issues/gender/reports/ku57pq00002hdv3w-att/phi_2008_summary_en.pdf

42 Isabel Kristine M. Valdez, et al. "Violence against women in the Philippines: barriers to seeking support." *The Lancet regional health. Western Pacific* vol. 23 100471. 3 May. 2022, doi:10.1016/j.lanwpc.2022.100471

43 From a Messenger Chat conversation with Dr. Ces Estera, Medical Director of Shalom Paanakan Birthing Center in Antipolo.

44 Limos, "Remote Work."

45 Limos, "Remote Work."

46 Rambo Talabong, "Trans Woman Arrested after Being Blocked from Using Women's Restroom in Cubao," Rappler, August 13, 2019, https://www.rappler.com/nation/237698-transgender-woman-arrested-after-blocked-using-women-restroom-cubao/

47 Clarissa Delgado, in Co, 2021.

48 Carlos Antonio Anonuevo, "An Overview of the Gender Situation in the Philippines," *Friedrich-Ebert-Stiftung Philippine Office*, September 2020, accessed October 4, 2023 from https://library.fes.de/pdf-files/bueros/philippinen/50069.pdf.

49 "Filipino Women in Leadership: Government and Industry," *Investing in Women,* accessed October 5, 2023 from https://investinginwomen.asia/knowledge/filipino-women-leadership-government-industry/

50 Carolyn Custis James, When Life and Belief Collide: How Knowing God Makes a Difference (Grand Rapids, MI: Zondervan, 2001), p. 182.

51 James, p. 181.

52 "Filipino Women in Leadership: Government and Industry," *Investing in Women,* accessed October 5, 2023 from https://investinginwomen.asia/knowledge/filipino-women-leadership-government-industry/

53 Carolyn Custis James, *Half The Church: Recapturing God's Global Vision for Women* (Grand Rapids, MI: Zondervan, 2010).

54 Sadiri Joy Tira and Enoch Wan, "The Filipino Experience in Diaspora Missions: A Case Study of Christian Communities in Contemporary Contexts," Commission VII: Christian Communities in Contemporary Contexts Edinburgh Commission, June 12-13, 2009, p.9.

55 Tira and Wan, p. 9.

56 Tira and Wan, p. 9.

57 Ibid.

BIBLIOGRAPHY

"A Brief History of Gender (In)equality," *Future Learn.* University of Exeter. https://www.futurelearn.com/info/courses/understanding-gender-inequality/0/steps/66837, accessed April 14, 2022.

Anonuevo, Carlos Antonio. "An Overview of the Gender Situation in the Philippines," *Friedrich-Ebert-Stiftung Philippine Office*, September 2020, accessed October 4, 2023 from https://library.fes.de/pdf-files/bueros/philippinen/50069.pdf.

Banks, James, ed. "Cultural Hybridity." *Encyclopedia of Diversity in Education*, 2022. https://sk.sagepub.com/reference/diversityineducation/n166.xml.

Bayeh, Endalcachew. "The Role of Empowering Women and Achieving Gender Equality to the Sustainable Development of Ethiopia." *Pacific Science Review B: Humanities and Social Sciences*, Volume 2, Issue 1, 2016, Pages 37-42, https://doi.org/10.1016/j.psrb.2016.09.013.(https://www.sciencedirect.com/science/article/pii/S2405883116300508)

Co, Ryanne. "Gender Parity In the Philippines: Is the Country Truly as Progressive as It Seems?" *Tatler Asia*, August 7, 2021, https://www.tatlerasia.com/power-purpose/ideas-education/gender-parity-in-the-philippines.

Cohick, Lynn. "Episode 138: God's Purpose" in *God Hears Her*, presented by Our Daily Bread Ministries, podcast, accessed October 6, 2023, at https://www.godhearsher.org/podcast/gods-purpose?fbclid=IwAR1k6uZHRT_7aa-LeS-gQpzMfoWv6lSR1pemM_Vugrkc8eMQRaKks3c3M6p8

Dilli, Selin, Sarah Carmichael, and Auke Rijpma. "Introducing the Historical Gender Equality Index." *Feminist Economics* 25, no. 1 (2019). https://doi.org/10.1080/13545701.2018.1442582.

Eugenio, Ara. "On Ricci, Andrea: How Public Proposals Can be Problematic for Women." *Reportr*, April 14, 2022. https://www.reportr.world/news/ricci-rivero-andrew-brillantes-proposal-explainer-a4713-20220414-lfrm?fbclid=IwAR11IMzTJXg_n5o5GRE7xWdCzD4TDFRxt-68NUnUEsENko4AR4eyvIWWua6s.

Gacila, Wilfred. "The Power of Pinays – A Short Essay," *SOMA Pilipinas*, accessed October 4, 2023 at https://www.somapilipinas.org/community-1/powerofpinays#:~:text=At%20its%20core%2C%20Philippine%20society,default%2C%20become%20the%20family%27s%20treasurer.

"Gender Profile of the Philippines." https://www.jica.go.jp/Resource/activities/issues/gender/reports/ku57pq00002hdv3w-att/phi_2008_summary_en.pdf

Gilbert, Asha. "Penn Swimmer Lia Thomas Becomes First Trans Woman to Win NCAA Swimming Championship." *USA Today*, May 18, 2022. https://www.usatoday.com/story/sports/college/2022/03/18/lia-thomas-trans-woman-win- ncaa-swimming-championship/7088548001/

Jackson, Jesse. "Two Years Later, Beth Moore Addresses John MacArthur Telling Her to 'Go Home." *Church Leaders*, February 4, 2022. https://churchleaders.com/news/416530-two-years-later- beth-moore-addresses-john-macarthur-telling-her-to-go-home.html.

James, Carolyn Custis. *Half The Church: Recapturing God's Global Vision for Women* (Grand Rapids, MI:Zondervan, 2010).

James, Carolyn Custis. *When Life and Belief Collide: How Knowing God Makes a Difference* (Grand Rapids, MI: Zondervan, 2001).

Kristoff, Nicholas D. and Sheryl WuDunn, *Half the Sky: Turning Oppression into Opportunity for Women Worldwide* (New York: Vintage Books, 2009).

Limos, Mario Alvaro. "Remote Work Is a Heavier Burden on Filipino Women Than Men, According to Study." *Esquire*, March 3, 2021. https://www.

esquiremag.ph/life/women/filipino-women-work-opportunities-linkedin-a00293-20210303-lfrm?utm_source=Facebook EsquireMoney&utm_medium=Siteshare&utm_campaign=20220414-fbnp-life-filipino-women-work-opportunities-linkedin-a00293-20210303-lfrm-fbold&fbclid=IwAR1z-rpKrnCksvhGmSkTeFY63YaZvrVdh0FQG1u2aw-wk-PjMXw6n079B3sE

Mahone, Regina. "Half the Sky: Turning Oppression into Opportunities for Women Worldwide." *Review of Half the Sky*, by Nicholas Kristof and Sheryl WuDunn. *Philanthropy News Digest*, April 15, 2016. https://philanthropynewsdigest.org/features/book-reviews/half-the-sky.

Mowczko, Marg. "Partnering Together: Paul's Female Coworkers." Marg Mowczko: *Exploring the Biblical Theology of Christian Egalitarianism*, May 1, 2019. https://margmowczko.com/paul-romans-16-women-co-workers/.

Philippine Commission on Women. "Philippines Drops 8 Places in Gender Equality, Remains Top in Asia." December 28, 2019. https://pcw.gov.ph/philippines-drops-8-places-in-gender-equality-remains-top-in-asia/

"Post-modern Feminism." *Tutor2u*, May 26, 2019.https://www.tutor2u.net/politics/reference/post-modern-feminism.

Rodriguez, Leah. "The 10 Best and Worst Countries to be a Woman in 2021," *Global Citizen*, October 22, 2021. https://www.globalcitizen.org/en/content/best-worst-countries-for-women-gender-equality/

Sheth, Sonam, Madison Hoff, Marguerite Ward and Taylor Tyson. "These 8 Charts Show the Glaring Gap between Men's and Women's Salaries in the US." *Insider*, March 15, 2022. https://www.businessinsider.com/gender-wage-pay-gap-charts-2017-3.

Statistics Times. "Gender ratio in the world," August 26, 2021. https://statisticstimes.com/demographics/world-sex-ratio.php.

Talabong, Rambo. "Trans Woman Arrested after Being Blocked from Using Women's Restroom in Cubao." *Rappler*, August 13, 2019. https://www.rappler.com/nation/237698-transgender-woman-arrested-after-blocked-using-women-restroom-cubao/

Tan, Nigel. "Filipinas Who Were First in Philippine History," *Rappler*, March 21, 2014, https://www.rappler.com/newsbreak/iq/53470-filipinas-first-ph-history/

The Global Gender Gap Report 2023, June 2023 (p. 5), *World Economic Forum*, https://www3.weforum.org/docs/WEF_GGGR_2023.pdf

Unitarian Universalist Association. *Handout3: Position–Muslim Women Are Not Equal.* https://www.uua.org/re/tapestry/youth/bridges/workshop14/185708.shtml

United Nations. "Gender Equality." https://www.un.org/en/global-issues/gender-equality. Accessed April 14, 2022.

Valdez, Isabel Kristine M et al. "Violence against Women in the Philippines: Barriers to Seeking Support." *The Lancet Regional Health. Western Pacific* vol. 23 100471. 3 May. 2022, doi:10.1016/j.lanwpc.2022.100471

"What Does Gender Equality Look Like Today?" *UN Women*. October 6, 2021. https://www.unwomen.org/en/news/stories/2021/10/feature-what-does-gender-equality-look-like-today

World Economic Forum. "Global Gender Gap Report 2021," March 30, 2021. https://www.weforum.org/reports/global-gender-gap-report-2021.

World Economic Forum. https://www3.weforum.org/docs/WEF_GGGR_2021.pdf,

"Women's Rights and Gender Justice." *Oxfam*. https://www.oxfamamerica.org/explore/issues/womens-rights-and-gender-justice/.

DISCIPLESHIP PERSPECTIVES FOR *DANGAL* HONOR / *HIYA* TRANSFORMATIONS OF THE GREAT COMMANDMENT IN THE GOSPEL OF MARK

Narry F. Santos

Have you ever wondered how we, as Filipino Christians, can understand the Great Commandment in Mark 12:29-31 (i.e., to love God with our whole being and to love our neighbors as ourselves), in light of our Filipino culture and for the purpose of growing in discipleship? Is it really possible to grasp this biblically Christian concept with cultural sensitivity, without diluting its being Christian or its being cultural?

In this chapter, we will see how to move In this direction of cultural sensitivity to our biblical understanding. We will use functional links between the Filipino concepts of *dangal* ("honor") and *hiya* ("shame"), and the biblical text in the Gospel of Mark. Through these functional links,[1] we can transform our perspectives in bridging the two important worlds of the Bible (particularly in Mark's Gospel) and our Filipino culture (particularly, *dangal* and *hiya*) in relation to discipleship.

DISCIPLESHIP USE OF "HIYA"
TO LOVE OUR "KAPWA"

The first perspective that prepares us for cultural transformation relates to a basic view on *hiya2* and its implications for discipleship. We can understand *hiya* as a positive Filipino concept.[3] When we see *hiya* as positive, we begin to discover the honor that lies behind it. When we extend this positive understanding to other cultural concepts in our Filipino value system, we spark a change of perspective that helps us to appreciate more deeply who we are and to believe more in what we can do as a people.

To begin with *hiya* as positive is not for the sake of mere positive thinking. It is recognizing *hiya* for what it is. To view *hiya* as negative is to misunderstand it altogether. In reality, what people call negative *hiya* are the *labis* ("too much") and *kulang* ("too little") extreme misuses of this cultural concept, not *hiya* itself. We need not feel ashamed of our *hiya*; instead, we can rediscover (and recover) the honor in our *hiya*. However, as a positive concept, *hiya* poses a challenge for us. As Filipino Christians, how can we wisely use *hiya* in its *tamang pamantayan* ("right standard") to maximize it in our sensitivity to others' *damdamin* ("feelings"),[4] and to harness it in the service of our *kapwa-tao* ("fellow-human"), *kapwa-Pilipino* ("fellow-Filipino"), and *kapwa-Kristiyano* ("fellow-Christian")?

In light of Mark's Gospel, we can widen our understanding and deepen our appreciation of our *kapwa* (literally, a "fellow" who is valued as our equal),5 the *damdamin* of our *kapwa*, and our *hiya* toward our *kapwa*. Using perspectives and principles found in the Gospel, we can also think reflectively on how to wisely use, maximize, and harness our *hiya* cultural concept. Mark challenges each disciple of Jesus to become a "servant of all" (Mark 9:35) and "slave of all" (10:44), to "deny oneself" (8:34), and to "lose our life" for the sake of Jesus (8:35). In addition, Jesus modeled being a servant of others (10:44): "For the Son of Man came not to be served but to serve, and to give his life a ransom for many" (10:45). He also showed how to relate to people to meet their needs with compassion. In his teaching, he even affirmed the need for the second part of the Great Commandment: "You shall love neighbor as yourself" (12:31a).

SHOWING LOVING GESTURES OF HIYA

As Filipino Christian disciples, how can we contextualize becoming servants and slaves of all, losing our lives, and compassionately loving our neighbor as we love ourselves? One way is to show loving gestures of *hiya* or sensitivity to others' *damdamin* in our *pakikipagkapwa* ("relating with each other as fellow-humans" and as equals). Specifically, our exercise of *hiya*'s sensitivity to our *kapwa*'s feelings, sentiments, needs, and struggles indicates our compassion for them. Our practice of *hiya*'s commitment to harmonious relationships and its high regard for people show our desire to love them as we love ourselves. Our demonstration of *hiya*'s desire for *pakikipagkapwa* in our *kagandahang-asal* ("good character") and *kabutihang-loob* ("goodness within [or from the heart]") displays our obedience to Jesus' command to be slaves and servants of all. In other words, we can use *hiya*, the basic twofold function of which is to show sensitivity to the *damdamin* of our *kapwa* and to show consideration in building harmonious relationships with them, as the Filipino expression of our Christian commitment to love others as ourselves. We can use our *hiya* to love our *kapwa*.

The metaphors of *mukha* ("face") and *balat* ("skin") vividly picture our own sensitivity and our *damdamin*. This fragility of feelings leads us to physically and figuratively protect or save our face and care for our skin. These acts of protecting and caring form part of our cultural shield, intended to fortify ourselves from being embarrassed or shamed through public exposure. As expressed by one respondent in a fieldwork study in the Philippines regarding our cultural shield:

> *The face mirrors our inner selves...it must be protected at all cost. It must be saved from all kinds of "social dirt," which*

could stain our moral character and color other people's regard for us. Similarly, the skin is the protective cover of the body. If it is peeled off, our body becomes vulnerable to fatal diseases. Moreover, the skin bleeds when cut; and the wound causes pain. Thus, it must also be taken care of by all means.[6]

As a people, we are committed to protecting or savIng our face and carIng for our skin. We do not want to "lose our face" or be *mapahiya* ("be put to shame"). We also do not want to be called *makapal ang mukha* ("thick-faced") or to be *balat-sibuyas* (literally, "onion-skinned", overly sensitive). In a sense, this is how we carefully protect ourselves or naturally love ourselves. This natural protection and love for ourselves leads us to also protect and love others. Just as we protect our own *mukha* and *balat*, we also desire to protect the *mukha* and *balat* of our *kapwa*. Just as we go to great lengths not to be *mapahiya* ("experience shame"), we also go to great lengths not to give our *kapwa* any *kahihiyan* ("shameful experience"). In this sense, we can say that to use *hiya* toward others is our way of protecting others or of loving them as ourselves. As Filipino Christians, we are then able to fulfill the command of Jesus to love our neighbors as ourselves in the cultural context of *hiya*, supported by the biblical virtues of compassion and service for those in need.

When I think about how Filipino Christians can show *hiya's pakikipagkapwa* and kabutihang-loob, along with being a servant with compassion, as an expression of loving our neighbor, I remember a Christian brother, who upon seeing street kids in Luneta Park had compassion on them. The next time he went there, he brought bread for them. He kept coming quite often to see them, resulting that he saw the need to have a bread factory to feed them.

His desire to help them did not stop with simply feeding the kids with bread. He also thought of feeding them with the Word of God when he would visit them. So, he learned Bible stories, studied how to creatively present these stories to kids, enlisted others to help him, and bought a small truck to carry the bread. He even redesigned the side of the truck to serve as a stage while teaching the Bible to the street kids.

His weekly ministry has expanded to the extent that he has bought a few other trucks and has recruited several teams to regularly visit the kids in various points in Metro Manila. What started with a gesture of *pakikipagkapwa* and kabutihang-loob, coupled with Christian love and service, has now grown to bless more street kids, who seem to have been regarded as insignificant and treated as *nakakahiya* ("shameful") in society. Yet, because of one person, they have been regarded as significant and treated with *dangal*. May we have more Filipino Christians like him.

As Filipino Christians, how must we view our *hiya*? We need to view our *hiya* as our expression of loving our neighbors as ourselves. How do we accomplish that? First, we can emphasize this functional link in our relationships and ministries by looking at *hiya* as our loving attitude, being sensitive and concerned for others, and as our loving commitment to build relationships of harmony with our *kapwa*. Since *hiya* is positive, and since it is our way to love our neighbors as ourselves, we can use this concept to enhance our regard for others and to deepen our *pakikipagkapwa-tao* ("relating with our fellow-humans"), our *pakikipagkapwa-Pilipino* ("relating with our fellow-Filipinos"), and our *pakikipagkapwa-Kristiyano* ("relating with fellow-Christians").

MODELING TAMANG PAMANTAYAN OF HIYA IN CONCRETE ACTIONS

Aside from showing loving gestures of *hiya*, we can model the *tamang pamantayan* of *hiya* in terms of loving others as ourselves in concrete actions. Others will then know that *hiya* is positive and is an expression of love in action through our concrete examples of sensitivity and harmony toward them. We can also encourage our Filipino *kapwa-Kristiyano* to show *hiya's tamang pamantayan*, as we commit to do it in loving ways to them and with them. We can also be accountable to one another in not going to any of the *labis* and *kulang* misuses of *hiya*. But in cases when we find ourselves or others in any of these *labis* or *kulang* sa *hiya* misuses, we can graciously come alongside one another, and then seek or give help. That is love in action.

How do we help in cases when we or other Filipino Christians are plagued with the *labis* sa *hiya* extreme use of *balat-sibuyas*, or being self-critically inferior? We can try to help others (and ourselves) through a renewal of the mind. The *balat-sibuyas* tendency may be present due to an excessive sense of inferiority. To help overcome this feeling, we can dwell on how special we are in God's sight. We can help others to see that they are loved by God. We can use examples from the Gospel of Mark to show how special we are in God's sight and how loved we are by him. We can claim the following truths of God's high regard for us: Jesus relates with us in compassion, just as he did for the needy ones (1:41; 10:21); Jesus gave his life for us as a ransom, just as he did for the disciples (10:45); Jesus has made us members of his new family, just as he did with his followers (3:35); Jesus enables us to be with him and to do his will (3:14-15), just as he did for the Twelve; Jesus wants to use us to powerfully serve others, just as he did for the struggling disciples (6:7-13).

Since we are special in God's eyes and since he loves us greatly as his children, we need not be plagued with thoughts and feelings of inferiority or with sentiments of *pagkabalat-sibuyas*. We are important before God. We are special in his sight. We are loved with a love quite deep. We can share these thoughts to them with clear expressions of compassion and love, showing acceptance of them and affirming their importance to us through our gracious attitudes and loving actions.

On the other hand, our importance before God does not give license for us to be *mayabang* ("arrogant") or *nagbubuhat nang sariling bangko* (literally, "lifting one's own bench"; "boastful"). That is another misuse of *hiya*, the *kulang* sa *hiya* ("lacking in shame") extreme. In the Gospel of Mark, these excesses are evident in the "old" value system that needs to be transformed. For example, there are those in the Gospel who seek to save themselves (8:35), who want to be the first without being "last of all" (9:35), and who wish to great without being a servant (10:44). The problem here is not wanting to be first or wishing to be great. Jesus does not rebuke his disciples for having these good desires. What Jesus rebukes is the means of asserting the self in order to be first or great. Jesus' way is the opposite: the way up is the way of humility with sacrificial service. He modeled this highest form of humble and sacrificial service at the cross.

If we (or others whom you know) are infected with the tendency to be *mayabang* or *nagbubuhat nang sariling bangko*, we can have a reversal of our mind by remembering two things. First, we can remember Jesus' teaching on humility by being "last of all" and "slave of all." His way of humility leads to honor, while our own way of pride leads to dishonor. Second, we can recall Jesus' model of humbling himself at the cross as the ransom on our behalf. His death on the cross for our sake speaks volumes about his humility that turns our shame into honor. His humble model in the Gospel of Mark is presented for us to follow, not to disregard through *yabang*.

I know of a Filipino Christian whose humility is commendable. He is president of a Bible seminary and a previous professor in my New Testament classes. We were assigned to the same church ministry together. One evening, we arrived at the church quite early. I observed that there were four chairs placed side by side in one corner of the room. So, I asked him, "Why are the chairs arranged that way?" He replied, "I slept there late last night." "Why?" "Because I waited for the parents of one of our first-year students in this church. I volunteered to drive them to the bus station. I felt sleepy as I waited for them, so I slept for 30 minutes there." I further asked, "Did you know them before?" "No."

He truly amazed me. He was the seminary president, who was willing to serve a first-year student and his parents whom my friend did not even know. He was willing to wait for them late in the night, and drive them to a distant bus station (and with no complaints).

GOD'S DANGAL AND HIYA AS MOTIVATIONS FOR A LIFE OF DISCIPLESHIP

Aside from *hiya* as a positive concept in loving our *kapwa* in discipleship, a second key perspective to keep in mind is the importance of taking *dangal7* ("honor") and *hiya* together in our cultural value system. As a Filipino people, we already see the value of being motivated to think, feel, speak, decide, and act, in light of what is shameful.[8] We need also to see the value of being equally motivated to think, feel, speak, decide, and act, in light of what's honorable. In other words, we can use *dangal* and *hiya* as key motivations for a life of discipleship, with God as our court of reputation.

The concept of *dangal* includes knowing what is morally right, feeling what is morally good, and acting in a way that is morally desirable. Knowing what is morally right means going out of our way to know more about the real situation before making decisions. In addition, feeling what is morally right answers the question, "How much do we care about others?" Moreover, acting in a way that is morally desirable means making right choices and acting for the good of oneself, others, and the community.[9]

Dangal (our moral standard) relates well with *damdamin* (our emotional standard) and *kapwa* (our relational standard). *Dangal* synthesizes the meaning and significance of both *damdamin* and *kapwa* into an integrated whole. To have *dangal* is to have commendable character – firm in conviction and fair in judgment. People who are marangal do not violate the *kapwa* principle; they do not hurt the *damdamin* of others. They show genuine concern for the welfare of their *kapwa*-tao. Since *dangal* and *hiya* are both influenced by *damdamin* and *kapwa*, we can observe and relate the dynamics of *dangal* and *hiya* together. The joint scrutiny of *dangal* and *hiya* can help us appreciate our study of the honor-shame contents and concepts in our cultural context.

When perspectives of both honor and shame shape our vision, we can rightly be motivated to think and feel according to what is right. When principles of both honor and shame guide our path, we can be rightly motivated to speak and live according to what is right. More importantly, we can also begin to experience more balanced ways of living together and more harmonious ways of relating with one another in discipleship.

SHIFT IN DISCIPLESHIP FOCUS
ON THE HONORABLE JESUS

In the Gospel of Mark, we can see that Mark uses the honor-shame concepts of the first-century Mediterranean culture in clear and concrete ways.[10] In fact, Mark has refashioned the cultural concepts of his day by elevating the honor-shame values to a higher level.[11] Mark basically has shifted focus from what's honorable in society to what's honorable in God's sight. Similarly, he has shifted attention from what's shameful in the human point of view to what's shameful in God's point of view.

The primary shift regarding honor in discipleship throughout Mark's Gospel is focused on Jesus, the honorable one. Jesus is represented as the full embodiment of honor. His name is honorable; his life is honorable; his words are honorable; his mission is honorable; his death is honorable; and his resurrection is honorable. Everything that he taught and performed is honorable. Thus, what Jesus has declared as honorable is now our basis or standard for honor in discipleship.

What does this new discipleship focus on Jesus as the model of honor imply to our concept of *dangal*? It implies that our motivation to do what is marangal ("honorable") in relation to others in society needs to be for the honor of Jesus. Our desire to now live with *karangalan* ("status of honor") is because we want to honor Jesus. In other words, as Filipino Christians, we are to continue seeking ways to apply our *dangal* concepts in our relationships and service to others in the new family of Jesus, in our own family, and in other groups. We need still to keep our *kapurihan* ("purity" in personal honor) intact[12] show *pitagan* ("high esteem") to others,[13] and take opportunities for *kawanggawa*14 ("benevolence," "philanthropy").[15] We need still to fortify our *karangalan* with words and deeds of *malasakit*16 ("selfless service") and *katapatan*[17] ("loyalty") to people. Especially in the household of faith, we need still to demonstrate mutual *pagkabahala* ("concern, responsibility") for the good of others, gracious *paggalang* ("respect, deference") to their person and views, and grateful and generous *utang-na-loob* (literally, "debt of gratitude," moral obligation) in our reciprocal interactions.[18]

Sadiri Joy Tira

But there is one clear difference for us now: we are to do these same deeds of karangalan for the sake of Jesus, not our own; to please Jesus, not our family or friends; to submit to the authority of Jesus, not just our society. We are to do the same actions (just like before), but with a different motivation (not like before). In other words, the functional link between our cultural concept of *dangal* and the biblical concept of honor is this: God's *dangal* is an important motivation in our life of discipleship.

REASONS FOR THE SHIFT IN DISCIPLESHIP FOCUS TO JESUS

Why must Jesus have that sole place of *dangal* in our life of discipleship? Why must he be at the center of all our efforts for karangalan? First, Jesus has instructed us to do things for his sake. Here are some instances when Jesus honors those who do things for his sake: (1) "... those who lose their life for my sake and for the sake of the gospel, will save it" (8:35b); (2) "Truly I tell you, there is no who has left house or brothers or sisters or mother or father or children or fields, for my sake and for the sake of the good news, who will not receive a hundredfold now in this age–houses, brothers and sisters, mothers and children, and fields with persecutions–and in the age to come eternal life" (10:29-30); (3) "As for yourselves, beware; for they will hand you over to councils; and you will be beaten in synagogues; and you will stand before governors and kings because of me [or "for my sake"], as a testimony to them" (13:9); and (4) "And you will be hated by all because of my name [or "for my name's sake"]. But the one who endures to the end will be saved" (13:13). Thus, we need to live honorably for the sake of Jesus in our discipleship.

Second, it is because it is only Jesus who has lived to the full what it means to be marangal. Only Jesus has kept his kapurihan intact at the cross, when his disciples denied, betrayed, and deserted him. Only Jesus has shown pitagan for others, even though they mocked him, spat on him, struck his face, flogged him, and crucified him. Only Jesus has taken a lot of opportunities for kawanggawa through his exorcisms, healings, and miracles on behalf of the needy and insignificant in society. Only Jesus has fortified his karangalan with words and deeds of malasakit and katapatan, forgiving his disciples and initiating reconciliation with them though they have no katapatan. Only Jesus has demonstrated pagkabahala for others, paggalang for their person, and grateful utang-na-loob to the heavenly Father. Only Jesus deserves to receive all honor.

Thus, our motivation to live with karangalan must now be to honor Jesus. In a similar way, our motivation to do what displays positive shame and to shun what shows negative shame must be for Jesus' sake. In the Gospel of Mark, shame in all its aspects has been changed and focused on Jesus. Jesus and his standards have now become the measure by which any thought or deed of shame is to be measured. Jesus has declared what Is shameful and what Is not. He has defined what we must be ashamed of and what we must not. In other words, we can use this additional functional link between our cultural concept of *hiya* and the biblical concept of shame: our *kahihiyan* before God is an important motivation in our Christian life. As his children, we do not want to be *kahiya-hiya* in the presence of the honorable heavenly Father.

Let us take one example of what is now clearly shameful in the eyes of God. In Mark 8:38, we hear the words of Jesus, "Those who are ashamed of me and my words in this adulterous and sinful generation, of them the Son of Man will also be ashamed when he comes in the glory of his Father with the holy angels." Being ashamed of Jesus and his words on earth now means to be shamed in the presence of the heavenly Father in the future. Since God's *hiya* is the most important motivation, we are to avoid falling into the trap of openly or secretly disassociating ourselves from Jesus and his words, and of directly or indirectly distancing ourselves from anything that has to do with Jesus and his work on earth. If we disassociate ourselves from him and distance ourselves from his words and work, it's *kahihiyan* in the sight of God and *kahiya-hiya* before God.

Therefore, one way that we can show God our love for him with our whole being (12:30) is to not be ashamed of Jesus and his words (8:38). Another way to love God with all our heart is to honor him in doing what he wants us to do for the sake of Jesus (8:35b; 10:29-30; 13:9, 13). Thus, using *dangal* and *hiya* together in our functional links, we have the following connection: God's *dangal* and *hiya* are our most important motivations in our life of discipleship.

CONCLUSION

As Filipino Christians, is it possible for us to see the Great Commandment as our way of growing in discipleship, using our *dangal* and *hiya* concepts? Can we fulfill the first part of the commandment (i.e., loving God with all our being) by viewing God's *dangal* and *hiya* as the most important motivations in our life of discipleship, with the most honorable Jesus as the main focus of our being? Finally, can we fulfill the second part of the commandment (i.e., to love our neighbor as ourselves) through the use of *hiya* as our way to love our *kapwa*, so that we can grow in our life of discipleship by deepening our *pakikipagkapwa-tao* ("relating with our fellow-humans"), our *pakikipagkapwa-Pilipino* ("relating with our fellow-Filipinos"), and our *pakikipagkapwa-Kristiyano* ("relating with fellow-Christians")?

----

1 "Functional links" are helpful tools that build bridges between the twenty-first century *dangal* and *hiya* in light of their related Filipino cultural concepts, and the biblical honor-shame teachings in the Gospel of Mark and in light of the first-century Mediterranean honor-shame value system. For information on "functional links" ("functional equivalence" or "dynamic equivalence") as applied to cultural transformations using the "dynamic equivalence" method of translation, see Charles H. Kraft, "The Church in Culture – A Dynamic Equivalence Model," in John R. W. Stott and Robert Coote (eds.), *Down to Earth: Studies in Christianity and Culture* (London: Hodder and Stoughton, 1981), pp. 211-30.

2 *Hiya* is a norm (or rule of conduct) that supports the emotional standard of *damdamin* ("feelings") in seeking not to hurt the feelings of others and in minimizing (if not avoiding) conflicts. As a norm, *hiya* prescribes how we should behave in relation to one another in a specific situation or condition, so that we do not offend each other's feelings. Through hiya, we are not just concerned for others' feelings but also for maintaining good relations with them.

3 *Hiya*, as a positive value, is reflected in the expression *tamang pamantayan* ("right standard"). However, if *hiya* is abused or misused as a positive value, it is violated either through *labis sa hiya* ("excessive in shame" to a fault) or through *kulang sa hiya* ("lacking in shame"). *Labis sa hiya* can be seen in a person's being *balat-sibuyas* (literally, "onion-skinned", over-sensitive), or being self-critically inferior. *Kulang sa hiya*, can manifest itself in at least four ways of expression, I.e.,

(1) *makapal ang mukha* (literally, "thick faced," insensitive); (2) *nagbubuhat ng sariling bangko* (literally, "lifting one's own bench") and *mayabang* ("boastful"); (3) *walang delicadeza* (literally, "no proper behavior"); and (4) *walang hiya* (literally, "no shame," shameless). In our cultural system, neither *labis sa hiya* nor *kulang sa hiya* represent the *tamang pamantayan*.

4 F. Landa Jocano considers *damdamin* as the emotional standard of the Filipino value system (*Filipino Value System: A Cultural Definition* [Quezon City: PUNLAD Research House, Inc., 1997]), 69.

5 The concept of *kapwa* reveals the value we give to harmonious relations. For Virgilio G. Enriquez, *kapwa* is so crucial that he calls it a core concept in Filipino social psychology ("Kapwa: A Core Concept in Filipino Social Psychology," *Philippines Social Studies and Humanities Review* 42 (1978), pp. 100-118).

6 Jocano, *Filipino Value System*, 42.

7 Jocano explains the indigenous concept of *dangal* from the viewpoints of native informants who were interviewed during fieldwork studies. Popularly used as social honor and dignity, *dangal* is actually a moral value that characterizes our identity with, pride in, and commitment to revered ideals, principles, and people around us. As a moral standard, *dangal* means honor, dignity, integrity, nobility, position of respectability, good reputation. Cf. Jocano, *Filipino Value System*, 79-83, and Jocano, *Filipino Worldview*, 123-34.

8 An example of a common comment meant to influence behavior based on shame is this: *Huwag kang gagawa ng anumang kahiya-hiya sa atin* ("Do not do something that will bring us shame").

9 Jocano, Filipino *Value System*, p. 80.

10 For the way Mark clearly and concretely used the honor-shame cultural concepts of his day, see Narry F. Santos, *Turning our Shame into Honor: Transformation of the Filipino Hiya in the Light of Mark's Gospel* (Manila, Philippines: LifeChange, 2003), 99-140.

11 For a view of how Mark transforms honor and shame in Mark's Gospel, see Santos, *Turning Shame into Honor*, 141-226.

12 *Puri,* as personal honor and dignity, is highly valued among us. We also use puri as a reference to chastity, good name, and reputation. We may hear from our parents two common statements on *puri*: (1) *"Ingatan mo ang iyong puri"* ("Take care of your honor or reputation [in the case of females, chastity]"); and (2) *"Huwag mong sirain/dungisan ang puri ng ating pamilya"* ("Do not destroy/stain the good name of our family"). These common statements show our moral standard in moving toward good behavior before others.

13 *Pitagan* means "worthy of high respect, esteem, or reverence." People whose behavior is *kapita-pitagan* are usually *magalang* ("respectful"), *matapat* ("honest, loyal), maginoo ("honorable"), and *mapagmahal* ("loving"). The people who consistently demonstrate these *kapita-pitagan* virtues are valued as *marangal* in the public estimation of others.

14 The notion of *kawanggawa* centers on compassionate benevolence. It means "putting the interests of the community, an office, or public service over one's own personal interests." People who are *mapagkawanggawa* are available and able to help in the time of troubles. They have a self-imposed moral obligation to help, even without being told or pushed.

15 The moral aspects of *dangal* are usually seen in three basic elements; namely: (1) *kapurihan* (personal honor, as in chastity); (2) *pitagan* (high esteem or reverence); and (3) *kawanggawa* (benevolence; philanthropy).

16 The concept of *malasakit* shows concern and service for others. This is the highest virtue in community life and the basis of harmony in group relations. *Malasakit* comes from the two words *malasin* (i.e., "to look at intently," "to notice," "to take note carefully," "to focus attention with much concern") and *sakit* (i.e., "pain due to physical, emotional, or mental hurt," "suffering due to misfortune in life"). So *malasakit* means being concerned for someone who has sorrow

or pain. We generally consider a person with *malasakit* as *marangal*. Cf. Jocano, Filipino Worldview, 128.

17 This concept of *katapatan* includes loyalty, honesty, integrity, and uprightness. We need *katapatan* because it validates the genuineness of *malasakit*. If *katapatan* Is absent, the act of *malasakit* may be taken as *pakitang-tao* lang ("only showing off"), or, as our idiom says, *kaplastikan* lang (literally, "being plastic," or "insincere"). If one were not *matapat* (taken from the root word *tapat* [literally, "in front"], meaning "open" or "transparent"), we would interpret that person's acts of *malasakit* as not real "selfless services," but as self-serving deeds. The term we use here is *pagsasamantala* ("taking advantage [of others in times of crisis]"). Such an act of opportunism is not *dangal* nor *katapatan* nor *malasakit* at all.

18 The three supporting norms or rules of conduct of *dangal* are *pagkabahala* ("concern, responsibility"), *paggalang* ("respect, deference"); and *utang-na-loob* ("debt of gratitude, moral obligation"). These norms motivate us to act with *karangalan*.

BIBLIOGRAPHY

Enriquez, Virgilio G. *"Kapwa*: A Core Concept in Filipino Social Psychology." Philippines Social Studies and Humanities Review 42 (1978): 100-118.

Jocano, F. Landa. *Filipino Value System: A Cultural Definition*. Quezon City: PUNLAD, 1997.

___. *Filipino Worldview: Ethnography of Local Knowledge*. Quezon City: PUNLAD, 2001.

Charles H. Kraft, "The Church in Culture – A Dynamic Equivalence Model." In *Down to Earth: Studies in Christianity and Culture*, edited by John R. W. Stott and Robert Coote, 211-230. London: Hodder and Stoughton, 1981.

Santos, Narry F. *Turning our Shame into Honor: Transformation of the Filipino Hiya in the Light of Mark's Gospel*. Manila: LifeChange, 2003.

GLOCAL MISSIONS AND THE LOCAL CONGREGATION

Juno Wang

INTRODUCTION

Over the years, the center of the global Christianity has shifted from the North to the South, and people are on the move with interconnections between their host country and homeland. Our world is "glocalized." With this in mind, the vision and mission of PCEC is to transform individuals and communities under the Lordship of Jesus Christ. Its mission is to promote cooperation of missionaries and Overseas Filipino Workers (OFW) around the world.

In 1989, the *Manila Manifesto* of the Second Lausanne Congress on World Evangelization (LCWE) in the Philippines deliberated on the prospects for the fulfillment of the Great Commission, and it was accepted by an overwhelming majority of the participants (LCWE 1989). I would like to express my gratitude to Filipino churches and Christians who participated and supported my late godfather, Dr. Thomas Wang, the International Director of the Second LCWE, in every way. Six years later, with the passing of the OFW Act in 1995 to protect Filipino migrant workers (Senate of the Philippines Legislative Reference Bureau 1995), the outflow of Filipinos around the world increased significantly (MacroTrends 2023).

As the world has become glocal, so must our missions. Glocalization not only provides local congregation with the opportunities to evangelize and disciple global diasporas who live in our community, but also connects and sends Filipino diaspora Christians, including OFWs, from the congregation to the world for glocal missions. Will our global missions and local missions be integrated for glocal missions? The purpose of this paper is to present how a local congregation can be involved in glocal missions when the opportunity presents itself.

DEFINITION OF KEY TERMS:

Diaspora: Diaspora means "a scattering," used to describe the large-scale movement of people from their homeland to settle permanently or temporarily in other countries (Lausanne Committee for World Evangelization Issue Group No. 26 A and B 2004).

Glocal Missions: Global in scope but local in action and in sequence (Wan 2017) because of the seamless integration between the local and the global (Roberts 2007, 24), which means local evangelistic outreaches have global ripple effects (Tira 2010).

Missions: Ways and means of accomplishing "the mission" which has been entrusted by the Triune God to the Church and Christians (Wan 2003).

MIGRATION SITUATION

According to the World Migration Report 2022, it is estimated that in 2020, there were about 281 million international migrants worldwide. That means that 1 in 30 people in the world was a migrant, and more than 40% were born in Asia. Asia and Europe experienced the most remarkable growth from 2000 to 2020 and comprised 61% of the global international migrant population (International Organization for Migration 2022). Some diasporas have become permanent residents or even citizens in their host country; some are temporary diasporas such as international students, business people, contract workers, and travelers; while others are displaced people who are refugees or asylum seekers.

In the Philippines, there were 219,000 immigrants in 2017, with the majority from the US, China, and South Korea (Statista Research Department 2022). While international tourism is recovering from the COVID pandemic, 8.26 million international tourists including non-resident Overseas Filipinos (OF) visited the Philippines in 2019, and 70% came from South Korea, China, the US, Japan, and Taiwan (Department of Tourism Philippines 2019). In 2020, 24.2 % of nearly 80,000 foreign citizen residents were from India (Republic of the Philippines: Philippine Statistics Authority 2023).

As for Philippines emigration statistics, there was a 53.41% increase from 1995 to 2000 (MacroTrends 2023). The United States was the top destination country (Statista Research Department 2022), and nearly 10% of Filipinos were in diaspora, living in more than 200 countries and territories (Integral Human Development). In some instances, the Filipino diaspora has been the impetus for effecting changes of legislation in their host countries regarding their welfare, such as those enacted in relation to immigration and domestic violence in Australia in the 1990s (Roces 2021). In 2021, the total of OFWs was 1.83 million, with the top five destinations being: Asia (78.3%, which includes Saudi Arabia, 24.4%, and the United Arab Emirates, 14.4%), Europe (9.3%), the Americas (8.9%), Australia (2.2%), and Africa (1.3%) (Republic of the Philippines: Philippine Statistics Authority 2022). Labor OFWs, referred to as modern-day heroes, have contributed significantly to the Philippine economy for many years, and the value of migrant remittance inflows ranked fourth globally (Statista Research Department 2023). Although the Philippines limited the annual number of health professionals to send abroad, more nurses are seeking to work abroad since the pandemic (Cinco 2022).

During the pandemic, it was a daunting challenge to attend to the needs of OFWs. The learned lesson is that it will require the whole of society to help OFWs and their families build a life at home (Scalabrini 2020). In July 2023, lawmakers proposed a unique pension and social security system designed specifically for OFWs which acknowledges their vulnerabilities abroad (Adel 2023). The Church needs to get involved in assisting returned Filipino diaspora Christians including OFWs as they are the local missionaries sitting in the pews, and to send Filipino diaspora Christians, including OFWs, from the congregation to the world as global missionaries to integrate local and global missions for glocal missions.

In mid-2021, only 18.2% of non-Christians around the world personally knew a Christian (Johnson and Zurlo 2021)--so we could be the first Christian friend to our global diaspora neighbors wherever we are. In fact, it is God who controls movements of people and uses them for his purposes (Lausanne Committee for World Evangelization Issue Group No. 26 A and B 2004). He has turned the magnitude of the diaspora population into a mission opportunity (George 2017), and it is a primary part of God's mission and redemptive purposes (Lausanne Committee for World Evangelization 2009). We need to rely on our relationship with God to manifest his nature of love, glory, and sending for our engagement with global diasporas (Wan 2007), both locally and globally. As such, the need is for us to reorient our missional eyes from a global perspective to see from a glocal perspective, and to mobilize local congregations for glocal missions in order to expand God's Kingdom.

GLOCALIZATION, CHURCH, AND MISSIONS

Nowadays, the world has blurred the boundaries between the local and the global. Glocalization means the interconnection of the local, contextual, and homogenous with the global, universal, and heterogenous. The global and local enable each other, and reciprocally form each other. They are deeply and inextricably connected, are interdependent, and are not opposing forces (Hill 2016, 26).

Since the impacts of our missions task are glocal, the Church needs to have at glocal vision. The Church must see and understand the interconnection of the local and global aspects of church and missions. They are both to be considered equally important (Gravaas 2011,

208). What is global is our universal faith, and what is local is contextualization. People live locally, not globally; therefore, the global mission strategies must focus on local realities and local methods (Schnabel 2011, 30). Glocalization is about discourse, learning, and partnership (Hill 2016, 26), and so are our glocal missions. The Cape Town Commitment calls church and mission leaders in host countries to recognize and respond to the diaspora missional opportunities in strategic planning, training, and resourcing of workers among them, and to witness in word and deed (The Cape Town Commitment 2016, 142-3).

THEOLOGY

Our God is a missional God, and mission is *"missio Dei* within the Father, the Son, and the Holy Spirit." The foundation of missions begins with sending among the Trinity, where the Father sends the Son to all peoples (Rom 10) who are created in his image, and also the Spirit whom he sends in Christ's name (John 14) to all believers. That mission is now extended to us (John 17:4). We need to see diasporas in our midst from God's perspective, recognizing that it is he who has moved our diaspora neighbors here so that they might know him.

The Great Commission clearly includes the mission of the Church to win people into the Kingdom everywhere in the world, and this work must see that God's will is done on earth outside the Church and to declare his glory among all peoples (Winter 2009). The promise of the presence of the Holy Spirit is given after the Great Commission to enable all disciples to obey his commandments (Matt. 28:18-20). Jesus modeled his life to the disciples, but they were not transformed to be his witnesses until the coming of the Holy Spirit at Pentecost (Acts 2), after they had obeyed his command not to leave Jerusalem, but to wait for the Holy Spirit God promised (Acts 1:4). A Christian does not truly believe until he obeys; he is still being born again because his faith is dead without obedience (James 2:14-17) (Patterson 1981, 10).

God gives us a spirit of love, of power, and of self-discipline (2 Tim. 1:7) to extend his Kingdom. A Spirit-filled church is a mission-minded church in which evangelism should arise spontaneously (The Lausanne Covenant 2016, 48). We need to see diasporas in the full scope of their humanity rather than as simply targets of our religious marketing (Looney 2015, 87). God invites us into his fellowship life (Hill 2016, 414), as humans are created to be in a unique relationship with the Creator (Glasser et al 2003, 35). The horizontal reconciliation in Ephesians of age, class, gender, and race comprises the "love your neighbor" commandment, which itself is merely a reflection of the greatest commandment of the vertical reconciliation of sinners to God (Eph. 2:1-10) (Yeh 2016, 26).

Being a World Christian means to have a global perspective with local and cultural awareness (Park 2010, 92). However, missions without an orientation outward and to others conceives an ingrown, complacent, and ethnocentric church (Roembke 2000, 1). Being a missional Filipino church is an obedience issue because we will get out of our comfort and safety zones and engage the world as Jesus did if we love like Jesus (Roberts 2007, 146).

DIASPORA MISSIOLOGY IN BRIEF

As the creation in the image of God, our existence, and our ability to know and undertake in missions are all dependent on God (Acts 17:28), who is the great I AM (Exod. 3), and it is God-centered (Wan 2014). What people most desperately need is peace with God, and what can be powerful enough to carry us far away from our comfort zones to be his witnesses is a deep sense of divine calling (Lorance 2015). When we know who God is, and who Jesus is, we would want to witness for our God (Wright 2006, 66-7). Our Triune God is relational, and we are created as relational beings. Wan calls for action to engage in diaspora (glocal) missions and to integrate the Great Commission with the great commandment relationally (Wan 2010).

Diaspora missions requires us to practice strategic stewardship for our relational accountability to God and the unsaved (Wan 2010). It is missions to every person outside his Kingdom everywhere and supplements the traditional missiology (Wan and Tira 2010).

Traditional missions is polarized or dichotomized in focus, and territorial with a sharp distinction between here and there; and movement is lineal, meaning goes one way. It is geographically divided and compartmentalized as a discipline (Hesselgrave 2005, 348). It may exist under the possible influence of functionalism in which all aspects of a ministry practically serve as functional acts for the survival of that ministry. Evangelistic efforts are to function for the purpose of evangelism. Conversion is always at the center of evangelism, and the number of converts at any evangelistic meeting determines its success (Wan and Nguyen 2014); therefore, the missional approach is pragmatic and managerial.

Diaspora missions focuses on holistic missions and contextualization, integrating evangelism and social concern. It is de-territorialized and simultaneously local and global in concept. With the connecting links with homeland, the gospel can be the part of the communication traffic between those at home and those in "exile" (Ingleby 2007). In perspective, it is not geographically divided but borderless, transnational, and global (Wan and Tira 2010). Missions is practiced at both the institutional career-missionary level and also the personal level of all believers, and it is not a matter of either-or (Wan 2010).

Diaspora missions must be intentional because cross-cultural missions is almost always against our human nature. God has given us his Holy Spirit as a powerful resource to help us overcome any obstacles and challenges. By the empowerment of the Spirit, we tear down the barriers of my people, my place, my plan, and my comfort and pleasure to serve the people in our neighborhood with a Kingdom mindset. We need to submit ourselves to the Lord and get down from our Tower of Babel of self-centeredness because the biggest barrier we face is ourselves. When we focus on the Kingdom, the Church becomes less cultural, and missions goes glocal because the world has gone glocal (Roberts 2007, 29). Once we open our missional eyes and see our diaspora neighbors from God's perspective, we see opportunities.

The two key points for diaspora missions mobilization are that the calling is for every believer to love our neighbors and that it requires our obedience in doing His will for the Kingdom out of our close relationship with God. The Spirit will bear witness about Jesus when we witness of truth and love from the Scriptures (John 15:26).

GLOCAL ADOBO AND GLOCAL WITNESS

When I had my first authentic adobo at a Filipina friend's home, I immediately fell in love with the dish. Not only it is colorful, aromatic, and tasty, but it can also go beautifully with rice, quinoa, or mashed potatoes to make it a glocal adobo! It reminds me how my dear Filipino Christian friends are God's glocal witnesses by bearing the fruit of the Spirit for the colors (Gal. 5:22-23), having the knowledge of Christ for the aroma (2 Cor. 2:14-16), and staying salty for the taste (Matt. 5:13) locally and globally.

There are various adobo recipes, and the main difference is the secret ingredients. The secret ingredients for glocal missions are the empowerment of the Holy Spirit, allegiance to our King, and love and relationships with God and neighbors thus to live out a transformed life. Evangelism is the daily witness of every church member in their regular contacts (Patterson 1981, 31). There are four types of diaspora missions for our glocal witnesses, and they are cyclical (Wan 2014). The missions requires partnership among local transformed individuals, communities, congregations; returned Filipino diaspora Christians; missionaries; and global Filipino diaspora Christians and missionaries in planning, training, and resourcing.

MISSIONS TO THE DIASPORA

In general, Filipinos are known for their adaptability and flexibility, English proficiency, humor and positivity, and strong family ties. A research study of the difference in acculturation among Russian immigrant nurses in Israel and Filipino nurses in the US shows that the Filipino nurses have a higher level of acculturation because of their familiarity with the English language and American culture before their immigration to the U.S. (E. Ea et al. 2010). That means a local congregation has some cross-cultural skills to reach a large population of American immigrants, residents, and tourists in the Philippines. In addition, Filipino culture is a group culture which is the majority culture of the world. Filipinos know the importance of honor and shame, ingroup and outgroup factors, hospitality, and building trust and relationships to reach other ethnic groups, including Chinese, Indians, and Koreans in the Philippines. In particular, the shared migrant experience helps returned Filipino diaspora Christians not only to empathize and understand our diaspora neighbors, but also to help them find their new identity in Christ and the Kingdom.

When we minister to members of a diaspora community through social and spiritual dimensions for the Great Commandment as a pre-evangelistic and holistic outreach, it is "missions to the diaspora" (Acts 1-7), the first type of diaspora missions. Let the Gospel flow naturally along relationship lines while we live out a missional lifestyle to be a good steward of our time, talents, and treasures (Carter 2011). The lost need to meet Jesus in flesh and blood (Davis 2015, 102-3) through transformed individuals and communities under the Lordship of Jesus Christ.

MISSIONS THROUGH THE DIASPORA

Diaspora missions begins at a local level and proceeds to be global in perspective (Wan 2010). With real time communication, diasporas connect with family and friends back home on a regular basis. Therefore, as a friend of a person in diaspora, we could become a family friend locally and globally. Once people in diaspora see, hear, and experience the gospel from Filipino Christians here locally, it will be shared within their networks globally. Our Christian witness then, is local and global all at the same time. When local diasporic individuals and congregations are to be mobilized and empowered to fulfill the Great Commission in their homeland and elsewhere, it is "missions through the diaspora" (Acts 8-12) (Wan and Tira

2010). From this type of diaspora missions, global Filipino diaspora Christians from the local congregations could be the connecting people and partners for missions in our diasporic neighbor's homeland and elsewhere.

MISSIONS BY AND BEYOND THE DIASPORA

The apostle Paul used his bi-cultural diasporic roots to be sensitive both to ministry and message contexts (Caldwell 2015). Moreover, the shared memory of the diaspora experience can give all diasporas a shared unity of identity and experience (Rubesh 2010). When people in diaspora have accepted Christ and acquired the language and are adjusted to the Filipino culture with the shared migrant experience, they are the natural bridge for "missions by and beyond the diaspora" (Acts 13-28) to reach out to other ethnic groups in the Philippines. Once they accept the Lord, local congregations and global Filipino diasporic Christians could reach their homeland and global networks through them (Downes 2015).

MISSIONS WITH THE DIASPORA

As we have limited resources, we can partner with other ethnic churches and mission organizations to be a faithful and obedient steward to our King. Through partnership between a diaspora group and others focusing beyond one diaspora group to serve other diaspora or non-diaspora people is "missions with the diaspora" in Kingdom ministry (Wan 2014). Partnership is also because the other meaning of the Church is the Whole Church, which is the body of Christ, the kingdom of the Lord, including all churches in his family that truly believe in the Lord Jesus.

Most ethnic churches have been involved in the first two types of diaspora missions, but mostly in order to reach their own ethnic group. Filipino churches would be a great model of these four types of missions for others to follow. After this type of partnership for glocal missions comes the beginning of a new mission cycle from "Missions to the Diaspora" to reach another diaspora community in or outside the Philippines.

Above all, the most important thing is not our doing and knowing, but it is our being the right person as a witness. It is about being transformed by the Spirit through our willingness to grow and change, and through our obedience to Jesus' commands and his Lordship (Wang 2021). It takes time to form cross-cultural relationships, and it cannot be agenda driven (DeYmaz and Li 2010, 47). We pray and trust the Spirit to bear fruit in his time.

CONCLUSION

The torch of the 1989 Lausanne Manila Congress began its relay journey from Jerusalem and ended in Manila. It could also be seen as a symbol of passing the baton of glocal missions to Filipino churches. The Filipino diaspora have been involved in global missions, and now is the time for local congregations to integrate their local missions with global missions.

Local congregations need to recognize that it is God himself who brings the global diasporas to us (Acts 17:25), and everyone at church needs to understand what God is doing at the global level and involve themselves at the local level. We need to have a breakthrough in our ethnocentric thinking and adjust our missional vision and directions for glocal missions. We must overcome the temptation of using our calling as an excuse for not reaching out, but to think of it as an opportunity to draw closer to the Lord (Yi 2019). Our first calling is to worship God (The Lausanne Covenant 2016, 15), and the local congregation's mission is to invite global diasporas into the present Kingdom through our witness, and to enjoy adobo at the Messianic banquet with us in the future Kingdom.

BIBLIOGRAPHY

Adel, Rosette. "New Bill Bats for Creation of OFW Pension System." *The Philippine Star.* July 7, 2023. https://www.philstar.com/headlines/2023/07/07/2279401/new-bill-bats-creation-ofw pension-system (accessed July 11, 2023).

Caldwell, Larry W. "Diaspora Ministry in the Book of Acts: Insights from Two Speeches of the Apostle Paul to Help Guide Diaspora Ministry Today." In *Diaspora Missiology: Reflections on Reaching the Scattered Peoples of the World*, edited by Michael Pocock and Enoch Wan. Evangelical Missiological Society Series no 23, 91-105. Pasadena, CA: William Carey Library,2015.

Cameron, Judith E. M., ed. *The Lausanne Legacy: Landmarks in Global Mission.* Peabody, MA: Hendrickson, 2016.

Carter, Alan and Katherine Carter. "The Gospel and Life Style." In *Theology and Practice of Mission: God, the Church, and the Nations*, edited by Bruce Riley Ashford, 128-43. Rev. ed. Nashville, TN: Academic, 2011.

Cinco, Maricar. "Focus: As Pandemic Eases, More Filipino Nurses Set to Seek Work Abroad." *Kyodo News*, November 6, 2022. https://english.kyodonews.net/news/2022/11/5b6fee89a1f6-focus-as-pandemic-eases-more-filipino-nurses-set-to-seek-work-abroad.html (accessed July 17, 2023).

Davis, Charles A. *Making Disciples Across Cultures: Missional Principles for a Diverse World.* Downers Grove, IL: InterVarsity Press, 2015.

Department of Tourism Philippines. "Visitor Arrivals: January-December 2019." http://www.tourism.gov.ph/industry_performance/Dec2019/Visitor_Arrivals_Report_FY2019.pdf (accessed July 16, 2023).

DeYmaz, Mark and Harry Li. Ethnic *Blends: Mixing Diversity Into Your Local Church.* Grand Rapids: Zondervan, 2010.

Downes, Stan. "Mission by and Beyond the Diaspora: Partnering With Diaspora Believers to Reach Other Immigrants and the Local People." In *Diaspora Missiology: Reflections on Reaching the Scattered Peoples of the World*, edited by Michael Pocock and Enoch Wan. Evangelical Missiological Society Series no 23, 77-88. Pasadena, CA: William Carey Library, 2015.

Ea, E., M. Itzhaki, M. Ehrenfeld, and J. Fitzpatrick. "Acculturation Among Immigrant Nurses in Israel and the United States of America," *International Nursing Review 57*, no. 4 (December 2010):443-448.

George, Sam. "Is God Reviving Europe Through Refugees: Turning the Greatest Humanitarian Crisis of Our Times into One of the Greatest Mission Opportunities." *Lausanne Global Analysis* 6 no. 3 (April 28, 2017). https://www.lausanne.org/content/lga/2017-05/god-reviving-europe-refugees (accessed October 27, 2021).

Glasser, Arthur F., Charles E. Van Engen, Dean S. Gilliland, and Shawn B. Redford. *Announcing the Kingdom: The Story of God's Mission in the Bible.* Grand Rapids, MI: Baker Academic, 2003.

Gravaas, Hans Aage. "Mission and Globalisation: Some Lessons to be Learned—A Brief Summary." In *The Church Going Glocal: Mission and Globalisation,*" edited by Tormod Engelsviken, Erling Lundeby and Dagfinne Solheim. Eugene, OR: Wipf and Stock Publishers, 2011: 207-211.

Hesselgrave, David J. *Paradigms in Conflict: 10 Key Questions in Christian Missions Today.* Grand Rapids, MI: Kregel Publications, 2005.

Hill, Graham. *Global Church: Reshaping Our Conversations, Renewing Our Mission, Revitalizing Our Churches.* Downers Grove, IL: InterVarsity Press, 2016.

Ingleby, Jonathan. "Postcolonialism, Globalization, Migration and Diaspora: Some Implications for Mission." *Encounters Mission Ezine*, no. 20 (October 2007).

Integral Human Development. "Country Profile: The Philippines." https://migrants-refugees.va/country-profile/the-philippines/ (accessed July 17, 2023).

International Organization for Migration. "World Migration Report 2022." https://worldmigrationreport.iom.int/wmr-2022-interactive/ (accessed December 16, 2021).

Johnson, Todd M. and Gina A. Zurlo. eds. *World Christian Database.* Leiden/Boston: Brill, 2021.

Lausanne Committee for World Evangelization. "Manila Manifesto." https://lausanne.org/content/manila-1989-documents (accessed July 15, 2023).

___. "The Seoul Declaration on Diaspora Missiology." (November 14, 2009), LCWE Diaspora Educators Consultation 2009. https://www.lausanne.org/content/statement/the-seoul-declaration-on-diaspora-missiology (accessed October 27, 2021).

Lausanne Committee for World Evangelization Issue Group No. 26 A and B: Diasporas and International Students. "Lausanne Occasional Paper 55: The New People Next Door." In *2004 Forum Occasional Papers* (September 29-October 5, 2004). Edited by David Clayton, 2005. https://lausanne.org/content/lop/diasporas-and-international-students-the-new-people-next-door-lop-55 (accessed October 27, 2021).

Looney, Jared. *Crossroads of the Nations: Diaspora, Globalization, and Evangelism,* edited by Kendi Howells Douglas and Stephen Burris. Portland, OR: Urban Loft Publishers, 2015.

Lorance, Cody C. "Reflections of a Church Planter Among Diaspora Groups in Metro-Chicago," In *Diaspora Missiology: Reflections on Reaching the Scattered Peoples of the World,* edited by Michael Pocock and Enoch Wan. Evangelical Missiological Society Series no 23, 259-84. Pasadena, CA: William Carey Library, 2015.

MacroTrends. "Philippines Immigration Statistics 1960-2023." https://www.macrotrends.net/countries/PHL/philippines/immigration-statistics:~:text=Philippines%20immigration%20statistics%20for%202010%20was%20208%2C599.00%2C%20a,2000%20was%20

318%2C095.00%2C%20a%2053.41%25%20increase%20from%201995. (accessed July 7, 2023).

Park, Hyung Jin. "The Journey of the Gospel and Being a World Christian." *Torch Trinity Journal* 13, no. 1 (May 30, 2010): 83-98.

Patterson, George. *Church Planting Through Obedience Oriented Teaching.* Pasadena, CA: William Carey Library, 1981.

Republic of the Philippines: Philippine Statistics Authority. "Foreign Citizens in the Country (2020 Census of Population and Housing)." July 4, 2023. https://psa.gov.ph/population-andhousing/node/177054 (accessed July 11, 2023).

___. "Overseas Workers From the Philippines - Statistics & Facts." December 2, 2022. https://psa.gov.ph/statistics/survey/labor-and-employment/survey-overseas-filipinos (accessed July 7, 2023).

Roberts, Bob Jr. *Glocalization: How Followers of Jesus Engage a Flat World.* Grand Rapids, MI: Zondervan, 2007.

Roces, Mina. "Filipino Migrants are Agents of Change." Lowy Institute. November 2, 2021https://www.lowyinstitute.org/the-interpreter/filipino-migrants-are-agents-change (accessed July 11, 2023).

Roembke, Lianne. *Building Credible Multicultural Teams.* Pasadena, CA: William Carey Library, 2000.

Rubesh, Ted. "Diaspora Distinctives: The Jewish Diaspora Experience in the Old Testament." *Torch Trinity Journal* 13, no. 2 (November 30, 2010): 114-136.

Scalabrini, Maruja M.B. Asis. "Repatriating Filipino Migrant Workers in the Time of the Pandemic." In I*nternational Organization for Migration*: Making Migration Work for All. Migration Research Series no. 63 (2020). https://publications.iom.int/system/files/pdf/mrs 63.pdf (accessed July 7, 2023).

Schnabel, Eckhard J. "Global Strategies and Local Methods of Missionary Work in the Early Church: Jesus, Peter and Paul (Brandtzaeg Memorial Lecture)." In *"The Church Going Glocal: Mission and Globalisation,"* edited by Tormod Engelsviken, Erling Lundeby and Dagfinne Solheim. Eugene, OR: Wipf and Stock Publishers, 2011: 20-46.

Senate of the Philippines Legislative Reference Bureau. Republic Act No. 8042. https://issuanceslibrary.senate.gov.ph/legislative%2Bissuances/Republic%20Act%20No.%20802 (accessed July 11, 2023).

Research Department. "Number of Immigrants Philippines 2005-2017." May 12, 2022. https://www.statista.com/statistics/698033/philippines-number-of-immigrants/ (accessed July 17, 2023).

___. "Philippines: Countries with the Highest Number of Filipino Emigrants." July 7, 2022. https://www.statista.com/statistics/1033910/countries-with-the-highest-number-of filipino-emigrants/(accessed July 7, 2023).

___. "Overseas Workers from the Philippines - Statistics & Facts." January 27, 2023. https://www.statista.com/topics/8943/labor-migrants-from-the-phil-ippines/topicOverview (accessed July 7, 2023).

Tira, Sadiri Joy. "Glocal Evangelism: Jesus Christ, Magdalena, and Damascus in the Greater Toronto Area." *Lausanne World Pulse*, (06-2010). http://www.lausanneworldpulse.com/perspectives-php/1291/06-2010 (accessed October 27, 2021).

Wan, Enoch. "Global People and Diaspora Missiology." Plenary paper, *Tokyo 2010 Global Mission Conference*, Tokyo, Japan, May 11-14, 2010. http://tokyo2010.org/resources/Tokyo2010_Plenary_Enoch_Wan.pdf (accessed November 11, 2017).

____. "Introduction." In Diaspora Missiology: Theory, Methodology, and Practice, edited by Enoch Wan, 3-10. 2nd ed. Portland, OR: IDS-USA, 2014.

____. "'Mission' and 'Missio Dei': Response to Charles Van Engen's 'Mission Defined and Described.'" In *MissionShift: Global Mission Issues in the Third Millennium*, edited by David J. Hesselgrave and Ed Stetzer, 41-50. Nashville, TN: B&H Publishing Group, 2010.

____. "Relational Paradigm for Practicing Diaspora Missions in the 21st Century." In Diaspora Missiology: Theory, Methodology, and Practice, edited by Enoch Wan, 191-203. 2nd ed. Portland, OR: IDS-USA, 2014.

____. "Relational Theology and Relational Missiology." *Occasional Bulletin 21*, no. 1 (Fall 2007). https://www.westernseminary.edu/files/documents/faculty/wan/Relat_theol_missio_OB_21_1.pdf (accessed October 27, 2021).

____. "Rethinking Missiology in the Context of the 21st Century: Global Demographic Trends and Diaspora Missiology." *Great Commission Research Journal* 2, no. 1 (Summer 2010). http://journals.biola.edu/gcr/volumes/2/issues/1/articles/7 (accessed November 11, 2017).

____. "Rethinking Missiological Research Methodology: Exploring a New Direction." *Global Missiology*, (October 2003). http://www.enochwan.com/english/articles/pdf/Rethinking%20Missiological%20Research%20Methodology.pdf (accessed October 27, 2021).

Wan, Enoch and Sadiri Joy Tira. "Diaspora Missiology and Mission in the Context of the 21st Century." *Global Missiology English* 1, no. 8 (October 2010). http://ojs.globalmissiology.org/index.php/english/article/viewFile/383/994 (accessed October 27, 2021).

Wan, Enoch and Tin V. Nguyen. "Towards a Theology of Relational Mission Training: An Application of the Relational Paradigm." *Global Missiology* 2, no. 11(January 2014). http://ojs.globalmissiology.org/index.php/english/article/view/1626/3600 (accessed December 22, 2021).

Wang, Juno. *Multi-ethnic Outreach in the Silicon Valley: A Chinese Diaspora Reaches Out to Multi-ethnic Diasporas*. Silicon Valley: Juno Wang, 2021.

Winter, Ralph D. "Three Mission Eras and the Loss and Recovery of Kingdom Mission, 1800-2000." In *Perspectives on the World Christian Movement: A Reader*, edited by Ralph D. Winter and Steven C. Hawthorne, 263-78, 4th ed. Pasadena, CA: William Carey Library, 2009.

Wright, Christopher J. H. *The Mission of God: Unlocking the Bible's Grand Narrative*. Downers Grove, IL: InterVarsity Press, 2006.

Yeh, Allen. *Polycentric Missiology: Twenty-First-Century Mission from Everyone to Everywhere*. Downers Grove, IL: InterVarsity Press, 2016.

Yi, Kevin. "The Temptations of Using Your 'Calling' as an Excuse." *Sola Network*. July 10, 2019. https://sola.network/article/temptations-calling-as-excuse (accessed December 27, 2021)

SOUTH ASIANS IN THE PHILIPPINES

Mark Edward Sudhir

In the supreme plan of God, the movement of people from one corner of the globe to another has become a significant and un-avoidable trend. All parts of the globe now have people in diaspora communities from many nationalities, people groups and religious groups. The Philippines has become a hub of international communities in Asia. In the last decade, it has grown even more rapidly. Mr. Chugani, an old-timer Indian, says, "We have been moving to the Philippines since the time of the partition of India, but the flocking in of Indians and other South East Asians has been mind-blowing."[1] Indeed, there has been a rising number of South Asian immigrants in the Philippines.

My wife and I have a definite call from God to reach out to our own peoples and plant churches among them both in native and diaspora contexts. We are from two different countries whose bilateral relationship are not good, so that we cannot go to each other's country easily. We were looking for a third country where we could live safely and serve God with the same vision both of us have to reach out to our own people. God opened the door miraculously for both of us to come to the Philippines and do pastoral ministry to the Indian church which had been there for two decades but was looking for a long-term Indian pastor. Responding to the call, we arrived in the Philippines. Though the existing church among the

Sindhi community brought me, that became a platform to extend the work of God among other people groups and religious groups.

There are four major categories of Indian diaspora in the Philippines: the Sindhi people group, Punjabi people group, Information and Technology expatriates, and medical students. They are found in every region of this country and the population of South Asians is almost a million. In 2008, "According to National Geographic, 3% of the average Filipino's genes are of South Asian origin, which equates to nearly 3,300,000."[2] My vision is to make disciples and plant churches among them throughout the Philippines.

This chapter aims to describe the presence, role, and relationships of South Asians in the Philippines as well how the church has affected and been affected by the South Asian diasporas. It will also discuss the challenges and opportunities of making disciples and report on the status of the ongoing gospel work among the South Asian diaspora communities. This chapter will not concentrate on socio-political aspects but rather focus on ministry aspects.

THE PRESENCE OF SOUTH ASIANS IN THE PHILIPPINES.

South Asians primarily are from India, Pakistan, Bangladesh and Sri Lanka. They are a minority group in the country, but they have been growing in number since the pandemic. "Their presence in the Philippines can be traced back several centuries, with historical records indicating that South Asians began arriving in the Philippines long before the Spanish colonization."[3] They were engaged in trade and cultural exchange between the Indian subcontinent and the Philippines, leading to the exchange of goods, ideas, and people. Among all of these countries, India contributes the highest number of its population in the Philippines. Indians have been contributing in many ways to the Filipino society in various fields. It is noticed that huge numbers of South Asians are arriving to the Philippines.

The arrival of South Asians started with the "Madrasis"[4] who sailed with the British through the East India company. They were obliged to the company to carry out their vision. These people were ill-paid and ill-treated. The payment they received was very low, and it was given to their families in India because the offices were in India. Indian workers in the Philippines often lived on the charity of their British superiors. Even after the British pulled out of Manila, a considerable number of sepoys and laborers working with the British East India company did not return to India. Many who remained were or had drifted into the bush to escape miserable living conditions at the garrison camp. A large group converged in the small town of Cainta. Their Dravidian physical features and dark complexion earned them the nickname of "Bombays," but they retain no memory of their Indian past.

Later, a group of business people came to the Philippine shores in the closing years of the nineteenth century; they were traders from Sindh, who pioneered in the establishment of business houses in various British colonies. During the time of the partition of India, these Sindhis were in the province called Sindh, which became part of Pakistan. Muslims at that time were forcing everyone who wanted to stay in the newly formed Pakistan to embrace Islam. But these Sindhis did not want to become Muslim. They had to leave their houses, businesses, and any property they had. They fled to different countries around the world and some of them arrived in the Philippines. There they developed high-scale businesses.

A different type of business people started to arrive in the Philippines in 1902, namely, the Punjabis. The first Punjabi who came to Manila learned that the Philippines had been acquired by America as a colony and that there were job opportunities there. Then, after his arrival. his friends and people from the province called Punjab started coming to the Philippines. They were not well-educated but worked as farmers and potters. These people groups were comfortable living in the outskirts of the cities, and they managed to retain the peculiarly rural traits which characterize their communal and social life in the Philippines. They are generally conservative, cautious, and hardworking.

Among the South Asian community, another group that has grown spectacularly more recently is made up of medical students.

During the past decade, more Indian and other South Asians than ever before have come to the Philippines for their medical studies. One of the main reasons for them to choose Philippine medical universities is that financially they are much more reasonable than in India. One medical student, Jibi, says, "With the donation amount for admission in the medical college that we need to pay in India, we can finish our four years of studies here in the Philippines."[5]

With the growing healthy biliteral relationship between India and the Philippines, another group of South Asians coming to the Philippines are the Information and Technology experts. Engineers of different fields are coming to contribute and develop infrastructures. They now number in the thousands. Though they are here for a short term, they bring in plenty of influence on the local society,

The Roles and Contributions of South Asians in the Philippines. South Asians have played a significant role in the cultural diversity and historical development of the Philippines. Following are some areas where they have made others feel their presence by contributing significantly.

Religion and Culture: South Asians are mostly Hindus, Muslims, Sikhs, and Buddhists. They bring their religions with them to the Philippines. The number of Hindu temples, Sikh temples, and Muslim mosques is increasing throughout the country[6] In 2010, when I first came to the Philippines, Hindu and Sikh temples and Muslim mosques were very few and were found only in selected cities. Ajit Singh Rye points out, "Philippines-Indian cultural links developed, over a long period of time, prior to the spread of Islam in Southeast Asia." Brahmanical and Buddhist influence spread through the intervening culture areas to the islands of Borneo, as well as Mindanao and Visayas in the Philippines."[7] Today there are traces of Indian cultural and religious influence in the Philippines, such as the worship of Hindu deities, Sikh religious processions, Muslim festivals and holidays and the presence of Buddhist artifacts. Hindu festivals such as Ganapati festival,[8] Diwali,[9] and Holi[10] have become great crowd-gathering and attracting events in the Philippines. More Filipinos are also joining the religious festivals and celebrations.

Today, many Filipinos like Indian food and buy Indian groceries as well as watching Indian Bollywood movies. These are a very strong display of how the culture of the Philippines has been shaped. A taxi driver greeting me in the Indian language greeting *Namaste*[11] and saying *Shukriya*[12] is such a warm experience. Indian cuisine has left a lasting impact on Filipino food culture. Dishes like curry and kare kare (a Filipino stew with a peanut sauce) have Indian origins or influences. Some South Asians, especially the Indians, have made significant contributions to the country in fields like politics, entertainment, and sports.

Economic Sector: South Asians are involved in various businesses including textiles, jewelry, electronics, medicines, and restaurants. They are one of the major suppliers to the malls and businesses in the Philippines. Their contributions are very visible in the markets. When one goes to the downtown area, it is obvious that many wholesale shops belong to South Asians. On the other hand, the Sikh community, which counts highest among the Indian population in the Philippines, is involved in micro-financing businesses, which are locally called "five-six" businesses. In these. they lend the customer at their doorsteps money or things without any collateral and collect the money little by little from their doorsteps on a daily basis. Many Filipino vendors and small-scale businesspeople as well as local people borrow money from the Indians. Some of them don't get their money back, and they put their lives at stake due to the risk of an angry customer or fellow competitors; nevertheless, on a daily basis Indian Sikhs from the province of Punjab are coming to the Philippines.

Social Sector: South Asians in the Philippines up to a certain level have made very good friendships with the local Filipinos. There are many inter-marriages taking place. Throughout the Philippines, the number of Fil-Indian families is multiplying. These integrated families are bringing the Indian influence to their extended families and that is affecting the lives of everyone. In social settings, many practices that were only seen in Indian before are now seen in Philippine families and society. The distance between the two cultures is becoming shorter. Interactions with other communities and ethnic groups have been growing with the South Asian community.

While South Asians constitute a small minority in the Philippines, their presence is more pronounced in urban areas, particularly in cities like Manila, Cebu and Davao. Many South Asians have integrated into Filipino society and have become part of the cultural tapestry of the country.

RESPONSE OF THE FILIPINO CHURCH AND SOCIETY TOWARDS SOUTH ASIANS.

The response of Filipino churches and society towards South Asians is similar to that toward other countries around the globe. Since Filipinos remember Spanish colonialism (1565-1896) and American colonialism (1898-1946), their response towards South Asians is one of suspicion and maintenance of distance. The reception they receive in Filipino society is often influenced by their socio-economic status and the nature of their interactions with local communities. As in many parts of the world, South Asians in the Philippines may occasionally be stereotyped and face prejudice, particularly if they are seen as outsiders. However, these attitudes are not uniform and vary among individuals. Some common attitudes are mentioned below.

Uninformed of the Culture or Religion: Filipino churches and society are not very familiar with the religions and culture of South Asians. Filipino society is mostly Catholic and has had little exposure to South Asian religions like Hinduism, Sikhism, Buddhism, and Islam. Moreover, South Asians in the Philippines come from diverse cultural and economic backgrounds, including professionals, entrepreneurs, and migrant workers.

Assuming Missions Only across Borders: The evangelical churches in the Philippines, like in many other countries, have the understanding that missions means going across borders. Lately, some churches are understanding the new dimension of the mission, but the traditional view of mission still is predominantly that, when we go out of the country as a missionary to reach out to other nationalities, then that is the mission. Many overseas foreign workers are going as tentmakers to different countries of the South Asian subcontinent, and many churches are supporting them, but the concept of reaching the South Asians here in the Philippines is not usually considered by the majority of churches. That nearby South Asian diaspora communities can be potential church planting locations is understood by very few local churches. It is recorded by the Philippines Mission Association that not even 100 churches are involved in reaching out to Hindus and Sikhs.[13]

Difficult to Reach: Although there are some churches engaged in reaching out to the South Asian diaspora, the perception of Hindus and Sikhs in the Filipino churches is they are hard to connect to. Lack of thorough knowledge about these religions makes it difficult for Filipino churches. The Hindu and Sikh cultures are so complex that it becomes hard for the locals to understand. For a Hindu or Sikh to make the decision to follow Jesus may not be possible in a short time, and it may take years. Due to cultural and family ties, community and social pressure, religious beliefs and practices, religious persecution, and personal convictions, the South Asian in diaspora context seems virtually unreachable for Filipino churches.

Challenges to Reach out to South Asians in the Philippines.

Reaching out to South Asians in the Philippines can be challenging due to various factors. Some of them that I have personally experienced and observed by the ministries of some Filipino churches are now mentioned.

Panentheism: Most of the South Asian diaspora are from Hindu and Sikh religion followers. For them, God is immanent in the world, which means that God is present within all things, guiding and sustaining the universe. At the same time, God transcends the world, being greater and beyond the physical universe. It is not limited to a single religion or belief system. For them to add Jesus as one of the many gods is not a problem, but to make Jesus the only God becomes the issue.

Little Awareness by the Local Church: Despite the dramatic growth of the South Asian diaspora in the Philippines, the awareness to reach out to them and make disciples is very low. There are several reasons for varying levels of engagement and awareness. Some factors that may contribute to the little awareness by Filipino churches in reaching out to Sooth Asians are limited exposure, cultural and linguistic barriers, focus on other priorities, lack of information, fear of insensitivity, and the historical and political context. Not many churches are even aware of themselves being capable to reach out to the South Asian diaspora.

Limited Manpower: Not only Filipino churches but also Indian churches which have been planted in the last decade are finding that one of the many crucial challenges is lack of effective and available workers. We have been working on training and raising up leaders who will carry out the ministry among the South Asian diaspora, but compared to the population and its spread in all the regions, we have very little manpower. People who are biblically grounded, culturally oriented, speaking the languages of the target people groups, passionate, and adequately resourced are needed for ministering to the Hindus and Sikhs in the Philippines. Raising committed indigenous missionaries is the priority, but their involvement in their businesses, work, and studies creates very tough challenges. For new Christians to grow into maturity takes time. On the other hand, the training of Filipino churches is also time consuming.

Time Factor: Among all the categories in the South Asian diaspora, Indian medical students are in the Philippines for four to five years. This is also true of the Sikh businessmen who come to the Philippines to equip themselves in the English language and accumulate some finances in order to prepare themselves to settle in countries like the United States of America, Canada, and Australia. It is extremely important for the churches to reach out to them while they are in the country. The medical students come from the upper class and middle class of Indian society. To ignore them or delay in reaching out will cause them to finish their time span here in the Philippines and move out without hearing the gospel.

OPPORTUNITIES TO DISCIPLE
THE SOUTH ASIANS.

Every difficulty can become an opportunity for the gospel among the unreached communities. Discipling the South Asian diaspora in the Philippines does have a few opportunities in the midst of the various challenges. Most of the opportunities are found in the deep-down core issues that they are facing.

Less Social Pressure: India and South Asian culture is typified by close family bonds. Extended families are closely associated and involved in each other's lives. That also creates social pressure on a person's decisions, hobbies, and careers. Everyone walks in the standards and cultures of their society. South Asian cultures often place a strong emphasis on family values and obligations. Religious and cultural norms can exert pressure on individuals to observe customs, rituals, and practices within their communities. Deviating from these norms can lead to social stigmatization. The growing number of persecutions in South Asian contexts are due to someone's conversion to Christianity. In the decision-making process of a person, society plays a huge role. Society and family interfere in the life of people.

By contrast, in the diaspora context, due to the absence of family members and other people from the same community, and busy with their own work in a Christian country like Philippines, people in diaspora have less possibility of anyone interfering with them following their personal choices. Compared to their home countries, social pressure is very low. Every day they have access to Catholic and Christian culture. In our ministries we have seen that many people make decision without the fear of social pressure.

Legal Issues: Among the Indian diaspora the majority are the Punjabi Sikh community. Many of them are illegal and less-educated immigrants. They are involved in a type of business which is very risky. They put their lives at risk and practice the money-lending business. We have witnessed many cases of kidnaping for ransom, shooting deaths, holdups and various other situations that trouble them. Due to their minimal educational backgrounds and illegal presence in the country, they fall in the traps of fake agencies and people who offer them solutions for high amount of money. They end up paying everything they have earned and many still have no solutions. Many Indian medical students come to the Philippines with false promises and agreements with the agencies and have paid them huge amounts of money, but when the students arrive here in the Philippines, schools completely deny the agreements they have come with. They are stuck with no school and no visa. For them to get into a school and acquire a visa is next to impossible. That has caused many to be depressed and commit suicide.

Their rough situations create an opportunity for us to get involved and share the gospel with them, while at the same time directing them to the right path to make themselves legal and overcome the difficult situations they are in. We have ministered to huge numbers of people who were in these types of problems. A majority of them have encountered Christ in the process of dealing with their situations. They have experienced that the fear that they were living with is gone when they come to know Jesus Christ and pray in His name.

Marital Problems: Unlike many other countries, the Philippines doesn't offer jobs for foreigners. The only solution to acquiring a valid visa they find is through having a Filipino spouse. Some South Asians get married on paper by paying a significant amount so they can obtain their visas. The marriages for the purpose of visa ends up in their staying together. However, most of them are already married in India. When the spouse in India finds out about their marriage here in the Philippines, it creates havoc in the family. Likewise, when the already-existing marriage comes to the knowledge of the Filipina spouse, that becomes a life-threatening and legal issue here. In many families, the spouse from India comes to the Philippines, too. So, then the man stays in one house with his Indian wife and keeps the Filipina wife in her place. This causes huge family problems.

Often in these situations, addiction to alcohol, domestic violence, financial problems, and depression are the result. A Punjabi counselor in the Philippines named Jimmy says, "There are so many families are broken due to having no proper guidance on what type of visa they should have when one comes from India, in order to avoid future jeopardy."[14] This unhappy situation gives the church an opportunity to bring peace and reconciliation through solutions that are biblical. We have been guiding the people when they come to the Philippines on how to acquire a visa which will not lead them to family problems. Added to that, we have started counseling ministries to the affected families to help them live in unity and peace. In the process of reconciliation, they are given Bibles and the gospel of Jesus.

Young and Secular Mindset: Those who are arriving now from South Asian contexts, or are born in South Asian diaspora families or are medical students are all young. Therefore, their mindset in secular and global. It is often observed that young individuals, with their open and inquisitive mindset, can be receptive to new ideas and beliefs, including the gospel of Christian faith. Older people are very strong in their Hindu and Sikh religions. In contrast, the young people are naturally curious and open to exploring Christian beliefs. Their openness to information already gives them some ideas on Christianity and that is supplemented by the Christian culture in the Philippines.

Vicky, a young man whom we visited in his house in Taytay, said, "I was wondering how I could meet with Indian Christian people to know about Christianity, as I have been seeing churches around whenever I go out for work."[15] He not only heard the gospel himself but also invited his relatives and friends because it was the very first time we were visiting him. Since then, they have showed interest in coming to the church though they live far from where our church is located.

Christian Atmosphere: The majority of the South Asian diaspora are out there in the streets and marketplace every day. They see churches everywhere; people are either Catholics or Christians. Some of their business clients and customers are born-again Christians. In terms of medical students, many of their professors are good Christians. They have access to the Christian atmosphere. The long Christmas celebration in the Philippines gives them opportunities to hear Christmas messages in various places and forms.

When we present Jesus to them, they don't reject him up front because they have already been influenced by the Christian culture.

The friendly and generous culture of the Philippines demonstrates good influence of Christians. They find great differences between Indian and Filipino culture in good ways. They find Filipinos are very helpful, understanding, and easy to be friends with, whereas, in India, competition and jealousy are everywhere. Indians come from a classification based on caste and financial status, but in the Philippines, everyone is considered equal. This creates a good opportunity to share Jesus with them, since their hearts are prepared to be receptive.

BIBLICAL MODELS FOR EFFECTIVE STRATEGIES.

To reach out to the South Asian diaspora in the Philippines, biblical strategies are very effectively helping us to plant churches. Below are some strategies that are working in the Philippines.

Contextualization: Contextualization in Christian mission is becoming effective in all parts of the globe. It is the process of adapting the message of the gospel to the cultural, social, and linguistic context of a particular group of people.[16] In the context of South Asians in the Philippines, we are presenting the message of Christ in a way that resonates with Hindu and Sikh cultures while remaining faithful to the core teaching of the Bible.

The Apostle Paul's speech on Mars Hill in Athens (Acts 17:22-31) provides an example of contextualization. He engaged with the local philosophers by referencing their altar to the "unknown god" and used it as a starting point to introduce them to the true God. Following John 1:14, the concept of incarnation, where the Word became flesh and dwelt among us, is a foundational model of our contextualization.

In the parables Jesus conveyed spiritual truths in terms that were familiar to His audience. Likewise, we are bringing them to their scripture and letting them understand how it is directing them to Christ. We use the language they speak in our worship, and give them Bibles, testimonies, and music in their heart languages. In the church we serve vegetarian food, keep the shoes on, and our and men and women sit separate. Women cover their heads while worshiping. We use Indian instruments in our worship. When people from South Asian cultures come to our church, they are finding belongingness.

Welcome the Strangers: Welcoming strangers is a biblical principle that encourages hospitality and care for immigrant businessmen, Indian medical students, and all foreigners. It is rooted in the Bible, emphasizing the importance of compassion, kindness, and inclusion toward those who are new to a community. Leviticus 19:33-34 says, "When a foreigner resides among you in your land, do not mistreat them. The foreigner among you must be treated as your native-born. Love them as yourself, for you were foreigners in Egypt. I am the Lord your God."[17]

We in our ministries provide care, counseling, and compassionate assistance when they are in troubles, bankrupt, or depressed. They are far from home and looking for help in their time of difficulties. One Pakistani Catholic family came to the Philippines as refugees. They obtained papers to stay legally, but they had no any help financially for their shelter, food, and daily expenses. They were living in difficulty and misery, and they had no one to hear their case when the Philippines was going through a long pandemic lockdown. We extended our helping hands towards them for their survival every month, and eventually, when the lockdown was slowly loosened, we were able to assist them to open a small canteen near the medical college where Indian medical students are. Now they are in a good shape and they got to know the importance of a personal relationship with God through Jesus alone.

Another two Sikh men were going through bankruptcy and all the doors for them were closed. During our outreach activities we met them. One of them had tried to commit suicide three times, but according to him, he was unsuccessful. God in His perfect plan for these two men enabled us to help them through counseling, financial help, and mentoring them with prayer and Bible studies. They are now living confidently and with faith in Jesus. People and friends of theirs who were looking down on them have now been surprised by the transformation that has happened in these two men's lives.

Power Evangelism: One of the key strategies that is working effectively among the South Asian diaspora is power evangelism. John Wimber writes that power evangelism "emphasizes the supernatural power and demonstration of the Holy Spirit as a means of sharing the Gospel and ministering to others."[18] It often involves practices such as healing and other miraculous manifestations to convey the message of Jesus.

South Asians are very religious in their context and always looking for a tangible experience of God. For them to choose only Jesus as their Lord and Savior out of 33 billion gods and goddesses requires spiritual interventions that are truly supernatural and miraculous. For a Hindu, Muslim, or Sikh mindset to understand and embrace only one to be their God, power evangelism is very instrumental and successful. When they experience a more powerful God than what they have been hearing of in their religious background, it becomes easy to pause and think and know more about Jesus.

A very rich and strong Hindu tried everything that he could by visiting good hospitals, temples, catholic centers, and faith healers but nowhere experienced any breakthrough from the evil spirit's trouble to one of the family members. The whole family was very tired and scared. Someone met them and talked about us, suggesting that they meet with Indian pastor, and that he might know what to do about this. When we met and prayed for the demon-possessed person, the evil spirit started demonstrating its various appearances and power. When I started asking the evil spirit about its purpose, existence, and reality it started sharing why it is scared of Jesus and where they are from and where they bring people who worship them and all the others except Jesus. The evil spirit admitted they came from hell and they bring all to hell. The family was listening to everything. In fact, the evil spirit gave the gospel to the family indirectly. The family understood and decided to believe in Jesus. We cast out demons and the entire Hindu family put their faith in Jesus and now they are all very strong Christ followers.

God healed a man who was on a ventilator; another family had a child born normal when four doctors had done ultrasound and said there was water in the head of the baby in the womb and no brain; and another women was completely healed from all her kidney stones. There have been many miracles of healing, family reconciliation, and businesses sustained. Associate priests and scripture readers from other faiths have come to Christ by seeing the miraculous work of Jesus in the lives of their family members and friends. These are not things that we promote as our work but as God's work of bringing people when we are eager to reach out to the South Asian diaspora with the Gospel.

SUGGESTIONS AND CONCLUSION.

The population of the South Asian diaspora is growing rapidly in the Philippines. In the next few years there is a possibility that it will grow more. The work of the gospel among these communities needs to grow faster than now. Here I would like to bring a few suggestions for the churches, missionaries, and mission agencies to consider in order to have a healthy and effective ministry towards making disciples and planting churches among the South Asians.

Mobilize the local churches: When more churches get involved in engaging with South Asians in the Philippines, the work will grow and pick up speed. Today, not many churches are informed enough to be involved, and there are many who think they are not ready, so very few churches are making any attempts to learn about these communities. More Filipino churches need to be mobilized and given orientation about South Asian religion, culture, and effective ways to reach them. Seminaries need to equip theologians to be able to reach out to the South Asians. Churches of all denominations and in every region must be mobilized to engage in doing kingdom work among South Asians. Visiting the churches, bringing awareness in conferences, conducting missional Bible studies in the churches, letting Filipino churches visit and observe the South Asian churches in the Philippines and other simultaneous steps are needed to mobilize the local churches.

Raise More Indigenous Workers of the Gospel: A very important step we need to take is to raise leaders, evangelists, missionaries and pastors from the South Asian background. They speak their language, they know their worldview and mindset, they can connect well with their life-changing testimonies, and they are aware of their religious teachings and practices. Raising a Filipino or non-South Asian for ministry to South Asians may take a long time and is less effective. There are some advantages but comparatively more disadvantages in enabling them to appropriately and effectively communicate the gospel with the fellow South Asians.

We have observed that the churches that are growing in different places do so because of the first-generation Christ followers who are sharing their testimonies to their families and friends in different regions. They are opening their minds to hear about Jesus and perhaps be part of our services in person if they live nearby, or online if they are living far from where our churches are located. We have been challenging and motivating our people to serve God to win their own people for Christ.

This is effective in reducing the costs and time spent in preparing workers for the South Asians. Out of seven Indian churches, three churches are run by indigenous leaders who are first-generation Christ followers. Four leaders are now under training. There is need to raise more indigenous leaders who will serve the huge South Asian population to be discipled in the Philippines.

More Evangelistic Materials and Resources: Materials and resources are very crucial in strengthening evangelism and making disciples. Printed materials, audio visuals, social care equipment, resourceful and skilled persons, finances, and all kinds of evangelistic materials that are effective need to be created or multiplied.

Bringing in materials from India takes time, but producing them in the Philippines makes it more practical and makes it possible to print or record the local South Asians' testimonies. We have tried printing evangelistic materials in the Hindi and Punjabi languages, as well as recording and shooting some life-changing testimonies from Hindu- and Sikh-background Christ followers. Those are very effective and handy in our ministries to the South Asians in the Philippines.

Connect South Asian Ministers Globally: The more partnerships grow globally, the stronger ministry among South Asians will become locally. For South Asian minds, that which is emphasized and followed by people from their own background in countries like the USA, UK, Canada, and so on will attract them more. They are inspired by a South Asians who lives in America but is following Christ and try to do the same. It always has great advantages.

Connecting as much as possible with South Asian Christ-followers around the world gives them courage to declare their faith in Jesus boldly. When we started connecting some of our new believers with Christ-followers in Canada, Australia, and Singapore, they started growing more in the Lord. They feel like they are not alone and that no one can discourage them. A strong network of South Asians will help South Asians around the world to grow, witness, and plant churches. It will not only help churches to grow in the Philippines but in other parts of the world as well.

We are in a strategic time of world history to expand the church planting movement in the diaspora context for diasporas are everywhere now. My prayer is to see a church among South Asians in every barangay of the Philippines where they are found, and all around the world. India is rising up as a global power, so the Indian church must also grow globally, experiencing and spreading the revival to make disciples and plant churches among all nations. I believe South Asians will become powerful gospel bearers throughout the world.

----

1 Interview with Mr. Chugani, July 21, 2023, 1:30PM

2 https://www.findeasy.in/indian-population-in-philippines/, October 1, 2023. 8:30PM.

3 Gowing, P. G. Muslim Filipinos: Heritage and Horizon, New Day Publishers, 1988. p. 89

4 People from South India used to be called "Madrasi" after the name of the city Madras; now it is called Chennai, the capital city of Tamil Nadu, India.

5 Interview with Jibi Thomas, September 12, 2022, 4:00PM

6 D. J. Fernandez, "The South Asian Community in the Philippines: A Sociodemographic Study" in *Population Review*, 54 (1), pp 15-34.

7 Ajit Singh Rye, "The Indian Community in the Philippines: A Profile" in *Asian Studies: Journal of Critical Perspectives on Asia*, https://asj.upd.edu.ph/mediabox/archive/ASJ-19-1981/singhrye.pdf, September 20, 2023.

8 *Ganapati* festival is a major Hindu festival to worship a Hindu god called *Ganapati* or *Ganesh,* the elephant-head god, son of the third head in Hindu trinity. They perform idol worship publicly

for three or five or seven days, then deposit the idol in the ocean or river on the final days of worship.

9 *Diwali* is one of the big festivals for Hindus. It is a new year's celebration of victory of good over evil, and they celebrate the goddess Lakshmi believing that they will receive a blessing of wealth by her visitations if they light the candle and different types of lights at the entrance of their homes.

10 *Holi* is the color festival that is celebrated for three to four days, observed by greeting each other with sweets and colors in the belief that spreading of colors will bring unity.

11 *Namaste* is an Indian greeting, which literally means "greetings to you." It originates from the Hindu scripture Vedas as salutation to divinity.

12 *Shukriya* is an Urdu and Hindi word for "thank you."

13 Lalano Badoy, *Presentation on Mission of the Philippine Churches*, BLTC, Bible Society, Manila, October 12, 2023, 3PM.

14 *Interview with* Jimmy Singh, on September 12, 2023, 2:30pm. Jimmy is a senior Indian Punjabi who is staying in the Philippines for last three decades and knows many Indians here. He is contacted for help by fellow Punjabi Indians for their problems.

15 Vicky Singh, Taytay, Metro Manila, September 8, 2023, 6:15pm.

16 A. Scott Moreau, Contextualization in world Missions: Mapping and Assessing Evangelical Models, (Grand Rapids: Kregel Publications, 2012), P. 122-123. Also read Paul G. Hiebert, Transforming Worldviews: An Anthropological Understanding of How People Change, (Grand Rapids, Baker Academic, 2008), p.23.

17 Also read in Matthew 25:35, Hebrews 13:2, 1Peter 4:9, Romans 12:13, and Deuteronomy 10:18-19.

18 John Wimber and Kevin Springer, Power Evangelism, (California: Regal from Gospel Light Ventura, 2009), 78-79.

CHILD PROTECTION: SOCIO-THEOLOGICAL REFLECTIONS AND MINISTRY IMPLICATIONS

Nativity A. Petallar

INTRODUCTION

I am a minister who helps in my local church. One night, one of our lay pastors called me and reported to me that one of the girls in our Bible Study outreach had been sexually abused by her grandfather. I was at a loss on what to advise her. We have a Child Protection Policy in our local church, but this case happened outside our church. What should I tell our lay pastor? Since this child is not a regular member of our local church nor is she registered in our childcare sponsorship program, we cannot implement the procedures that we have laid out in our Child Protection Policy against this alleged abusive grandfather. So, after considering the problem, I told our lay pastor to do the following: first, make sure the child was safe. Take her out of the abusive situation. Second, report the incident to the Barangay Child Welfare Desk. She did all these things and was rather successful in preventing the abuse from happening again. Now the child is attending our regular childcare sponsorship ministry. How many churches today are equipped to respond to disclosures of abuse?

This article aims to discuss socio-theological perspectives on child protection and identify practical ministry applications.

WHY CHILD PROTECTION?

Davao City. An Overseas Filipino Worker (OFW) came home to bury her two-year-old son who was beaten to death by his guardians.[1] What was the reason for the beating? The guardians got angry after the child urinated in his pants.

Manila. Another boy was beaten to death by other wards in a Manila shelter for street children. Observers described this government-run rehabilitation center as a concentration camp because of its cases of negligence and maltreatment.[2]

Cebu City. Six children—most under age 7—were sexually exploited in images and video broadcast online to customers in over 19 countries on four continents! This was reported by the International Justice Mission (IJM).[3] Two girls who were not quite eight years old were made to do sexual acts with minors as well as adults. These included intercourse as well as acts involving sex toys. This happened in Metro Manila as reported by ABS-CBN news.[4]

Worldwide, there are nearly 2 million children in the commercial sex trade.[5] Manila is one of the most lucrative destinations for traffickers. The Philippines, in general, is a major hub of a billion-dollar global child cybersex industry.[6] Women and children from the provinces are lured to the capital with the promise of a better life. But these women and children mostly end up in the sex trafficking industry, both in the entertainment clubs as well as in cybersex, the modern-day form of slavery. Now we ask the question: what happened to the Philippines—the largest Christian country in Asia, with over 89% of the population identifying as Christians? Why are our children deprived of a happy childhood and are suffering, sometimes in silence?

Child protection is part and parcel of caring for children in a holistic way. Child protection is a broad term to describe philosophies, policies, standards, guidelines and procedures to protect children from both intentional and unintentional harm.[7] Brewster and McCloud call it, "protecting children from ourselves."[8] To know the essence of child protection we need to identify who the child is and the vital reasons why the child should be protected, using research as well as existing statutory policies both within the Philippines as well as in the international context.

WHO IS THE CHILD?

When a child comes into this world, a plan has already been set in motion in the heart of God. A child does not come into this world by accident, though some parents may think that one or two of their children came out unplanned. In the church, when a child passes through our doors, we have to be aware that a thousand possibilities are before us! How astounding to be part of the journey of this person, fearfully and wonderfully crafted by the Creator Himself! To be able to protect this child, one needs to know the nature of this person.

Let us look at the child using three lenses, to wit, biological, cultural, and biblical, and let us identify some implications for child protection in the local church (Figure 1). This diagram presents the ways in which the nature of the child can be viewed. All these lenses contribute to how we view and consequently treat a child.

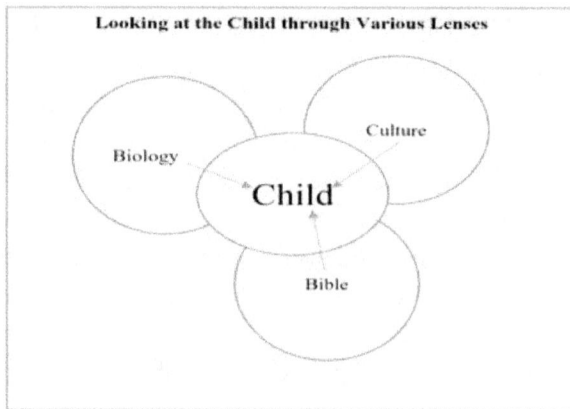

Figure 1: Looking at the Child Using Various Points of View

BIOLOGICAL VIEW ON THE CHILD

First, let us look at the child using the lens of biology. Davies writes, "A human child is the product of human conception, usually via sexual intercourse between an adult male and an adult female which results in the fertilization of the female ovum by the male sperm."[9] When a child is born, she is 100% human, capable of knowing, being, and doing. Post-modern researchers and child psychologists note that contrary to the belief of the Greek Stoics, Aristotle, Rousseau, and Locke a millennia or so ago—a newborn child is not born with a blank slate, or tabula rasa, but rather is a human being complete with her genetic code, preferences, and leanings. There are studies showing how newborns display knowledge of some form which they did not have to learn from the outside world. For instance, a study conducted by Van Heugtena and Johnson on infants showed that "infants begin to exhibit some ability to recognize variable word forms from speech very early on."[10] The "Baby Human" experiments found out that "the baby human comes into the world ready to communicate" and that the moment a baby is born, they are "attuned" to language.[11] Janet Werker, awarded for her research investigating infants' language acquisition concludes, "The more time you spend around infants and young children, the more you realize how organized the mind is from early in life."[12] This new development in research shows us that even before a baby is born into this world, God has already made her ready and so our responsibility starts right there and then especially in relation to child protection. Children develop from general motor, social, mental, and emotional characteristics to increasingly complex characteristics.[13] Our goal is for every child to thrive, to mature, to develop her God-given potential. A child's growth can be affected by many factors like nutrition, rest, exercise, illness, abuse, neglect, nurture, and a host of other elements. This is why in Christian education our ministries are designed from "the womb to the tomb." We aim to minister to the whole person.

CULTURAL ANALYSIS OF THE CHILD

Second, children may also be looked at through the eyes of culture. In the international community, one human rights treaty ratified by 196 countries is the United Nations Convention on the Rights of the Child (UNCRC). This international document defines 'child' as "every human being below the age of 18 years unless under the law applicable to the child, majority is attained earlier."[14] Culturally, the child is a member of a people group. In the Philippines, the child is considered to be "one of the most important assets of the nation."[15] Under this definition comes the following declaration of the Policy of the Child and Welfare Code: The child is not a mere creature of the State. This welfare code in the country is replete with injunctions on how to raise, protect, and nurture the child with the help of the State and other organizations in the country like the church or NGOs. Filipino anthropologist Landa Jocano commented that the majority of the Filipino people view children as "*biyaya ng Diyos*" (gifts from God).[16] This view reflects the biblical view of the child. Furthermore, Tomas Andres explains that children are signs of God's favor, the fulfillment of manhood and womanhood, and are gifts from above.[17] Filipinos in general place a high value on children.

BIBLICAL UNDERSTANDING OF THE CHILD

Finally, the Bible, the textbook for our education in the local church, describes the child using the following unique descriptions among many others: (1) created in the image of God (Gen. 1:26-31; 2:18-25; Ps. 139:13-14); (2) heritage from the Lord (Ps. 127:3); (3) included in God's covenant (Deut. 29:10-15, 31:12-13); and (4) crown to the aged (Prov. 17:6). These Scripture references show how special a child is in the eyes of God and the biblical writers. Furthermore, children have the following capacities as noted in Scriptures: (1) to glorify God (Matt. 21:15,16); (2) to come to Christ (Mark 10:13-16); (3) to understand Scripture (2 Tim. 3:15); (4) to receive the promises

(Acts 2:39); (5) to believe (Matt.18:6); (6) to receive training (Eph. 6:4); and (7) to worship in God's house (1 Sam. 1:24,28).[18] As such, the local church has the joy, responsibility, and opportunity to nurture them in the knowledge of God until they "reach unity in the faith and in the knowledge of the Son of God and become mature, attaining to the whole measure of the fullness of Christ" (Eph. 4:13, NIV).

Zuck writes: "Children are not an afterthought in the Bible. The word "child" is used 121 times; children—448 times; son or sons—2,700 times; (not counting the references to Jesus as the Son of God); firstborn— 100 plus times; boys and girls—196 times. There are also dozens of stories about or including children. All together the child and family-related words occur more than 8,000 times."[19] This shows how the Bible portrays the importance of children.

Cadwallader, a reflective Catholic scholar observes, "Frequently in the Bible and in Christian tradition, children appear as little more than objects of adult writing and that not always favourably. Speech by and to children in the NT is miniscule, possibly ten instances in each case. By contrast children are spoken about (whether in direct speech, narrative or epistolary address) numerous times, at least 82 times, 45 in direct or indirect speech."[20] Cadwallader is emphasizing that the church needs to put children on equal footing with adults and that unless children are "factored inextricably into Christological and theological exposition, actual children will remain marginalised and forced to be dependent on fashions of adult concern and attention."[21]

To enrich this discussion, the Lausanne Occasional Paper (LOP) created by the Lausanne Issue Network for Children at Risk presents a high view of children and a high view of Scripture using the biblical story of young Samuel.[22] Using this approach, the following are some biblical principles that emerge: (1) all children should be holistically nurtured throughout childhood; (2) God uses whom God will, including those on the margins of life, where many children find themselves; (3) children can be called by God and hear God's voice; (4) children can be active participants in worship and service to God; (5) the people of God are to respect, listen to, envision, and empower children as vulnerable agents of God's mission. These principles provide a framework which allow the church to nurture and protect children as well as empower and release them as agents of God's mission. This framework also provides boundaries so that children are not placed in situations of spiritual abuse by the adults who try to release them to be part of the *missio Dei*. This gives us the unifying theme that children are important because they are created in the image of God and that they need our care and attention.

CHILD PROTECTION IN THE BIBLE

God in His sovereignty has entrusted the care of children to adults. When God created the world, we read in Genesis chapter 2:7, "Then the Lord God formed the man of dust from the ground and breathed into his nostrils the breath of life, and the man became a living creature" (ESV). Then Genesis 2:15 says, "The Lord God took the man and put him in the garden of Eden to work it and keep it" (ESV). Then when we go back to Genesis 1:27-28, the Bible says, "So God created man in his own image, in the image of God he created him; male and female he created them. And God blessed them. And God said to them, 'Be fruitful and multiply and fill the earth and subdue it, and have dominion over the fish of the sea and over the birds of the heavens and over every living thing that moves on the earth'" (ESV). Finally, we find in Genesis chapter 4:1 that Adam and Eve had children. The fruit of the relationship of Adam and Eve is children. This implies that God intends for children to be cared for by persons who are in a relationship with one another in the context of a loving family.

CHILD PROTECTION IN THE OLD TESTAMENT

Looking at Deuteronomy 6, there is a mandate for the family and the whole congregation of Israel to teach the laws of God in a total curriculum of experience. The teaching of the law is emphasized so Israel can flourish in the Promised Land into which they are about to enter. Within the context of God's law, there is protection. The foreigner, the orphans, and the fatherless are protected under the law of God. Thus, when Israel observes God's statutes, no one is to be treated badly, especially the children. The community of faith has the mandate to provide this environment of loving and caring. In like manner, New Testament believers are mandated to go and teach the Gospel of Jesus Christ, which also encapsulates loving God and one's neighbor (Matthew 18 and Matthew 22), just like what Moses taught Israel as written in the book of Deuteronomy.

CHILD PROTECTION IN THE NEW TESTAMENT

Jesus shows His care for children by providing a space for them to come to Him (Matt. 19:14). When little children were brought to Him, Jesus placed His hands on them (Matt. 19:13). John Wesley commented that the laying on of hands was a rite which was very early used in praying for a blessing on young persons.[23] Jesus also mentions the horrible punishment of someone who causes little ones to sin. He says, "Whoever causes one of these little ones who believe in Me to sin, it would be better for him if a millstone were hung around his neck, and he were drowned in the depth of the sea" (Matthew18:6, NKJV). This punishment was practised by the Greeks, Syrians, and Romans at the time. A millstone is a large circular rock used to grind wheat and other kinds of grain into flour. This is then turned around by either a human being or an ox. If a person is thrown down into the sea with this kind of millstone, that person, even though he or she knows how to swim would still die by drowning due to the fact that the weight of the stone would not allow him or her to swim to the surface. Jesus cautions His audience on the importance of making sure that the little ones are brought up in a gentle and healthy environment.

In this particular verse, namely, Matthew 18:6, "little ones" in Greek is "mikros mikroteros," meaning "small in size." Keener writes, "The most powerless members of ancient society were little children.

In Jewish culture, children were loved, not despised; but the point is that they had no status apart from that love, and no power or privileges apart from what they received as total dependents on their parents."[24]

In the Hellenistic context, Gundry-Volf explains,

> *Childhood was viewed largely negatively as a state of immaturity to outgrow . . . people considered children fundamentally deficient and not yet human in the full sense. They were physically small, underdeveloped, and vulnerable. They were mentally deficient and ignorant; they spoke nonsense and failed to think and plan rationally; they were capricious, foolish and quarrelsome. In a word, they lacked the prime Roman virtue of reason and could not participate in the rational world of Roman citizens.*[25]

But Jesus modeled a different kind of attention to the "little ones." Jesus placed a great value on the children. Children as created in the image of God possess intellect, reason, spirituality, feelings, beauty immortality, and creativity. As created in the image of God, children are also capable of righteousness. As such they have to be respected and treated as persons, not as property or objects that anyone can dispose of. Children have to be respected for who they are, not for who or what adults want them to be.

The church needs to make parents fully aware that there is a need to respect the dreams, goals and life choices of their children. The church needs to emphasize to the parents not to live vicariously through their children's lives but instead to provide opportunities for children to choose what they want to become and support, guide, and journey with them until they become what God intends them to be. This does not mean that parents go to the extreme and just allow their children to do whatever they want apart from godly values. There needs to be guidance, gentle prodding, and some discipline in the journey.

In the home and in the ministries of the church, children's voices need to be amplified. They have to be consulted in decisions that affect their wellbeing and happiness. The church can respect the rights and voices of children in the following ways: (1) by studying the nature, characteristics, rights and responsibilities of children; (2) by amplifying their voices through creative activities that allow children to express their preferences, like drawing, casual conversations, journaling, or by providing, for example, a "free wall," where children write their wishes, prayer requests, or other thoughts; and (3) by letting them participate on matters that affect them, e.g., asking them what lessons and activities they would prefer to be included in their curriculum for Sunday school or other children's programs, what kinds of outdoor activities are meaningful to them, how the church should be structured to fit their physical, socio emotional, and spiritual needs, and what kinds of opportunities they desire for service, missions and outreach .

WHO SHOULD PROTECT THE CHILD?

Child protection is a cooperative effort among many individuals and systems. Kevin Bales, professor of Contemporary Slavery at the Wilberforce Institute for the Study of Slavery and Emancipation writes that slavery can be eliminated in our lifetime. He asserts, "Slavery has been and *is* coming to an end."[26] He discusses the historical perspective of slavery and emancipation—how individuals and governments have been successful in eradicating slavery with collaboration and strong political will.

There is a model that could be used in our efforts towards collaboration to ensure the safety of children in our midst. There are many possible models, but this theory is unique since it has included religious organizations in the development of the child. This is called Bronfenbrenner's Ecological Systems Theory. Bronfenbrenner has a unique definition of development. He writes, "Development is a lasting change in the way in which a person perceives and deals with his environment."[27] This implies that if one desires to study a child, he needs to consider not just the child's immediate environment, but also the influences of the larger system that directly or indirectly affect the development of the child. These systems have continuing impacts on an individual's development.[28] For Bronfenbrenner, the ecological environment is conceived topologically as a nested arrangement of concentric structures, each contained within the next. These structures are referred to as micro-, meso-, exo-, and macrosystems and can be defined as follows:[29]

A microsystem is a pattern of activities, roles, and interpersonal relations experienced by the developing person in a given setting with particular physical and material characteristics.

A mesosystem comprises the interrelations among two or more settings in which the developing person actively participates such as, for a child, the relations among home, school, and neighborhood peer group. For an adult, this includes family, work, and social life.

An exosystem refers to one or more settings that do not involve the developing person as an active participant, but in which events occur that affect, or are affected by, what happens in the setting containing the developing person.

The macrosystem refers to consistencies in the form and content of lower-order systems (micro-, meso-, and exo-) that exist, or could exist, at the level of the subculture or the culture as a whole, along with any belief systems or ideology underlying such consistencies.

Macrosystem
e.g. government policy on
employment and working conditions

Exosystem
e.g. parents' conditions
of employment

Mesosystem
of links
between
e.g. home
microsystem

e.g. school
microsystem

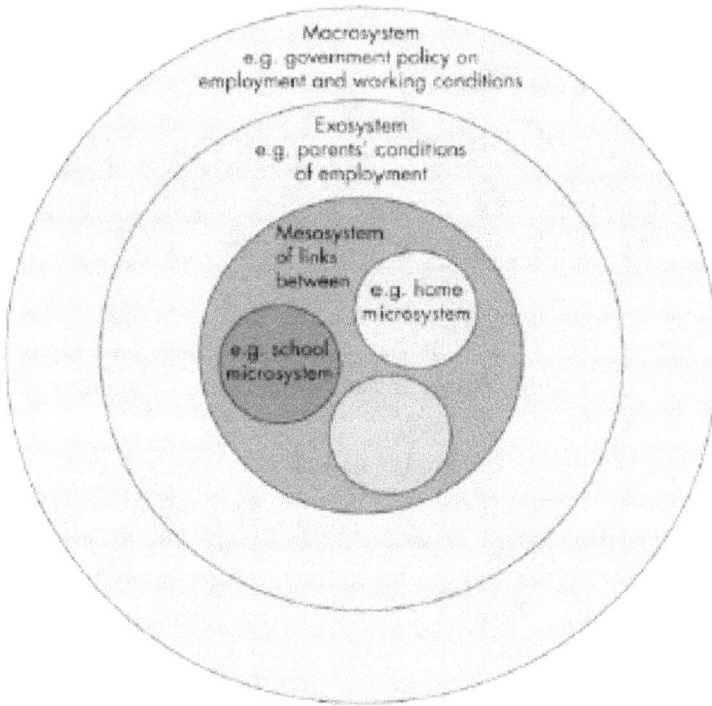

Figure 2: Bronfenbrenner's (1989) Ecological Framework30

The illustration above captures how the various systems in a child's life contribute directly and/or indirectly to her holistic development. In Figure 2, the church is part of the microsystem together with the family, peers, and school—the world the child revolves in most of her life. If the church fails, the world of the child could capsize. Without the presence of religious training, the child would have little or no input on things that could nurture her fully in terms of spirituality. Michael Vail, the series editor for the Clergy Development of the Church of the Nazarene made use of Bronfenbrenner's framework. In one of the lessons, he writes in relation to the settings that affect the self-image of the child: "The factors in the innermost ring are the most directly influential in the child's life. They also are the factors that tend to cause the most long-lasting effects in a child's life because they influence children's perceptions of how the world operates." This is just one example of how Bronfenbrenner's theory is accepted even by church educators.[31]

IMPLICATIONS OF THE ECOLOGICAL THEORY TO CHILD PROTECTION IN THE LOCAL CHURCH

1. Everyone in the church has the opportunity to be part of protecting children from abuse coming from different levels of society or the environment.
2. When the immediate setting of a child's defense is broken, i.e., the home, the church should be there to make up for the deficiencies. This would imply caring and nurturing programs and activities that would minister to the need for love that the child does not feel at home. Of course, nothing can replace the love that a family can give. However, the church can teach the parents how to provide love and affection within the home.
3. This also implies that the whole network of influences--the home, the school, and societal attitudes--should value child protection at all levels.

SUMMARY

This chapter has discussed the nature of the child as viewed through the lenses of biology, culture, and the Bible. Children are complex beings needing adult care, protection, and nurture so they can flourish and thrive. Children need all the help they can get from all sectors of society for holistic growth.

----

1 Bonna Pamplona, "OFW Comes Home to Bury Son Beaten Dead by Guardians," ABS-CBN News (November 20, 2016).

2 Nathaniel R. Melican, "Boy Beaten to Death by Other Wards in Manila Shelter for Street Children," ABS-CBN News," (March 12, 2015).

3 "Filipino Children as Young as 2 Rescued from Cybersex Trafficking," August 20, 2015.

4 Agence France-Presse, "2 Young Girls Rescued from Cyber-Sex Operators" (March 12, 2015).

5 International Justice Mission Fact Sheet."

6 Agence France-Presse, "2 Young Girls Rescued from Cyber-Sex Operators."

7 Elanor Jackson and Marie Wernham, *Child Protection Policies and Procedures Toolkit* (London: Consortium for Street Children, 2005), 9.

8 Dan Brewster and Heather McCloud, "Child Protection: Protecting Children from Ourselves," Presentation for Council of International Child Ministries, Holland (March 2001), n.p.

9 Maire Messenger Davies, *Children, Media and Culture* (Maidenhead: McGraw-Hill Professional Publishing 2010), 9.

10 Marieke van Heugtena and Elizabeth K. Johnson, "Infants Exposed to Fluent Natural Speech," *Journal of Speech, Language, and Hearing Research* 55 (April 2012): 554.

11 "To Talk," Baby Human videos, Janet Werker's Lab, University of British Columbia, Canada. In one of their experiments with a 12-hour-old baby, they found two amazing facts: (1) baby humans begin to learn the properties of language in the womb; and (2) at birth they prefer the rhythms of their native language to those of an unfamiliar one.

12 Dr. Janet Werker Honoured for Research Into Children's Language Acquisition," The University of British Columbia. Other child psychologists and theorists like Piaget, Erikson, and Vygotsky relate that even at an early age, infants already have the capacity to observe and assimilate the world around them. Vygotsky so believed in the power of the newborn that he wrote, "Learning and development are interrelated from the child's very first day of life" (Vygotsky, Mind in Society [Cambridge: Harvard University Press, 1978], 84); cited in Dialing, "The Impact of VNBC Elementary School Upon the Holistic Development of Its Selected Grade Six Students" (Thesis, APNTS, 2013), 31.

13 Verna Hildebrand, *Guiding Young Children*, chapter 16.

14 Convention on the Rights of the Child, 57.

15 "The Child and Youth Welfare Code."

16 F. Landa Jocano, Slum as a Way of Life: *A Study of Coping Behavior in an Urban Environment* (Quezon City: University of the Philippines Press, 1975), 56.

17 Tomas Andres, *Negotiating of Filipino Values* (Manila: Divine Word Publications, 1992), 46.

18 Biblical Cyclopedic Index," *The Open Bible*, expanded ed. (Nashville, TN: Thomas Nelson Publishers, 1983).

19 Roy B. Zuck, *Precious in His Sight* (Grand Rapids, MI: Baker, 1996), 1.

20 The figures are variable because of the 'age' and metaphorical expansiveness of 'child/children.' This is further discussed in Cadwallader, "Towards a Theology of the Child," (2013), 15.

21 Cadwallader, "Towards a Theology of the Child," 15.

22 Desiree Segura-April and others, "Mission with Children at Risk," *Lausanne Occasional Paper* (LOP) 66 (2014): 4.

23 *John Wesley's Explanatory Notes*, "Matthew 19."

24 Craig S. Keener, New Testament, The IVP Bible Background Commentary (Downers Grove, IL: 1993), 93.

25 Judith Gundry-Volf, The Least and the Greatest: Children in the New Testament (Grand Rapids, MI: Eerdmans, 2001), 31-32.

26 Kevin Bales, "Is It NaÔve to Think Slavery and Exploitation Will Ever Come to an End?" in Stopping the Traffick (Oxford: Regnum Book International, 2014), 14.

27 Urie Bronfenbrenner, The Ecology of Human Development: Experiments by Nature and Design (Cambridge: Harvard University Press, 1979), 3.

28 Bronfenbrenner, "Environments in Developmental Perspective" (Washington DC: American Psychological Association, 1999), 3.

29 Bronfenbrenner, The Ecology of Human Development, 3, 25-26.

30 Peter K. Smith, Helen Cowie, and Mark Blades, Understanding Children's Development, 6th ed. (West Sussex: John Wiley and Songs Ltd., 2015), 11.

31 Michael W. Vail, series curriculum ed. Developing Children's Ministry (Kansas City, MO: Clergy Development Church of the Nazarene, 2008), 4; cited in Tago, "Perceptions of Selected Parents on Parental Involvement in Light Of Epstein's Framework" (Thesis, APNTS, 2017), 67.

BIBLIOGRAPHY

Andres, Tomas. Negotiating of Filipino Values. Manila: Divine Word Publications, 1992.

France-Presse, "2 Young Girls Rescued from Cyber-Sex Operators" (March 12, 2015), available from http://news.abs-cbn.com/nation/metro-manila/03/12/15/2-young-girls-rescued-cyber-sex-operators.

Bales, Kevin "Is It NaÔve to Think Slavery and Exploitation Will Ever Come to an End?" In Stopping the Traffick: A Christian Response to Sexual Exploitation and Trafficking, eds. Glenn Miles and Christa Crawford. Oxford: Regnum Book International, 2014.

"Biblical Cyclopedic Index," The Open Bible, expanded ed. Nashville, TN: Thomas Nelson Publishers, 1983.

Brewster, Dan. Child Protection. Book 5: The Children and Families in the Bible Series Penang: Compassion International, 2014.

___, and Heather McCloud. "Child Protection: Protecting Children from Ourselves." Presentation for Council of International Child Ministries, Holland (March 2001), n.p.

Bronfenbrenner, Urie. The Ecology of Human Development: Experiments by Nature and Design. Cambridge: Harvard University Press, 1979.

___. International Encyclopedia of Education. Vol. 3, 2nd ed. Oxford: Elsevier Sciences,   Ltd., 1994.

___. "Environments in Developmental Perspective: Theoretical and Operational Models." In Measuring Environment Across the Life Span: Emerging Methods and Concepts, 1st ed., eds. Sarah L. Friedman and Theodore D. Wachs. Washington DC: American Psychological Association, 1999.

Cadwallader, Alan. "Towards a Theology of the Child." In Child Sexual Abuse, Societyand the Future of the Church, ed. Hilary D. Regan. Hindmarsh, SA: ATF Press 2013.

Convention on the Rights of the Child, 57, available from http://www.ohchr.org/EN/ProfessionalInterest/Pages/CRC.aspx.

Davies, Maire Messenger. Children, Media and Culture. Maidenhead: McGraw-Hill Professional Publishing 2010.

Dialing, Morita. "The Impact of Visayan Nazarene Bible College Elementary School Upon the Holistic Development of Its Selected Grade Six Students." MARE Thesis, Asia-Pacific Nazarene Theological Seminary, 2013.

"Filipino Children as Young as 2 Rescued from Cybersex Trafficking." August 20, 2015,available from https://www.ijm.org/articles/filipino-children-young-2-rescued-cybersex-trafficking.

Gaither, William and Gloria Gaither. 1975. https://mojim.com/usy123651x3x1.htm.

Gundry-Volf, Judith "The Least and the Greatest: Children in the New Testament." In *The Child in Christian Thought*, ed. Marcia J. Bunge. Grand Rapids, MI: Eerdmans, 2001.

Jackson, Elanor, and Marie Wernham, Child Protection Policies and Procedures Toolkit London: Consortium for Street Children, 2005.

Jocano, F. Landa. *Slum as a Way of Life: A Study of Coping Behavior in an Urban Environment.* Quezon City: University of the Philippines Press, 1975.

Keener, Craig S. *New Testament, The IVP Bible Background Commentary.* Downers Grove, IL: 1993.

Melican, Nathaniel R. "Boy Beaten to Death by Other Wards in Manila Shelter for Street Children," ABS-CBN News" (March 12, 2015), available from http://newsinfo.inquirer.net/651335/boy beaten-to-death-by-other-wards-in-manila-shelter-for-street-children#ixzz4sbjjE4Sv.

Pamplona, Bonna. "OFW Comes Home to Bury Son Beaten Dead by Guardians." ABS-CBN News (November 20, 2016), available from http://news.abscbn.com/overseas/11/20/16/ofwcomes-home-to-bury-son-beaten-dead-by-guardians.

Segura-April, Desiree et al. "Mission with Children at Risk," Lausanne Occasional Paper (LOP) 66, 014.

Smith, Peter K., Helen Cowie, and Mark Blades. *Understanding Children's Development.* 6th ed. West Sussex: John Wiley and Songs Ltd., 2015.

Tago, Pearl. "Perceptions of Selected Parents, Teachers, and Students of Christ's Commission Fellowship Life Academy Foundation, on Parental Involvement in Light of Epstein's Framework." MARE Thesis, Asia-Pacific Nazarene Theological Seminary, 2017.

"The Child and Youth Welfare Code," available from http://www.chanrobles.comchildandyouthwelfarecodeofthephilippines.htm#.Wa944sgjFPY.

"To Talk," Baby Human videos, Janet Werker's Lab, University of British Columbia, Canada. available from https://www.youtube.com/watch?v=-g464VAomog&list=RD-g464VAomog&t=54.

Vail, Michael W. *Developing Children's Ministry: Student Guide.* Kansas City, MO:Clergy Development Church of the Nazarene, 2008.

Van Heugtena, Marieke, and Elizabeth K. Johnson. "Infants Exposed to Fluent Natural Speech Succeed at Cross-Gender Word Recognition." Journal of Speech, Language, and Hearing Research 55 (April 2012): 554.

Wesley, John. John Wesley's Explanatory Notes, "Matthew 19," available from http://www.christianity.com/biblecommentary.php?com=wes&b=40&c=19.

Vygotsky, Lev Semyonovich. *Mind in Society: The Development of Higher Psychological Processes.* Cambridge: Harvard University Press, 1978.

Zuck, Roy B. *Precious in His Sight.* Grand Rapids, MI: Baker, 1996.

USING THE PRAXIS MODEL OF LOVE AND HONOR TO MINISTER TO ELDERLY CHINESE IN THE PHILIPPINES

Juliet Lee Uytanlet

1. WHO WILL EVANGELIZE THE ELDERLY CHINESE?

David Cheung challenged a group of college students and young professionals in a camp back in May of 1993 at Four Houses, Tagaytay. As the director of the Chinese Congress on World Evangelization, Philippines (CCOWE) then, he presented the case of the Chinese in the Philippines. He passionately advocated the importance of evangelism as the church faced AD 2000. In one session, he gave three reasons why the Chinese themselves are the best evangelists in reaching fellow Chinese in the Philippines. First, they know the language. The majority of elderly Chinese Filipinos still speak Minnanhua (also called Hokkien, Fukien, Amoy, Lannang-oe) and most of the Tsinoys who attended the camp understood and spoke the language.[1] Cheung reminded the youth that they did not need to learn a new language, as they already spoke the language. Second, they knew the culture. Again, speaking to the group of

Tsinoys who studied in Chinese schools and grew up in Chinese enclaves, they did not need to learn a new culture. They were living in the same culture. They understood that they were ethnic Chinese living in the Philippines. They knew both Chinese and Filipino cultures. Finally, Cheung pointed out that his listeners were living among the elderly Chinese. The Tsinoy Christians did not need to go abroad or move to faraway places to minister to them. They were living in the same city, neighborhood, and homes. The elderly Chinese were their parents, aunties, uncles, or grandparents. These reasons clearly showed that they were the best and most natural evangelists to these elderly Chinese.

Cheung entreated the group, saying, "Who then will share the gospel to the elderly Chinese in Ongpin and Binondo?" Three decades have passed since he gave that challenge. How many of these elderly Chinese have left this world without hearing the gospel message or experiencing the love of Christ? If heaven and hell are realities and not just some mystery or fairy tales, then where have all these souls gone? Have our hearts been so calloused with busyness and worldliness that saving the souls of our elderly grandparents, parents, relatives, or neighbors has been set aside and neglected for quite a long time? Is the lack of knowledge or methodologies on evangelizing and ministering to them the main reason? Or is the lack of Chinese pastors who can speak their language to be blamed?

This paper seeks to argue that the elderly Chinese in the Philippines are a minority among the minority ethnic Chinese. They represent eight percent of the Chinese Filipino population. Their numbers may be small and even dwindling, but they are still precious souls to be reached with the gospel message. Hence, there is an urgent need to evangelize and minister to these elderly Chinese. The author also wants to introduce the praxis model of love and honor as a way to reach out to and minister to these elderly Chinese.

2. WHO ARE THE ELDERLY CHINESE?

It is difficult to ascertain the exact population of Chinese Filipinos since there are many kinds of Chinese in the country. Moreover, the Philippine census does not include ethnic origin in its survey of Filipinos.[2] Tan and Palanca estimate that ethnic Chinese make up roughly two percent of the total population of the Philippines.[3] According to a press release in January 2013 by the Senate of the Philippines, the ethnic or pure Chinese comprise 1.35 million while Filipinos with Chinese ancestry number 22.8 million.[4] The 1.35 million figure probably does not include the waves of new immigrants at the turn of the new millennium or the Chinese mestizos that remained in the Chinese community. Hence, it will be safe to agree with Tan and Palanca that the number today is roughly two percent, i.e., around two million of the 112 million total population.[5]

Teresita Ang See estimated in 2004 that 90 percent of the Chinese in the country are 50 years old and below. That means the other 10 percent are 51 years old and above.[6] The demographic data from the Philippine Statistics Authority shows the following age structure in the country:

AGE DEMOGRAPHIC[7]			
2015		2020	
Age	Percent	Age	Percent
0-14	28.07	0-14	26.23
15-64	64.63	15-64	65.48
65-above	7.30	65-above	8.29

Note: The age group 15-64 is the largest group and is composed of "working age" and "economically active" persons.

This data also applies to the age demographics of the Chinese in the country.

Therefore, following these age groupings, the elderly Chinese for this paper refer to those 65 years old and above. They are the eight percent of the total Chinese population in the country, whether they be Chinese Filipinos, ethnic Chinese with no Filipino citizenship, or Chinese from the mainland.[8] These data coincide with the fact that the readership of Chinese newspapers in the country is declining.

Based on an interview with a representative of The World News in 2012, there were 20,000 subscribers of the said popular Chinese newspaper all over the country.[9] This is evidence that the majority of Chinese Filipinos prefer to read in English or Filipino, though they may speak in Minnanhua. They are the hybrid Tsinoys who were born and raised in the country, who mix Minnanhua, English, and Filipino in conversation, and who mix Chinese and Filipino cultures in their day-to-day life.[10] Moreover, the digital media that is widely available today is a default source for news more than the traditional paper-based material.

When the author did her fieldwork in 2012 for the book *The Hybrid Tsinoys*, the elderly Chinese she interviewed and interacted with were mostly old immigrants who mainly spoke in Minnanhua, though they often added some Filipino words like *kasi* (because), *tsaka* (also), *baka* (maybe), *paano* or *pa'no* (how), *sige* (okay), and *bahala* (whatever) every now and then as transitional words.[11] They have a strong affinity to their homeland, but circumstances such as famine, wars, and hardships led them to come to the Philippines. They have tried to maintain Chinese culture and language in their families as they plant roots in the host country that eventually became their home country. To the dismay of the elderly Chinese, they observed that the forces of the present environment contributed much to the inability of the Tsinoys to preserve the Minnanhua and Chinese culture and it is hard for them to compete with these.[12]

A decade has passed, and those informant Tsinoys in their 50s are now in their 60s and can be considered elderly. However, these elderly Tsinoys were born and raised in the country. They can speak Minnanhua (though fluency varies), Filipino (and/or other Philippine dialects), and English. Accordingly, there is all the more no excuse for not reaching them and ministering to them when language and culture are no longer issues or concerns.

In follow-up research on the hybrid Tsinoys entitled "The Intsiks, the Tsinoys, and the Chinoynials" in 2021 to 2022, the author discovered that the present Chinese Filipinos prefer not to be called 'Intsik'-- despite the fact that the word simply means Indio-Chino (*In-Chic*)--to differentiate them from the Filipinos, who were called

Indios during the late Spanish Period.[13] Furthermore, the meaning of 'Intsik' was even reconstructed to a more positive connotation after a century of negative usage of the word toward the Chinese in the Philippines during the American Period to the Postwar Period. The elderly Chinese reimagined how the word came about, saying, it means "your uncle" (*lin tsek*).[14] The survey also reveals that Chinese Filipinos prefer Chinoy to Tsinoy, possibly due to the change of the modern Filipino alphabet in 1987 and the popularity of the show *CHiNOY TV*.[15] Finally, they prefer Filipino-Chinese (trans. 菲華, a transliteration from the Chinese reference of Chinese in Philippines) over Chinese Filipino (Chinese as ethnicity and Filipino as the citizenship).[16] Identities in the 21st century remain an important cultural construct in finding meaning and belonging. Hence, the desired names or labels that the Chinese Filipinos identified with reveal their understanding of the meaning behind those words and their contexts and situations.

The present elderly Chinese aged 65 and above are not just the old immigrants; the new immigrants and Tsinoys who have reached 65 and above are also included in this category. Hence, it is important to take into account the different kinds of Chinese in the country as we do evangelism among them. It is important to know what language will be the best form of communication, what cultural practices they employ, and where they are. Evangelism is not just about proclaiming the gospel; it is a process of helping someone draw closer and closer to the knowledge of who God is and Jesus Christ whom he has sent (Jn 17:3). It is thus imperative, as St. Francis of Assisi says, "Preach the gospel at all times. Use words if necessary."

3. THE PRAXIS MODEL OF LOVE AND HONOR

Stephen Bevans' classic *Models of Contextual Theology* defines contextual theology as doing theology by engaging with two realities: the reality (or experiences) of the past as recorded in the Scripture and the reality (or experiences) of the present with specific contexts and situations. Bevans further explains that in the reality of present experiences, this includes "the individual and social experiences, secular or religious culture, social location, and social change."[17] Bevans presents the six models of contextualization, namely, the translation, anthropological, praxis, synthetic, transcendental, and counter-cultural models.

This research proposes the use of the praxis model in contextualizing the gospel message to the elderly Chinese. Bevans explains that the praxis model of contextual theology "focuses on the identity of Christians within a context particularly as that context is understood in terms of social change."[18] Virginia Fabella is referenced by Bevans as saying that the praxis model is a newer thrust in contextualization and that it is a dynamic process and very practical. It is the combining of words and action, an acceptance of changes, and a looking forward to the future. Bevans acknowledges that the praxis model is always associated with liberal theology. However, it can be said that this is a "practical theology." It is theology formed through intense knowledge that leads to reflective action.[19] As the apostle James urged,

> *What good is it, my brothers and sisters, if someone claims to have faith but has no deeds? Can such faith save them? Suppose a brother or a sister is without clothes and daily food. If one of you says to them, "Go in peace; keep warm and well fed," but does nothing about their physical needs, what good is it? In the same way, faith by itself, if it is not accompanied by action, is dead. But someone will say, "You have faith; I have deeds." Show me your faith without deeds, and I will show you my faith by my deeds. You believe that there is one God. Good! Even the demons believe that—and shudder (James 2:14–19 NIV).*

Bevans adds that the central insight of the praxis model is that theology is not simply constructing relevant Christian expressions but also a commitment to Christian action. The praxis model's methodology is knowledge as content and knowledge as activity. At its very core is that the truth is revealed at the "level of history, not in the realm of ideas." This model is committed to social change based on Christian principles and advocates for the poor, oppressed, and marginalized. Moreover, it is often equivalent to liberation theology. Nonetheless, Bevans seeks to continue to use the term praxis model instead of liberation theology since not all theologies start from a structural injustice but rather a reflective practical theology. This model goes beyond the liberation themes. Second, Bevans asserts that the model is not a theology for one particular theme, like the liberation model, though it perfectly fits that theme. It is a particular method of doing theology with "critical reflection on praxis."[20]

REASONS FOR USING THIS MODEL

The nature of the praxis model is low-key in terms of approaching the elderly Chinese with the gospel presentation. It does not exclude or avoid the message but provides the space for "appropriate readiness" to listen and understand the Word of God. It is important to realize that one has to earn the right to be heard. These elderly people will not just listen to anybody, especially those younger than them. Those who wish to reach them have to win their trust and their hearts to be able to speak to them with the Word. Second, the praxis model is an opportunity to do practical theology, literally "practical theology." It is using one's life to convey the love of God and the truth about his Word. In Chinese culture, action speaks louder than words. The deeds of a man determine his character and his personality. It is one thing to say God loves you, but it is much more effective for these people to understand what love is by our doing than only by saying. Third, the praxis model best suits the culture of the elderly Chinese since they put much emphasis on filial piety. Rituals and actions serve as visible evidence of one's respect, honor, and love for their parents. The praxis model opens the door for one to express filial piety fully and biblically. To expand on this and to be more specific, a love and honor theology is constructed to provide a methodology of doing evangelism and ministry among the elderly Chinese.

TWO PRINCIPLES OF LOVE
AND HONOR THEOLOGY

The Minnanhua concept of *hào sùn pń bú* 孝順父母, or filial piety, is honoring one's parents. It is the most important virtue that a Chinese must remember. Confucius taught it and he actually lived it. K. K. Yeo in his book *Musing with Confucius and Paul* narrates Confucius losing his father at age three and his mother at age seventeen. His childhood developed in him a filial love for both parents evident in his teachings. An interesting teaching Confucius has is the responsibility of the children to guide their parents to do the right thing when the latter get lost in their way. He writes in his *Analects*, "In serving your father and mother you ought to dissuade them from doing wrong in the gentlest way. If you see your advice being ignored, you should not become disobedient but should remain reverent. You should not complain even if you are distressed."[21] Indeed, as Christians, we must use the gentlest manner in helping them understand the truth of God's Word, something which they can best witness in our deeds rather than our words.

To illustrate Love and Honor Theology, two Chinese proverbs[22] will be used to present the two important principles in this proposed contextual theology for the elderly Chinese. First, the Minnanhua proverb 有耳沒嘴 (*u hi bo chhui*) means "have ears but no mouth." This is the principle of listening more and talking less. It is usually a reminder to children who love to reason out or interrupt an adult conversation. This "have ears but no mouth" principle can be a good method to show love and concern for them. Accordingly, this proverb can be reinterpreted to construct a theology for the elderly Chinese. The "have ears but no mouth" principle simply teaches us to listen more than talk. As children grow up, they tend to have their own opinions, own thinking, and own decisions. With this principle, it is important to remind ourselves that we need to take time to listen to what our parents, grandparents, and even uncles and aunties have to say. You may not fully agree and comply with their opinions, but finding the time to sit and listen shows how much you give importance to their thoughts and words. Listening shows our attention to them and that they are special and important to us. Secondly, if we want to show our love by listening, then we need to find time to spend with them. The more time we spend with them, the more we get to know them and the more we understand them. The more we understand them, the more we know how to best express our love to them.

I remember in high school as I grew in my faith journey, my utmost desire was to see my parents become Christians. I often asked our youth pastor to visit my parents and present the gospel to them. Many times, my father would hide in the bedroom and pretend to be sleeping. At times, I would go to him and plead that he get up and talk with the youth pastor. He usually just smiled and said he was too tired. My mother would just listen and smile to our youth pastor, but I knew she was simply trying to be nice. When the pastor left, she would scold me and ask why I joined such a group? What good could I get from it? Could I by joining earn money? There came a time when I became too actively involved in the student center, and my mother angrily told me to live in that center instead and make the pastor my grandma. At that time, we had a store and oftentimes extra helping hands were needed. But I opted to "serve God," for this is what I thought was the more spiritual way. My relationship with my mother got worse in my college days as I became more active in ministry. We argued a lot and I felt "persecuted" for my faith. In one prayer meeting, I asked for prayers that my mom and I would eventually have a better relationship. A visiting brother inquired how it all had happened. After hearing my story, he rebuked me and told me to spend more time with my mother to win her to Christ. For the first time in my life, I realized that I had dichotomized sacred and secular. I had failed to understand what true witnessing is all about. It is not just the gospel presentation; it is the life presentation of the gospel message.

From then on, I resolved to win back my parents' trust in me and to show how much I loved and honored them. The first thing I did was to cut down my ministry involvement. Second, I volunteered to watch our store on Sunday mornings. Most of my sisters wanted to go to church on Sunday mornings, but I also wanted my parents to relax on that day. I joined an afternoon service instead. Third, I found opportunities to talk and get to know my parents. Weird? Yes, but I wanted to know what they liked and what they wanted. The good thing on Sundays was that we did not usually have many customers. I got to chat and talk with my mother or father. Fourth, I started to spend time, more time with them. I would sit down and watch basketball with my father even if it did not interest me. I would help my mother prepare the rice for cooking by cleaning or removing small stones and unhusked grains. How I prayed I would not have to remove worms! Fifth, I expressed my love to my mother with hugs. The Chinese traditional family does not hug or kiss. They are very conservative and reserved. I remember being envious of the Americans as I watched the Hollywood movies' portrayal of the American family. The American parents are so sweet to their children. They hug and kiss. I remember during fourth grade, I was signing my classmate's "slum book" and came across the question "Who is your first kiss?" I wondered at that time if my parents actually kissed me when I was a baby. Nonetheless, I wrote "Father and Mother." Further, I observed that American parents are like buddies to their children. They play together and the children even share their secret crushes with their parents. How I longed for that intimacy and closeness with my parents. Yet this is so not Chinese culture for the elderly Chinese generation. Much of their parenting knowledge and skills are learned and patterned after their own parents. As a result, they are monocultural and very traditional. They are not expressive but I definitely know they love us dearly.

The pragmatism of the Chinese Filipinos extends to their familial life. The fact that they place a roof above your head, provide food and clothing, and give you education are more than enough proof of their love. Their children however are born and raised in the Philippines. They are exposed to Chinese, Filipino, and even Western cultures through education, society, and media. They are more open to Western thoughts and ideas. And so, when I tried to hug my mother, she initially refused my hugs and complained that it was hot and hugging made her feel even hotter. But one evening, as we sat down together to watch her favorite show, I hugged her and she hugged me back. Tears welled up in my eyes and I knew my mother had at last reciprocated. They did not convert to Christianity immediately after that. But they were more willing to join evangelistic meetings and church activities. Further, they gave their blessing when I decided to enter the seminary after I graduated from college.

The second Minnanhua proverb is 人要面, 樹要皮 (*lâng bè bin, chhiu bè phê*). Literally, this means a person wants a face and a tree wants bark. This saying shows the importance of face or honor as opposed to shame and bad reputation. Honor is the second element that we need to work on to reach out to the elderly. A Chinese child is never to embarrass their parents or put their family name to shame and give their parents no face to show to others. The Minnanhua word *bo bin* or "no face" literally means that one has caused so much shame that the person or his/her family has no face to show to the community. A Chinese must prove their loyalty and devotion to their parents by full obedience and sacrificial service. Moreover, they must ensure that they will take care of their parents even in the afterlife with ancestral worship. For this reason, Christians all the more need to show love and honor to their parents and grandparents. The fifth commandment teaches us to do exactly that. It seems not appropriate to rush into a gospel presentation in doing evangelism with the elderly Chinese. Not even using arguments and debates which can be misinterpreted as disrespectful and arrogant. Trust through time and an authentic Christian lifestyle will earn us their ears to listen. This is a way to establish the "appropriate readiness" for them to listen to what we want to say.

We can use debates and arguments to try to convince the elderly Chinese. For instance, using theories like *Shang Ti* and Monotheistic Early Chinese to prove that the early Chinese were actually monotheistic and acknowledged one Supreme Being who is the *Shang Ti*. We may utilize the controversial Genesis Coded in the Chinese Language argument to prove that there are certain Chinese characters that have encrypted messages of the Genesis narratives. The Chinese can also debunk Buddhism, Daoism, or even Confucianism by presenting the uniqueness of Christ and the message of the gospel. One can employ many other methodologies. But if they are not ready, we must not push it or we will just embarrass our parents by showing off our knowledge. Patience and perseverance are crucial virtues as we evangelize the elderly.

The Evangelism Explosion created by James Kennedy is a popular evangelism tool along with the Four Spiritual Laws of the Campus Crusade for Christ in the Philippines, both among Filipino churches and Chinese churches. When James Kennedy designed the Evangelism Explosion, the retirees living in Florida were the target people he had in mind. The two diagnostic questions are very straightforward and to the point. The Americans may have no problem with that. For the Chinese, it is very disrespectful to ask "If you were to die today, would you go to heaven?" In Minnanhua the elderly will say *"Di dè phà suey"* or "You are foretelling a bad omen." Chinese people are superstitious and fearful of death and the afterlife. It is not right to bring up the topic of death and dying. Hence, Chinese pastors in the Philippines will typically ask instead, "After one hundred years, where will you be?" Long life is considered a blessing for the Chinese. To wish for someone to live for more than a hundred years is to show honor. Unfortunately, the gospel presentation is too long and the illustrations are very Western. Moreover, during training, the gospel presentation had to be delivered verbatim, and changes were not allowed or encouraged. As for the Four Spiritual Laws, this approach is definitely not appropriate for the elderly Chinese as it may be for younger generation. Bill Bright's original audience was the college students who battled with faith and science at UCLA.[23] From my observation, Chinese pastors usually use a biblical passage and expound on it instead of using either of the two famous methodologies. And this is rightly so, since we need to contextualize the gospel message for the hearer to really understand.

4. ARE THEY WORTH OUR TIME AND EFFORT

It is a fact that the elderly Chinese who hold on to Buddhism or Daoism will definitely expect their children to do ancestral worship. When their children become Christians, they are alarmed and fear for their afterlife. This becomes a cause for disagreement and even discord in the family. The Christian child will be branded as disrespectful for abandoning the family beliefs and traditions. It is the children's responsibility to ensure their ancestors' well-being in the afterlife--consequently the importance of having children or posterity. The elaborate rituals and practices during funeral rites, annual observances, and festivities are also essential for their ancestors in the afterlife. When a son or a daughter becomes a Christian, it poses a threat to their ancestors' afterlife. Who will then burn incense and offer food to them? Who will burn paper money and all the other things they need in the afterlife? The gulf of conflict easily widens when one immediately uses arguments to disprove the traditions and beliefs of these elderly. This action can be viewed as being disrespectful and arrogant. Hence, showing love and honor while they are alive is the best way to apply filial piety, not when they are already dead and can no longer see or feel our efforts. Filial piety is a virtue and a practice that Christians should follow. Loving and honoring our parents throughout our lives by employing the two principles ("have ears but no mouth" and "upholding the parents' honor") can be a good evangelistic tool and mirror the love of God for them.

Finally, as Cheung reminded Chinese Filipinos of the urgency of evangelizing elderly Chinese, we in our time have no excuse, for we know the language, and we certainly can communicate with them in Minnanhua mixed with Filipino or English. We know the hybrid culture they have lived in, and we can navigate among these cultures, contextualizing our responses as we seek God's wisdom and guidance. Lastly, we have lived among them and are still perhaps living with them in the same house. The everyday encounters and everyday opportunities to witness by our actions will certainly speak louder than the one-time verbal gospel presentation.

----

1 "Minnanhua 閩南話 is Putonghua expression that refers to the language of the Hokkien people, who sometimes call the language *Emng oe or Banlam oe*. It is the lingua franca of the majority Chinese Filipinos. Minnanhua is known as Amoy by Westerners. Amoy is the English transliteration for Ûmng or Xi‡mÈn 廈門." Ninety percent of Chinese immigrants came from Fujian and Minnanhua is the language of these people. Juliet L. Uytanlet, *The Hybrid Tsinoys: Challenges*

of Hybridity and Homogeneity as Sociocultural Constructs among the Chinese in the Philippines (Oregon, Pickwick: 2016), 15 and 79.

2 There are six kinds of Chinese in the Philippines: old Immigrants, new Immigrants, Tsinoys, Chinese with Chinese citizenships, Chinese in inter-ethnic marriages, and the mestizos. Uytanlet, *The Hybrid Tsinoys*, 74–75. The *Tulay Monthly* classifies them as follows: ethnic Chinese, Philippine-Chinese, Filipino-Chinese, Chinese-Filipinos, and Alien-Chinese. *Tulay Monthly, Chinese-Filipino Digest* 1, no. 1 (June 1988): 3. See also, *Tulay Staff*, "The Chinese in the Philippines: Some Basic Facts," April 2, 2022, https://tulay.ph/2022/04/03/the-chinese-in-the-philippines-some-basic-facts/.

3 Michael L. Tan, "From Sangley to Tsinoy: Changing Identities among Ethnic Chinese in the Philippines," *Public Policy*, 11 (2013), 83. Ellen H. Palanca, "A Comparative Study of Chinese Education in the Philippines and Malaysia," *Asian Studies* 38, no. 2 (2002): 30, https://www.asj.upd.edu.ph/mediabox/archive/ASJ-38-2-2002/palanca.pdf. See also Edgar Wickberg, "Anti-Sinicism and Chinese Identity Options in the Philippines," in *Essential Outsiders: Chinese and Jews in the Modern Transformation of Southeast Asia and Central Europe*, edited by Daniel Chirot and Anthony Reid (USA: University of Washington Press, 1997), 164.

4 Since the report was made in January of 2013, it follows that the referenced population data should be that of 2012 which is 98 million. Hence, the Chinese Filipino population that are classified as "pure" ethnic Chinese are 1.37 percent of the total Philippine population. Pilar Macrohon, "Senate declares Chinese New Year as special working holiday," *PRIB*, (January 21, 2013), Office of the Senate Secretary, Senate of the Philippines, http://legacy.senate.gov.ph/press_release/2013/0121_prib1.asp.

5 The PSA or Philippine Statistics Authority projected that the total population of the country will be 112 million by 2023. PSA, "Updated Projected Mid-Year Population for the Philippines Based on the 2015 POPCEN Results: 2020 – 2025," https://psa.gov.ph/system/files/phcd/2022-12/Cities%2520and%2520Municipalities%2520Population%2520Projections_2015CBPP_Phils.pdf.

6 Teresita Ang See, *Chinese in the Philippines: Problems and Perspectives*, 3:21.

7 PSA, "Age and Sex Distribution Of Household Population In The Municipality Of Sigma (Based on the results of 2020 Census of Population and Housing)," May 22, 2023 https://rsso06.psa.gov.ph/sites/default/files/psacapiz/specialreleaseattachment/SR%202023-21%20Age%20and%20Sex%20Distribution-sigma.pdf.

8 The Philippines applies *jus sanguinis* not *jus soli* in relation to citizenship; hence, when a Chinese is born in the country, he/she does not automatically become a Filipino citizen unless the parents are already Filipino citizens. About ten percent of the Chinese in the Philippines remain Chinese citizens. The broad categorization of the term "Chinese citizens" includes nuances that they may be holding a Taiwan passport and not a China passport, or that they simply have Taiwan or China passports but not Taiwan citizen ID or China citizen ID.

9 Uytanlet, *The Hybrid Tsinoys*, 182.

10 Ibid. See also W. D. W. Gonzales, "Trilingual code-switching using quantitative lenses: An exploratory study on Hokaglish," *Philippine Journal of Linguistics* (2016), 47, 108–113, 126.

11 The old immigrants or *ji˘qi·o* 舊僑 (Putonghua) or *kukiao* (Minnanhua) are Chinese immigrants who entered from 1898 to 1975, while the new immigrants or *xinqi·o* 新僑 (Putonghua) or *sinkiao* (Minnanhua) refer to those who entered the country from 1976 to the present. Uytanlet, *The Hybrid Tsinoys*, 76–86, 110, 164.

12 Ibid., 152–155.

13 Richard T. Chu, *Chinese and Chinese Mestizos of Manila: Family, Identity, and Culture: 1860s–1930s* (Leiden: Brill, 2010), 69.

14 Juliet Lee Uytanlet, "An Analysis of Chinese Filipino Hybrid Identity from Postwar to Present: The Intsiks, the Tsinoys, and the Chinoynials," *Journal of Asian Mission* 23 (2022):38–40, 54–55.

15 "In 1987, the Modern Filipino Alphabet was introduced in classrooms. It consists of the original 20 letters with an additional 8 consonants to make Tagalog a more inclusive language as it became the national language called Filipino." Uytanlet, "The Intsiks, the Tsinoys, and the Chinoynials," 49–50.

16 The results from the snowball survey show "that there is no correlation between age and name preference. Each group was composed of all age ranges." Ibid., 50, 55.

17 Stephen B. Bevans, *Models of Contextual Theology* (New York: Orbis Books, 2010), xvi, 3–7.

18 Ibid., 70.

19 Ibid., 70.

20 Ibid., 72-73.

21 K. K. Yeo, *Musing with Confucius and Paul* (Oregon: Cascade Books, 2008), 13–14.

22 Proverbs are popularly used to exhort and to teach people how to live and how to behave. In Minnanhua we say, "怎麼做人/*ts‡i iu tsÚe l,ng?*" This literally means how to be human.

23 Richard Quebedeaux, I Found It (San Francisco: Harper & Row, 1979), 91–103.

WORKS CITED

Bevans, Stephen B. *Models of Contextual Theology*. New York: Orbis Books, 2010.

Chu, Richard T. *Chinese and Chinese Mestizos of Manila: Family, Identity, and Culture,* 1860s 1930s.Leiden: Brill, 2010.

Gonzales, W. D. W. "Trilingual Code-switching Using Quantitative Lenses: An Exploratory Study on Hokaglish." *Philippine Journal of Linguistics* (2016): 106–128.

Hiebert, Paul G., R. Daniel Shaw, and Tite TiÈnou. *Understanding Folk Religion: A Christian Response to Popular Beliefs and Practices*. Grand Rapids, Michigan: Baker, 1999.

Macrohon, Pilar. "Senate Declares Chinese New Year as Special Working Holiday." *PRIB*, (January 21, 2013), Office of the Senate Secretary, Senate of the Philippines. http://legacy.senate.gov.ph/press_release/2013/0121_prib1.asp.

Palanca, Ellen H. "A Comparative Study of Chinese Education in the Philippines and Malaysia." *Asian Studies* 38, no. 2 (2002): 29–62. https://www.asj.upd.edu.ph/mediabox/archive/ASJ-38-22002/palanca.pdf.

PSA. "Age and Sex Distribution Of Household Population In The Municipality Of Sigma (Based on the results of 2020 Census of Population and Housing)." May 22, 2023. https://rsso06.psa.gov.ph/sites/default/files/psacapiz/specialreleaseattachment/SR%20202321%20Age%20and%20Sex%20Distribution-sigma.pdf.

PSA. "Updated Projected Mid-Year Population for the Philippines Based on the 2015 POPCEN Results: 2020 – 2025." https://psa.gov.ph/system/files/phcd/202212/Cities%2520and%2520Municipalities% 2520Population%25 20Projections_2015CBPP_Phils.pdf.

Quebedeaux, Richard. *I Found It*. San Francisco: Harper & Row, 1979.

See, Teresita Ang. *The Chinese in the Philippines: Problems and Perspectives*. Vol. III. Manila: Kaisa Para Sa Kaunlaran, Inc., 2004.

Tan, Michael L. "From Sangley to Tsinoy: Changing Identities among Ethnic Chinese in the Philippines," *Public Policy* 11 (2013): 83–109.

Tulay Monthly. *Chinese-Filipino Digest* 1, no. 1 (June 1988): 3.

Tulay Staff. "The Chinese in the Philippines: Some Basic Facts." April 2, 2022. https://tulay.ph/2022/04/03/the-chinese-in-the-philippines-some-basic-facts/.

Uytanlet, Juliet L. *The Hybrid Tsinoys: Challenges of Hybridity and Homogeneity as Sociocultural Constructs among the Chinese in the Philippines*. American Society of Missiology Monograph Series, 8.Oregon: Pickwick, 2016.

___"An Analysis of Chinese Filipino Hybrid Identity from Postwar to Present: The Intsiks, the Tsinoys, and the Chinoynials." *Journal of Asian Mission* 23, no. 1 (2022):31–55.

Wickberg, Edgar. "Anti-Sinicism and Chinese Identity Options in the Philippines." In *Essential Outsiders: Chinese and Jews in the Modern Transformation of Southeast Asia and Central Europe*, edited by Daniel Chirot and Anthony Reid, 153–83. Seattle: University of Washington Press, 1997.

Yeo, K. K. *Musing with Confucius and Paul*. Oregon: Cascade Books, 2008.

A CLOSE ENCOUNTER WITH GRANDMA KWONG

Sadiri Joy Tira

"The whole Church, taking the whole Gospel, to the whole World."

- The Lausanne Movement

During the time that I served as Lausanne Catalyst for Diasporas[1] I had the honor of meeting men and women from all corners of the globe and from all walks of life dedicated to the Gospel of Jesus Christ. **Truly, I witnessed the Holy Spirit's moving through the whole Church to take the whole Gospel to the whole World.** This movement continues to be awe-inspiring, humbling me to give thanks to the Lord for his faithfulness to the Church, which is historically and spatially borderless.

GRANDMA KWONG

In 2019, my last year of service as Lausanne Catalyst, in Toronto, Canada—arguably the world's most multicultural city,[2] I was introduced to an extraordinary woman, "Grandma" Kwong (nee Fan Wai Lim), born in Guangdong province, China, on July 15, 1908, while the last emperor of China was still on the throne. Her grandson, Philip, and his wife, Amy--young partners of the Lausanne Movement--brought me to her. At 111 years old, Grandma's mind was clear, her grin was radiant, and in her prayer for Kingdom workers, for the Lausanne Movement, and for my family and me, her deep and life-long devotion to Jesus and his Kingdom was steadfast. I later learned that, well beyond her centenary year, Grandma continued to partner with the Lausanne Movement in both faithful prayer and in generous financial support. **As she held my hands in hers, I was moved by our fellowship in Jesus—it transcended physical, cultural, and linguistic borders, and I was struck by the fact that the Gospel of Jesus Christ has no age borders.**

On December 27, 2020, at 112 years old, she left her temporary earthly home and made her entrance into the Church Eternal. In celebration of her life, Philip writes:

Grandma deeply cared about mission, church growth and people believing in Jesus. She loved having visitors—the first thing she wanted to know was if they were believers. She would take the initiative to engage with the young adults (those who could handle some Chinese) and find out how she could pray for them or their families. In essence, Grandma was our young adult ministry partner—she kept her notes on them and would pray for them as a group and as individuals....

Phil recounts Grandma's last days with them: "True to her being missional, Grandma expressed her mission-mindedness in her reminders to us on praying and giving one last time. As always, Grandma never ceased to amaze or inspire us..."

I reflect on Grandma's life in the context of unique circumstances. In the early fall of 2019, when we first met, we could not have expected the "unprecedented" realities that 2020, the upcoming year, would bring. In February and March 2020, the COVID-19 pandemic closed down much of the globe's geographical borders. Migrants were urged to return to their home countries and people were encouraged to remain in the borders of their own homes. In July 2020, I suffered a severe stroke and for two months my family was told to await the long-term prognosis. By the time of Grandma's home-going in December 2020, I had lived five months within the borders of hospital walls, while the world had experienced nearly three-quarters of the year in isolation, and while COVID-19 claimed millions of lives.[3] In Canada, where I live, "deaths caused directly by COVID-19 disproportionately affected the elderly."[4]

Grandma Kwong in the church of her nursing home at the age of 109, accompanied by her grandson and granddaughter-in-law.

My extended stay in hospital care, with over two months in geriatric units, and then over three months in a hospital unit with primarily senior citizens in care, gave me a new perspective on senior citizens. Though I am not yet qualified for the honourific of "senior citizen," in their midst, I witnessed seniors in missions, and missions to seniors. There were senior citizen patients who prayed for me, for each other, and for the world.

Grandma Kwong in the church of her nursing home at the age of 109, accompanied by her grandson and granddaughter-in-law.

SENIORS IN MISSIONS & MISSIONS TO SENIORS

Further, in the midst of the global pandemic, while isolation seemed paramount, there were men and women, often times hospital staff, sometimes regular volunteers, who prayed for seniors as they washed them, fed them, braided their hair, pushed their wheel-chairs, brushed their teeth, organised socials, and wiped away tears for them. I cannot count the number of times I observed medical team members encourage seniors to press on, "because, even now, you are loved, and because there is always Hope." I even met an octogenarian gentleman, a former patient of the hospital, who after decades of weekends, continued to minister to the hospital patients on Sunday mornings. I asked him why he persisted in old age to lug over his saxophone and devote his Sunday mornings to the hospital. He replied: "Jesus loves me. He saved me. I owe Jesus everything." Truly, there are no successful borders limiting Jesus Christ's Gospel and Church, not even age.

The United Nations notes, "The global population aged 60 years or over numbered 962 million in 2017, more than twice as large as in 1980 when there were 382 million older persons worldwide. The number of older persons is expected to double again by 2050, when it is projected to reach nearly 2.1 billion."[5]

Grandma Kwong is representative of the many senior citizens—members of the whole Church—who are committed to bringing the whole Gospel to the whole World. **As the global pandemic raged on, and even since it waned, we must remember and support those on the edges of age and those who minister to them.** They continue to be Kingdom workers and continue to be a mission field. And, they are honoured and loved.

"The whole Church (including the aged), taking the whole Gospel, to the whole World (including the aged)".

This blog has already been published on internet August 23, 2022, with the permission of the author, Dr. Sadiri Joy Tira, is being published as a part of this book. https://outreach.ca/article/ArticleId/3984/A-Close-Encounter-with-Grandma-Kwong

----

1 The Diaspora Catalyst was formerly known as Lausanne Senior Associate for Diasporas. Sadiri Joy Tira served in this position from 2007-2019.

2 https://torontoglobal.ca/TG-Blog/March-2019/How-multicultural-is-Toronto-Let-us-count-the-way

3 At the time of writing, the World Health Organization had reported a global death toll of 2,232,233 (January 20, 2020-February 2, 2021). See "Overview" February 2, 2021 at https://COVID19.who.int.

4 https://www150.statcan.gc.ca/n1/daily-quotidien/201126/dq201126c-eng.htm

5 Quoted from https://www.un.org/en/development/desa/population/publications/pdf/ageing/5 WPA2017_Highlights.pdf. I do not know how the COVID-19 pandemic has adjusted these projections.

RE-IMAGINING RETIREMENT: RECOVERING AND VISION OF ELDERHOOD FOR THE GLOBAL CHURCH

Jeff Haanen

Greg Haanen, my father, recently turned 65 and retired from a career selling print advertising. For over 14 years, he lived in Minneapolis, while his wife Gayle ran Interlachen Inn, a small restaurant in Alexandria, Minnesota. Having lived apart from her for over a decade, he was ready to say good riddance to the two-hour commute every weekend, to spending nights alone, and to a life of hurry and obligation. They sold their house in Minneapolis and renovated their cabin with a deluxe fireplace, big screen TV, and farmhouse kitchen. He was eagerly awaiting a new season of rest and relaxation.

Yet his honeymoon period was short-lived. Less than three months after his retirement, his sister went in for another round of chemotherapy, having battled cancer for years. However, this time, she started to decline fast. In only weeks, he found himself coordinating hospice details, calling family, and moving her out of her apartment. As images of a carefree retirement on a beach slowly receded, he confessed to me, his son, "I feel like there's something more for me; but I'm just not sure what."[1]

My father is part of a larger, global trend. The world—and the Christian church—is aging quickly:[2]

- Roughly 10,000 Baby Boomers retire each day in the US,[3] and, this year, for the first time in American history, there will be more Americans over age 60 than under 18.[4]
- By 2050, the global population of adults over age 65 is expected to double to 1.6 billion.[5]
- The median age of Christians is also on the rise. In the US it is 53 (higher if you are in a mainline denomination); in the UK, 61. Pew reports that Christians, unlike Muslims, are dying faster in Europe than they are being born.6

Yet people are also living longer, which makes the current experience of retirement such an awkward fit for people like my father:

- For example, if you were born in 1947, you can expect to live to age 85.
- If you were born in 1967, your life expectancy is 91.
- For those born in 2007, life expectancy is now 103.[7]

In an age of human longevity, people are asking how they are going to spend what could be 20, 30 or even 40 years after official retirement.

Furthermore, governments are asking how they are going to foot the bill. In February of 2019, a *USA Today* staff editorial claimed, "*The Congressional Budget Office* estimates that in just ten years, half of all federal spending (except for debt service) will be benefits to senior citizens."[8] As global pensions are stretched (especially in Europe), promises of never-ending government benefits for retirees are looking thinner by the day.[9] One TIME magazine article made the case that China's aging population is a major threat to its future, largely due to its one-child policy and the imbalance of older to younger adults. Many believe an aging population is China's biggest economic problem.[10]

Globally, paradigms for aging are beginning to show cracks. The notion of sitting on the porch while living out one's 'golden years' is becoming less attractive to healthy, older adults.[11] Yet that ambition is tempered by the fact that most retirees have deep seated (and empirically founded) fears about affording the retirement 'dream'.[12] Why, then, in an age where people are healthier for much longer than at any time in modern history, does the idea of 'retirement' persist?

One reason is that retirement may be the most lucrative idea in the global economy. By one estimate, the US retirement industry alone is worth about USD 27 trillion.[13] While we have rarely connected the global economy and the notion of retirement, the primary reason most individuals invest in the stock market is that they are saving for retirement. Work, often laced with deep money-based fears, becomes a frenzy of activity all directed toward the goal of 'hitting your number' so that you can finally retire and 'be free'.

Have Christians been complicit in this narrative? What can be done to reform our views of work, rest, aging, and retirement in a new moment in global history?[14]

The time has come to change our views about retirement—not only for the sake of the global economy, but for the sake of the millions of men and women, like my father, who are longing to make a meaningful contribution with their lives, but live in a society that has relegated them to the margins.

Christians have started to reimagine retirement, but efforts to date are incomplete. Some Christians have attempted to baptize the idea of the retirement village, without a deeper view of age, rest, vocation, and elderhood. Several of these faith-based living communities exist around the world, yet look very much like secular retirement communities, complete with pools, shopping, happy hour, and golf courses. The only visible difference is more Bible studies.

Other leading voices are calling for Christians never to retire. "Lord, spare me the curse of retirement!", says John Piper, former pastor of Bethlehem Baptist Church in Minneapolis. Yet the problem with the 'never retire' stance is that people are tired—sometimes physically, almost always spiritually—from their careers. When we observe that 87 percent of the world is disengaged from their work[15] and that many have made their work their religion,[16] it becomes understandable that as soon as people are eligible to retire, they generally do.[17] What is needed is a recovery of the balance between work and rest, not a call to plough the thistles and thorns until you die (Gen 3:17-18).

Other proposals from Christians call for various versions of 'refirement' or 'renewalment'—calls to muster new energy in retirement—but fail to acknowledge that work can, and should, change as we age. The closest the Bible comes to the subject of retirement is Numbers 8:25: "And from the age of 50 years they [the Levites] shall withdraw from the duty of the service and serve no more" (ESV). Since hauling around the furniture of the tabernacle was hard physical labor, later in life Levites were commanded to "minister to their brothers in the tent of the meeting" (Num 8:26), a hint that God did not intend for our work to stop completely, but to morph and mature with age.[18]

Finally, many aging churches and denominations organize a 'seniors' ministry' for the 'elderly'; but can we do better than pulling older adults out of society and recruiting them to be door greeters?

Here are four practical ways to bring biblical hope to the millions of men and women approaching or experiencing retirement:

1. ENCOURAGE RHYTHMS OF REST, RENEWAL AND RE-ENGAGEMENT AS PEOPLE ENTER RETIREMENT.

What if Christian leaders across the world encouraged those entering retirement to take an intentional three, six, or twelve months of Sabbath rest, rather than planning for a vacation? Leviticus 25 and the Ten Commandments suggest that God intends not only for a day of rest, but seasons of rest, in order to reorient the heart to trust God, re-center one's identity in being God's people, and heal social divides.

Brad Hewitt, the recently retired CEO of Thrivent Financial, says: "After being in executive leadership for 25 years, I decided to take a sabbatical before the next season of service. I know I need to slow down before I jump into something else. This sabbatical season may be short, yet at the end I trust God will show me the next place or way to serve." Hewitt plans on a six-month sabbatical to pray, be silent, rebuild old relationships, and listen to God's call for his next assignment.

2. CHANGE THE CONVERSATION FROM ONE OF BENEFITS TO CHAMPIONING THE WORK OF ELDERS IN OUR COMMUNITIES.

Today, conversations around retirement are often embroiled in controversy. As pension funds buckle (like that of the state of Illinois, which has a USD 134 billion hole in its public pension system[19]), older adults are often seen as a problem to be solved. To call somebody 'elderly' is an insult. However, the Judaeo-Christian tradition shows us that elders were once associated with wisdom, character, and leadership ability, the assumed fruit of experience and age (Lev 19:32).

As older Americans re-engage in both paid and unpaid roles, the way to normalize this biblical notion of 'love your neighbor' through our vocations in the latter years is through storytelling. Marc Freedman, the talented CEO of Encore.org, is leading the way in telling these stories of intergenerational friendships, civic service, and the counter-cultural decision to work—even after 'retirement'.[20]

3. CHALLENGE FINANCIAL ADVISORS TO COUNSEL THEIR CLIENTS TO CONSIDER THE DIFFERENT SEASONS OF WORK OVER A LIFETIME.

The cultural caretakers of the idea of retirement are financial advisors, and they have a critical role to play in the future of an aging world. Rather than unthinkingly adopting secular notions of retirement as self-focused pleasure, what if they spoke with clients about seasons of work and rest over a lifetime?

Alongside encouraging generous giving, wise spending, prudent saving, and investing in businesses that align with God's good purposes for the world, financial advisors could be the key change agents in healing broken notions of vocation and elderhood for an aging world.[21]

4. ENCOURAGE INTERGEN-ERATIONAL RELATION-SHIPS IN THE CHURCH.

Elders have much to give a coming generation. Rather than practicing age-segregation, many churches are deploying the elders of their congregation for the well-being of a coming generation:

- Providence Mount St Vincent's Intergenerational Learning Center in Seattle—the subject of the documentary film The Growing Season—has excelled at spawning intergenerational relationships.[22]
- St John's-St Margaret's Church in Singapore has built Project Spring-Winter,[23] inspired in part by Zechariah's vision, "Old men and old women shall again sit in the streets of Jerusalem. . . and the streets of the city shall be full of boys and girls playing in the streets" (Zech 8:4-5 ESV).

A biblical picture of retirement is one of neither heroism nor hedonism, but listening to God's voice and responding in love as elders, intent on sharing wisdom and blessing with the next generation. It is simply a life of service, pointing beyond our self to the Servant in whose image we are made.

I recently called my father. He told me he was contemplating a new way to spend his retirement. After caring for his dying sister, and having always felt an acute concern for ailing family and friends, he told me that after a career in advertising he was going to attend a training session to become a hospice volunteer at Knute Nelson Hospice in Alexandria, Minnesota.

"I think I could do that, Jeff," he told me, contemplating a new vocation. "I visited my dying friend Hugh today. It was a powerful reminder of what a beautiful gift each new day is."

This article originally appeared in the November 2019 issue of the Lausanne Global Analysis (https://lausanne.org/content/lga/2019-11/reimagining-retirement) and is published here with permission. To receive this free bimonthly publication from the Lausanne Movement, subscribe online at https://lausanne.org/lga.

----

1 This story was adapted from my book *An Uncommon Guide to Retirement: Finding God's Purpose for the Next Season of Life* (Chicago: Moody, 2019).

2 Editor's Note: See article by Peter Brierley, entitled, "The Aging Church and Its Implications," in May 2016 issue of *Lausanne Global Analysis* https://lausanne.org/content/lga/2016-05/ageing-church-implications.

3 Glenn Kessler, "Do 10,000 Baby Boomers Retire Every Day?" *Wall Street Journal*, 24 July 2014, https://www.washingtonpost.com/news/fact-checker/wp/2014/07/24/do-10000-baby-boomers-retire-every-day/?utm_term=.b8f3e33fe0b1

4 Marc Freedman, "Building Bridges Across the Generational Divide," *Wall Street Journal*, 1 November 2018, http://webreprints.djreprints.com/4460340932488.html.

5 Marc Freedman, "Building Bridges Across the Generational Divide," *Wall Street Journal*, 1 November 2018, http://webreprints.djreprints.com/4460340932488.html.

6 Conrace Hackett and David McClendon, "Christians Remain World's Largest Religious Group, But They Are Declining in Europe," *Pew Research Center*, April 5, 2018, https://www.pewresearch.org/fact-tank/2017/04/05/christians-remain-worlds-largest-religious-group-but-they-are-declining-in-europe/

7 "No Matter Your Age, Ignore It At Your Peril," *100 Year Life* website, accessed on 28 December 2017: http://www.100yearlife.com/the-challenge/

8 "Social Security Plan Robs from Future to Pay for Past,' *USA Today*, 13 February 2019: https://www.usatoday.com/story/opinion/2019/02/13/democrats-social-security-plan-robs-future-pay-past-editorials-debates/2861184002/, emphasis mine.

9 John Mauldin, "Europe's Pension Funds Are Running Low as Boomer Retire," *Forbes*, 2 July 2018: https://www.forbes.com/sites/johnmauldin/2018/07/02/europes-pension-funds-are-running-low-as-boomers-retire/#329a34af63a0

10 Charlie Campbell, "China's Aging Population is a Major Threat to Its Future," *TIME*, 7 February 2019: http://time.com/5523805/china-aging-population-working-age/

11 Nancy Cook, "Will Baby Boomers Change the Meaning of Retirement?," *The Atlantic*, 18 June 2015: https://www.theatlantic.com/business/archive/2015/06/baby-boomers-retirement/396950/

12 Heather Gillers, Anne Tergesen and Leslie Scism, "A Generation of Americans is Entering Old Age the Least Prepared in Decades," *The Wall Street Journal*, 22 June 2018, https://www.wsj.com/articles/a-generation-of-americans-is-entering-old-age-the-least-prepared-in-decades-1529676033?mod=hp_lead_pos5

13 Nick Thornton, "Here's What the $27 Trillion US Retirement Industry Looks Like," *Think Advisor*, 2 January 2018, https://www.thinkadvisor.com/2018/01/02/heres-what-the-27-trillion-us-retirement-industry/?slreturn=20180714204623

14 *Editor's Note:* See article by Mats Tunehag, entitled, "Creating and Sharing Wealth," in May 2019 issue of *Lausanne Global Analysis* https://lausanne.org/content/lga/2019-05/creating-and-sharing-wealth.

15 "The Engaged Employee," *Gallup*, https://www.gallup.com/services/190118/engaged-workplace.aspx

16 Derek Thompson, "Workism is Making Americans Miserable," *The Atlantic*, 24 February 2019, https://www.theatlantic.com/ideas/archive/2019/02/religion-workism-making-americans-miserable/583441/

17 "Americans Project Average Retirement Age," *Gallup*, https://news.gallup.com/poll/234302/snapshot-americans-project-average-retirement-age.aspx.

18 Jeff Haanen, "Saving Retirement," *Christianity Today*, 15 February 2019, https://www.christianitytoday.com/ct/2019/march/cover-story-saving-retirement.html.

19 Amanda Albright and Danielle Moran, "Illinois Turns Warily to Bonds to Plug $134 Billion Pension Hole," *Bloomberg*, February 20, 2019, https://www.bloomberg.com/news/articles/2019-02-20/why-bonds-seen-as-fix-for-illinois-s-134-billion-pension-hole.

20 For more information, visit Encore.org.

21 Jeff Haanen, "A Manifesto for Financial Advisors," available at: https://www.uncommonretirement.com/financial-advisors.

22 The Growing Season, Trailer: https://www.youtube.com watch?time_continue=66&v=6K3H2VqQKcc.

23 Project Spring-Winter, http://psw.sjsm.org.sg. Thank you to Eunice Nichols for making me aware of both *The Growing Season* and *Project Spring-Winter*.

WORKS CITED

Amanda Albright and Danielle Moran, "Illinois Turns Warily to Bonds to Plug $134 Billion Pension Hole,"Bloomberg, February 20, 2019, https://www.bloomberg.com/news/articles/2019-02-20/why-bonds-seen-as-fix-for-illinois-s-134-billion-pension-hole

Peter Brierley, "The Aging Church and Its Implications," in May 2016 issue of Lausanne Global Analysis https://lausanne.org/content/lga/2016-05/ageing-church-implications.

Charlie Campbell, "China's Aging Population is a Major Threat to Its Future," *TIME*, 7 February 2019: http://time.com/5523805/china-aging-population-working-age/

Nancy Cook, "Will Baby Boomers Change the Meaning of Retirement?," *The Atlantic*, 18 June 2015: https://www.theatlantic.com/business/archive/2015/06/baby-boomers-retirement/396950/.

Marc Freedman, "Building Bridges Across the Generational Divide," *Wall Street Journal*, 1 November 2018, http://webreprints.djreprints.com/4460340932488.html.

Heather Gillers, Anne Tergesen and Leslie Scism, "A Generation of Americans is Entering Old Age the Least Prepared in Decades," *The Wall Street Journal*, 22 June 2018, https://www.wsj.com/articles/a-generation-of-americans-is-entering-old-age-the-least-prepared-in-decades-1529676033?mod=hp_lead_pos5.

Jeff Haanen, "Saving Retirement," *Christianity Today*, 15 February 2019, https://www.christianitytoday.com/ct/2019/march/cover-story-saving-retirement.html.

Jeff Haanen, "A Manifesto for Financial Advisors," available at: https://www.uncommonretirement.com/financial-advisors.

Conrace Hackett and David McClendon, "Christians Remain World's Largest Religious Group, But They Are Declining in Europe," *Pew Research Center*, April 5, 2018 https://www.pewresearch.org/fact-tank/2017/04/05/christians-remain-worlds-largest-religious-group-but-they-are-declining-in-europe/.

Wan He, Daniel Goodkind, and Paul Kowal, "An Aging World: 2015," *United States Census Bureau*, March 2016, https://www.census.gov/content/dam/Census/library/publications/2016/demo/p95-16-1.pdf.

Glenn Kessler, "Do 10,000 Baby Boomers Retire Every Day?" *Wall Street Journal*, 24 July 2014, https://www.washingtonpost.com/news/fact-checker/wp/2014/07/24/do-10000-baby-boomers-retire-every-day/?utm_term=.b8f3e33fe0b1.

John Mauldin, "Europe's Pension Funds Are Running Low as Boomer Retire," *Forbes*, 2 July 2018: https://www.forbes.com/sites/johnmauldin/2018/07/02/europes-pension-funds-are-running-low-as-boomers-retire/#329a34af63a0.

Derek Thompson, "Workism is Making Americans Miserable," *The Atlantic*, 24 February 2019, https://www.theatlantic.com/ideas/archive/2019/02/religion-workism-making-americans-miserable/583441/.

Nick Thornton, "Here's What the $27 Trillion US Retirement Industry Looks Like," *Think Advisor*, 2 January 2018, https://www.thinkadvisor.com/2018/01/02/heres-what-the-27-trillion-   us-retirement-industry/?slreturn=20180714204623.

Mats Tunehag, "Creating and Sharing Wealth," in May 2019 issue of *Lausanne Global Analysis* https://lausanne.org/content/lga/2019-05/creating-and-sharing-wealth.

"No Matter Your Age, Ignore It At Your Peril," *100 Year Life* website, accessed on 28 December 2017: http://www.100yearlife.com/the-challenge/.

"Social Security Plan Robs from Future to Pay for Past,' *USA Today*, 13 February 2019:   https://www.usatoday.com/story/opinion/2019/02/13/democrats-social-security-plan-robs-future-pay-past-editorials-debates/2861184002/

"The Engaged Employee," *Gallup*, https://www.gallup.com/services/190118/engaged-workplace.aspx.

"Americans Project Average Retirement Age," *Gallup*, https://news.gallup.com/poll/234302/snapshot-americans-project-average-retirement-age.aspx.

FLOATING CHURCHES: THE GLOBAL "PINOY" MISSIONARIES

Martin Otto

I magine...a church on a ship!

Close your eyes for a moment and visualize the seven seas. On these waters there are thousands of ships, large and small, all sailing somewhere. Look inside some of these ships and you will discover something you never noticed before.

On some of these ships, seamen meet regularly for worship. There is singing and praise, prayer, preaching, healing, encouraging, collecting of tithes, and baptisms. Such meetings are led by elders. And they are more than just meetings. These are the churches of Jesus Christ on the oceans of the world. He is among his people there and is carrying out the will of his Father. He calls and sends out; he glorifies himself through them. And these churches cannot be overcome by Satan. The members of these churches are also members of churches on land, having been sent out for service on the high seas. It is through these churches that the kingdom of God is growing from day to day!

A church on a ship? Why not? We have grown so used to the concept that 'church' equals a building, while the Bible teaches that church equals people. In English we have the further complication that we commonly use the same word ('church') for the gathering of God's people to praise God and also for the building in which they meet. This goes back to the sad deterioration from New Testament

Christianity, which was based on people, to a Constantinian Churchianity which was based on structures. Our concept of planting churches is more concerned with places to meet than with disciples to gather. No wonder this church- planting model does not fit the millions of nomadic peoples of the world who live much of their lives in movement – in deserts, steppes, forests, and oceans.

Over the last decades of the twentieth century, much more effort and thought were given to how to plant churches among the nomads of this world. We have seen astonishing growth among Roma or Gypsy peoples in Europe and the beginnings of success among such peoples as the nomadic Fulbe of West Africa, the Mongolians on the edge of the Gobi Desert, and the Sea Gypsies of Southeast Asia. But what of the millions of seafarers who spend the majority of their working lives away from home and in the difficult transient life on board commercial ships? For too long, ministry among them sought to address their social needs. It sometimes focused on evangelism, but to actually plant ship churches was hardly thought of. Yet so many of the major seafaring peoples of the world have many Christians– at least in name–such as the Pacific Islanders, the Filipinos, West Africans, and others. Could they not be used of God to reach out to the many Muslim seamen–Arabs, Somalis, Pakistanis, Maldivians, Indonesians? It is exciting indeed to think of the possibilities of a new generation of seamen's missionaries emerging with a vision not only to evangelize, but also to actually plant churches and link them to a network of shore bases where teaching and teaching materials are at hand, as well as to a network of ship churches that connects both seekers and Christians. Is not this vision something for the twenty-first century with all the tools we have in the internet, mobile/cell phones, Bible correspondence courses in print and online, and so on? Many missionaries who have served overseas could find a remarkable new outlet for using their skills and acquired language abilities to make this vision become a reality.

The body of Christ is vast. It consists of millions of Christians worldwide who love, obey, and worship Jesus Christ in thousands and thousands of churches with many different theological backgrounds.

But in order to continue to thrive and glorify God, these churches must multiply. And so, God equips his people to plant new churches.

Church planting is one of the most thrilling experiences in the world. And, as we see from the New Testament, planting churches is a biblical mandate. There are many books about church planting, and there are many different kinds of churches. There are small churches, house churches, and mega churches. Churches are planted in different ways, in different cultures, and at different locations. It has perhaps been most difficult to plant churches over the years in those countries where there has been no religious freedom. But believers are mapping out the globe and bringing the gospel to people everywhere–from prisons in Argentina to remote corners of the world, and churches are being planted in these places to the glory of God.

But what about the people we never see? What about people who make their living at sea? These are people you and I do not often think about. These are people who rarely, if ever, have a chance to visit a church on shore. Do those people not have a right to worship Jesus Christ in a church? Are they forgotten by God? Surely not! Christ died as much for seafarers as he died for anyone else. But where is their church?

There are about 1.6 million seafarers who spend between six and nine months at sea at a time. Following such a stint they generally spend about two months in their home countries, and then go out again for another six to nine months at sea. They desperately need a living church in which they can worship Jesus Christ.

In the nineteenth century, the Seamen's Christian Friend Society was formed to expand evangelism to this spiritually neglected group of people. They designed a special flag, which was hoisted on the main masthead when there was a church on board. They called it the Bethel flag. The word Bethel means 'house of God' and a Bethel flag indicated 'a ship fitted as a place of worship for sailors.'

God longs to see sailors worship him in his church. To fulfil this mission we need people, churches, and mission societies to minister to these forgotten people. Many of the seafarers are from the so-called 10/40 window. Many face all sorts of problems daily, from loneliness and difficulties with their superiors to sickness and communication problems. Because of these issues and the hard life they lead, many are very open to the gospel. You can meet with seafarers in international ports on all continents. Ships come to your country, to your ports. Do they hear the gospel there? Who is reaching out to these men? There are still ports in this world without an evangelical witness.

For more than 30 years I have seen that it is possible to have living churches on board ships. Some time ago I visited a huge passenger ship with many different nationalities on board – a thousand seafarers on just one ship – and I was asked to teach their congregation from the word of God during their time in Hamburg while the repairs on the ship were being finished. They met regularly for Bible study, prayer, and worship, and were eager to share the word of God. On another ship I met with a few believers who told me that they had even chosen elders and that they had communion regularly. This church met several times during the week, and they had developed a biblical structure, despite their difficult circumstances. They were a living testimony to the possibility of spiritual life on a ship. They were also a powerful witness to the other sailors on board. In Hamburg we have a small team and cannot visit all 'ship churches' regularly. But even if we cannot visit them all, we can inform other missionaries in other ports to see to them and nurture them. We can still support them by praying for them and by giving them Bible study correspondence courses, biblical CDs and books, and Christian music–all of which encourage their spiritual growth.

Whenever we meet at least two believers we encourage them to start a church on board. Of course, such a church is, in many cases, only temporary for the time the sailors are on board. But this should not prevent them from having a living church in which they can glorify God, and which will also minister to others on their ship. These sailors have the promises of God in the Bible. One of them that applies particularly to their situation is found in Matthew 18:20: "Where two or three come together in my name, there am I with them." Often these very small churches grow in numbers, and as a team we do our best to help and support them.

Jesus certainly has a big open heart for these men, and he wants them to worship him in a church body. If they have no chance to attend church at home because of their long absences, then they surely must find a way to worship God at sea. If a seafarer spends between 30 and 35 years at sea, he will only be home for about five years in total during that time. Where will he find fellowship and grow in the grace of our Lord Jesus Christ, if not in a church on board? Where will he find comfort and encouragement in times of difficulty, if not in a church on board? Where will he be able to practice his God-given spiritual gifts, if not in a church on board? It is therefore our goal and vision to plant as many ship churches as possible, as well as to nurture those that already exist. As the Holy Spirit establishes these ship churches among different nationalities, they will be a living testimony and a bright shining light to their fellow seafarers and to the glory of God.

The concept of churches on ships is not a new one. In fact, there have been churches in various forms on ships for many years. Unfortunately, we do not hear all the testimonies of churches on ships because some ships never come to our ports. The following is a report from a Christian newspaper in England. Years ago, the luxury liner *Queen Elizabeth 2* hit the headlines when disgruntled passengers complained about a refit not being completed in time. What the pampered passengers did not realize was that things might have been much worse if there had not been a group of mainly Filipino crew members praying for the ship and her passengers.

Fernando and Bert led a group of about 25 Christians in regular praise and worship meetings in the crew's library. Whenever the *QE2* berthed at Southampton, David Thomson, port chaplain of the Seamen's Christian Friend Society, was on board to encourage and help them. "It was tragic when a few years ago the *QE2* struck rocks and had to go to Hamburg for repairs," says David, yet God used the free time the crew had. "The port missionary in Hamburg, Martin Otto, held several group Bible Studies, explaining who Christ is and the need to take him into our lives as our personal Lord and Savior. I consequently saw the result of this when the ship came back to Southampton. Nine men spoke of how since they put Christ in first place of their lives, many aspects of their lives were changing. They spoke of beginning to see practical help in the Bible.'

The Seamen's Christian Friend Society's network of 'Port Links' around the world is a lifeline to the isolated Christian seafarer. These 'links' are often ordinary families living in the port area. A phone call to the family results in an invitation to come to their home and share a meal and the sailor does not have to join his shipmates wandering aimlessly through the town and being exposed to all sorts of temptations.

The *Royal Princess*, a large luxury liner, came to Hamburg several times. On board, I met many Filipino seafarers, and also crew members from Mexico, India, Portugal, Canada, England, and Nepal. I was always amazed to see how many people on board showed an interest in spiritual matters. When I last boarded the ship, I took a huge bag full of tracts, Bible study courses, Bibles, inspirational books, and Christian music (worship CDs). While I was sitting in the crew's mess room, I met Bernie, the pastor of the ship's church. Both Bernie and I were amazed that, after a short time, all the Christian material that I offered to the crew was gone. People were longing for more of God and were happy to buy a Christian music CD or a *Jesus* film. They were also delighted to receive the tracts, Bibles, and Bible study courses we provided for them. When I preached, people listened very carefully. I think they were so interested in spiritual matters because a Christian church had existed on this cruise liner for quite a long time. Some of the Christians told me that the church on *Royal Princess* meets at least three times a week, a gathering of between ten and fifteen Christians.

On Wednesdays they have a prayer meeting from 10:30 p.m. until 12 a.m. On Fridays they meet for Bible study from 10:30 p.m. until 12 a.m. On Sundays their worship service begins at 10:30 p.m. and sometimes lasts until 1:30 a.m. During this service, they listen to testimonies from various crew members, sing, pray, and also hear preaching–from a CD or from a fellow crew member. Their numbers peaked at about 30 a few years ago. Since then, many of the Christians had gone on vacation or moved to work on other ships. Some Christians on board cannot attend the church because they have to work during the meetings. "How does the church grow?" I asked the pastor.

Bernie answered, "First, we try to make sure that everybody is having a regular quiet time. Also, we meditate upon the word of God together. Third, we encourage members to share their faith with those they meet, and also, to share testimonies during our worship service. Fourth, we train people to start preaching or at least to share something from the Bible. And, lastly, we all listen to preaching CDs."

Bernie also told me that, in recent years, quite a number of seafarers have come to know Christ because of the evangelistic efforts of those involved in the church. They had elected two elders whose responsibility it was to lead the church. Every first Sunday of the month the church on board the Royal Princess breaks bread. They also take regular offerings, which they have used in the past to buy musical instruments and to support a missionary work in Chile. Bernie also told me that, each time an elder goes home on vacation, the church gives him US$100 for his local home church in the Philippines, to help build the church there.

"And what do the elders do when they go back to their home church?" I asked Bernie. "What would their position there be?"

"The elders go home as members of their local church," Bernie explained, "submitting to the eldership and leadership of their home church in the Philippines."

It is clear from the example of the *Royal Princess* and others that once a church is established on board, it has a positive influence on everyone. Christians involved in the church grow in their faith and develop loving and caring relationships with one another. Church members also pray for their mates and find they are much more willing to listen to the gospel if there is a church on board. A church can create a positive atmosphere that even non-Christians notice and appreciate.

The most exciting ship I've visited in the port of Hamburg is a luxury yacht belonging to a wealthy Saudi Arabian. People say that the owner is one of the advisers to the king. While the owner only visits his yacht every so often, when he does, he arrives in his own plane. He is transported from the airport in a huge Mercedes, escorted by his bodyguards. It is actually a sort of a secret ship–nobody is allowed to visit, and the crew is nervous when he is there. The ship carries neither cargo nor passengers but is essentially a showpiece of the "big man" from Saudi Arabia.

I did not, of course, know any of this when I approached the gangway to try to visit the yacht. The security officer who met me asked who I was and told me plainly that nobody was allowed to visit. So, I left, and our church prayed for God to give us an opportunity to visit this ship. Shortly after this time of prayer, I made one more attempt to visit the ship. A young second officer, who later told me that he was a born-again Christian too, met me and allowed me to enter.

In the mess room I met with about 20 Filipino seafarers who were delighted to see somebody from the seamen's mission. Several people were eager to have Bibles in their own language, which is Tagalog. As the ship stayed several weeks in dry dock, I had time to develop friendships with crew members. The captain of the yacht was not happy when I asked him whether I was allowed to hold Bible studies on board. He said that nobody would be interested and that the ship belonged to a Muslim. He did, however, allow me to meet with the seafarers in a nearby container. I met with the crew for Bible study, invited them to our home, and conducted personal Bible studies with individuals. Our time together was very encouraging, and before they sailed, two men gave their lives to Christ.

Three years later, the ship came back to Hamburg for some repairs. I boarded the ship and found that many of the crew were still there. There was also a very dedicated Christian Filipina seawoman who invited everybody for church meetings on board. And so, there and then, a church was started. They worshipped God, had Bible studies, and prayed together. There were between eight and ten crew members involved in this church (out of a Filipino crew of 20), and they were eager to tell the other crew members about Jesus Christ. They invited me to speak at their ship-church about prayer, and I enjoyed the wonderful fellowship with these brothers and sisters immensely.

It is always good to hear that a church on board a ship has gained official recognition. Following is an email message I received from a female information technology (IT) officer:

Hello, brother Martin, how are you? I'm very pleased to inform you that we are growing in numbers! Not only Filipinos, we also have Indian and South African members. Sadly, that was my last Bible study this contract, as I'm leaving for vacation on Saturday. But I'm glad to know that I'm leaving a great team ... and I know that the Lord is with this church, that he will bless them with more workers and speakers. Brother Melchor is on day shift next month, so he can be with them during fellowships. We were able to purchase a guitar–we have new members who have gifts in music. That's really exciting! Also, we already have on-board management's approval/permit for the cruise ship Boudicca–so we can gather at the crew day room officially, distribute flyers, and post invitations at the crew area. We really thank the Lord for all the blessings that he's giving us.

Most of the work we are engaged in through the seamen's mission focuses on commercial and cruise ships, but we also have an outreach to military ships. Following is an email from Thomas K. Hayden, on board the USS Nicholas:

On the second day underway one of my shipmates asked about getting involved in church services and sought help with his decision to 'turn over a new leaf'. By the third day underway I have had three people inquire about a Bible. On day four Jason informed me that one of our ship mates would be joining the service and bringing his guitar. The 'excitement' of what goes on with our group is spreading and I look forward to each day just to see who God is going to send my way. It has now been six days at sea and two more people have asked for Bibles. I am preparing my first Sunday service for the deployment and need your prayers. Week one is over, and another ship mate asked about receiving a Bible. I am almost out of Bibles! I sent an email regarding the lack of Bibles to David and Nancy in North Carolina, who passed my request to their friend in the Gideons. One of our upcoming ports is near a facility that should have Bibles I can pick up. If those options fail, I will let you know. I left my wife, Cindy, and daughters, Kayla and Kelsey, in Portsmouth, VA. ... I have a copy of the Naval Christian Fellowship (NCF) Hospitality List, but I don't see anyone for the areas we are going to. With regards to my Bible dilemma, I am anxiously awaiting an answer from my friends in North Carolina. I have the possibility of picking up Bibles from an upcoming port.

Today was my second Sunday at sea with an amazing attendance of 18 sailors this afternoon during Sunday service. We were able to pass out some Bibles and add some people to the list for the daily devotion that I send out. Each Sunday I am taking up a prayer list at the service to forward to praying friends. Sailors face a myriad of problems once we set sail from home, and it is my sincere hope and desire to help them through these problems by guiding them towards the strength of God. Currently the space I teach in holds 24 people. When we grow beyond that number, I will have to move to the mess decks which hold 40-plus people.

I wish you could see my excitement! My ship was visited by the admiral in charge of our entire battle group. He gave us a nice speech then opened the floor to questions, specifically asking if he could do anything for us. So, I raised my hand and simply stated, "I need Bibles." He asked what kind. I said, "Pocket size and regular, NIV and KJV." He then asked me how many I needed, and I said, "As many as you are willing." At that, he called in his aide and said, "Get Chief Hayden some Bibles. Get big ones, small ones, and a lot of them!" (Before I continue, let me give you a little background information. I am on my ship in the middle of the ocean. His ship is a long way off, somewhere else in the ocean.) By the time his helicopter came to pick him up a few hours later, he [had] delivered six boxes to me containing over two hundred new Bibles. There are hard-backed, paper-backed, small Bibles, NIV and KJV. Let us praise our Lord, for he is true to his Word ... "Ask and you shall receive." I thank everyone else for their offer to send Bibles, but now I am glad to say I no longer have room for anymore! Each day I stop by the place where I keep the Bibles and notice a few more have been taken!

First of all, I would like to thank you for the encouraging emails that you continue to send. I am a person that loves the company of family and friends and although my band of brothers is growing out here, it is still very comforting to receive correspondence from you. It doesn't surprise me to tell you that we have not only reached, but superseded, the capacity of the room we use for worship services. So it was with great pleasure that I announced today that our group would be moving to the mess decks because it holds over 40 people instead of only 24 people. In fact, we may even be adding another guitar player to our service which will bring us up to three guitars, one bongo and a keyboard. Your prayers are certainly helping with the momentum of God's work on this ship!!! I wish I had the words to describe to you [how] the level of enthusiasm for our Lord. Jesus is becoming a hot topic on board the USS Nicholas.

The only way for the word of God to spread at sea is via the lay leaders. Personally, I have found this to be a highly neglected duty on each of my ships upon arrival. It is nothing less than a burning desire for me to get sailors excited about Christ. On my first ship, USS Robert G. Bradley, I started a weekly Bible study and led Sunday service underway. On my first deployment, it was a huge challenge because although I was excited to do this, I had no formal or even informal training.

During my second deployment I had the advantage of lessons learned and some navy training from the chaplains on base. My wife bought me a keyboard so I could add some music to the *program, and I was blessed with a shipmate who could lead us in singing.*

By the time I started my third deployment I had a solid system down and a well-established group of believers and a regular attendance of 21 sailors. While I was on shore duty, I spent a great deal of time thinking of what I could do to make my next ship a fertile field for reaping a huge harvest for the Lord. To my surprise, when I arrived on the USS Nicholas, there was already a lay reader on board. So, I didn't try to assume that position. Within about a month I was personally asked by the captain to serve as the lay leader. The awesome thing about that is that I had not mentioned anything about my desires to fill that position.

I am convinced that God, who knows all, wanted me to get started with my plans for this ship. The one thing I learned from my last ship was that singing and music are vital to the service. It sets the stage for true worship and brings an aura of together-ness. I cannot lead the music by myself, so I immediately began a search for someone who was willing to do so. Thankfully, about three weeks before my first deployment on this ship, STG2 Jason Cash was transferred here at the last minute because we had a sudden loss of the personnel that can do his job. He is the son of a Christian music singer and has a natural talent for playing the guitar and singing. To my great surprise, he immediately volunteered to help. As a result, the entire deployment was a complete success. We established a wonderful fellowship and even created the Nicholas Praise Team. Jason and I have spent the last nine months praying and preparing for this deployment.

In January I started a daily devotion email distribution list. These emails included a morning and evening devotion and a list of Bible chapters to read each day in order to read the Bible in one year. At first, I had about 15 people sign up and now I am up to 45 people. My church at home has given me student guides and instructor lesson plans to teach Sunday service throughout the deployment. This has been well accepted by everyone who attends.

I also have an on-going prayer list that gets filled out every Sunday and disseminated via the distribution list. Our service usually runs anywhere from an hour to 1Ω hours. We have grown from about 16 people regularly attending to over 24 people. In fact, last Sunday we had almost 30 in attendance. The excitement of the group that I fellowship with seems to multiply each day. I don't have to walk far one way or the other on this ship without running into a brother in Christ. We are in a constant state of uplifting one another and praising our Savior. It is so awesome to see God work his way through this crew.

Jason changed our name from 'Protestant Lay Services' to N.P.C. (Nicholas Protestant Church). Everyone really liked that, I think. This is a wonderful blessing that I am truly honored to be a part of. I look forward with great anticipation each day as to what our Lord will do. We are called to tell others about Christ around the world. What better way than about a ship with a captive audience?

Imagine what could happen if the ship church was a training field for church planters worldwide. There are several maritime training academies in the Philippines led by born-again Christians. They teach seafarers the word of God. How wonderful it would be if they would also train them to start churches on the ships on which they will sail. In the same way, local churches could train their members who are seafarers, or who might be called to be seafarer missionaries, to be church planters on ships. If churches would assume this responsibility, they would make a huge contribution to world evangelization. Actually, the foundation of this vision is a triangle: the church at home, the seafarer and the port chaplain. These three should work together in different ways to see God's church established around the world. To God be the glory!

A REFLECTION ON MISSIONARY LIFE IN THE PHILIPPINES

Julie Ma

INTRODUCTION

I am honored and privileged to have served Filipinos as a missionary with my husband, Wonsuk Ma, for 27 years. My second child was born and raised in that country, while my older son was two years old when we went to serve in the Philippines. I spent more time in the Philippines than I did in my home country, Korea. As I lived longer in the Philippines, I became more at ease with the local people and culture. They were like my sisters and brothers.

I first studied Tagalog, the country's official tongue, and then Ilocano, the communication language among the mountain tribes. Even though each tribe has its own dialect, people may converse by understanding Ilocano. When we went to the mountain church, meals were served on coconut shells and banana leaves. No one used utensils like spoons or forks. Using my fingers to put the food in my mouth was difficult initially, but I kept trying. With a lot of work, I could put food in my mouth. I had fun doing it.

Even though we departed the Philippines after finishing our missionary work, we still have a lot of positive memories. Our primary mission projects included church planting, evangelism, helping mountain pastors, helping pastors' kids with school, and other things. In our mission, we worked with the local ministers as a team. More significantly, developing a solid relationship was critical. I greatly treasured and valued it. This essay will present one significant mission work we did among the tribal churches as well as some memorable stories from my missionary journey.

1. MISSIONAL CHURCH

It would take several pages to outline the significant time we spent teaching and training the local and mountain churches on the value of being a missional church and how the churches came to be missional.

We emphasized that a church must be a missional church by multiplying. We often encouraged churches to establish daughter churches in adjacent communities. We promised the churches that our collaboration would only be maintained if we attempted to multiply. When there isn't an existing house church that adheres to the Bible in the area, devotion to God typically motivates individuals to start one. Because they would foresee our great emphasis on reproduction, numerous churches had already started new activities before their church construction was dedicated.[1]

The Kankana-ey people live in the rugged hills of the northern Philippines. Small towns can only be reached by foot. The average lifespan is short since only poor medical care is available. Their long-standing religious customs, including sacrifices and funerals, can worsen their lives. Balili is the name of an old Kankana-ey "mother church" in this region. Members of the church who had moved away missed it as it grew, especially during the protracted wet season. As a result, the Sebang Church was founded. Miss Pynie Bacasen, a fresh graduate from Bible school, undoubtedly inspired a few young people in Sebang Church to pray for the highland Kalango-yas. Walking along the Spanish Trail, often frequented by Communist guerillas, was Pynie. She arrived in Cocoy after a five-hour trek and noticed the many little children scattered over the mountain settlements. As a result of her summer Bible school, a church swiftly grew in this firmly animistic area. Young people from Sebang traveled to Cocoy to assist the believers almost every week. Through prayer, many received healing and were freed from perilous dreams. Even with the adamant opposition of the village priest, the church continued to grow. Within a year, a ceremony was held to dedicate a new church edifice.

The young people of Cocoy began to pray for another nearby hamlet, Docucan, at this time because all the youngsters from Cocoy attended school in this town. On her weekly evangelistic excursions to Docucan, Pynie led a group of young volunteers, including those from Sebang and Cocoy. Throughout this time, the young people continued to regularly pray for healings and release from various physical and spiritual problems. Babili, Sebang, Cocoy, and Docucan residents worked together to construct the church. Even before the Docucan building was erected, the newest church was sending its young people frequently to the nearby village of Ambakbak. Six houses were already worshipping the Lord. Since then, four congregations have begun construction on their churches, transforming into "daughters" of the municipal church.

Tinuc is where this "chain of daughter churches" ends because it is the county's most central and vital Kalango-ya center. The good news is that the epicenter of this tribal region already has a Bible study. Again, this ministry involves participation from all the "mother" and "daughter" churches, including Babili, Sebang, Cocoy, Docucan, Ambakbak, and Kalango-ya.

Because Pentecostals and animists in tribal life shared a similar spiritual outlook, the gospel was successfully received. By receiving guidance and training to become missional churches, the tribal churches created daughter churches, intergenerational churches. This serves as a great example of a "full-circle mission." We can only truly make out a few distinct structures in God's plan's "multi-generation" progression over eight years. As a result of their Christian calling, it is not a surprise that churches have shown a strong interest in missionary work. This can be attributed to the members' exposure to Pentecostal teaching.

2. POWER ENCOUNTER

Most tribal communities in the majority world practice spiritism and ancestor worship. Priests, who are experts in religion, are critical to this kind of worship. They are thought to be able to connect people with (ancestor) spirits. This view holds that the ancestors' souls never detach themselves from reality; instead, they are always in a relationship with the living. The spirits can heal the sick, protect the family from harm, and prevent bad luck. Because of this, when a someone becomes ill, their family members will follow the priest's advice and provide a sacrifice to appease the spirit. In this religious environment, people must not neglect to pacify the ancestor spirits should catastrophe befall the family.

The first similarity between animistic faiths and Christianity in the majority world, especially among tribal nations, is the conviction that the spirit realm not only exists but also actively engages with the world of the living. In such cases, the ancestral spirits, for example, are never believed to live in a separate universe; instead, they coexist with their living descendants. They believe that the visible and invisible worlds are connected. Christians all concur that God is both transcendent and immanent. The Holy Spirit, who is within us, assists us when we are in need. He empowers believers to bear spiritual fruits such as love, joy, peace, patience, kindness, goodness, faithfulness, gentleness, and self-control (Gal 5:22–23). He gives both common and unusual gifts to Christ-followers (see, for instance, 1 Corinthians 12). In conclusion, the Bible demonstrates that God is involved in his children's lives.

The second link between these two ideologies is the conviction that supernatural beings, like the Holy Spirit, have the power to heal and bless. Because of their shared native worldview, Christians might be open to the magical power of the Christian God. Any supernatural manifestation, whether witnessed or experienced firsthand, becomes one of the prerequisites for accepting Christ.

Most Africans believe the spiritual world is essential to human experience and belief. Asians frequently share similar spiritual perspectives and experiences. These shared worldviews help partially explain the effectiveness of the Christian mission, and the frequently reported supernatural healings and exorcisms. The manifestation of God's power provides indisputable proof of God's majesty and the veracity of the Bible's assertions.

It is challenging to bring Christianity to the tribal people who live in the mountains because they have maintained their traditional Kanyao faith from generation to generation. However, the gospel of healing and blessing was favorably welcomed because of the comparable religious worldview mentioned above. A crucial contribution was the empirical proof of recovery from diverse illnesses.

In Tuding in 1954, Vanderbout held a once-weekly open-air service where she shared the gospel. Based on Mark 16:15–18, she declared during the ceremony that "they shall lay hands on the sick and they shall recover." She recognized these people's needs and asked her ministry team to pray for the ill out of a fundamental belief in the Word of God.[2]

A young boy, fourteen years old, developed leg ulcers. Witch physicians gave the youngster some treatment, but he could not recover. This youngster fell when he was seven, breaking his leg exactly where the knee should have been. His life became extremely tough during the next five years as the bones in his leg grew together and bowed throughout the healing process. He was unable to straighten his leg because it was stiff. His foot failed to touch the earth; he was unable to move. He hopped along with the aid of a stick or crawled on the ground as he strained to walk, and he undoubtedly led a horrible life.[3]

Because of the boy's illness and because she trusted in God, the boy's mother converted to Christianity. The boy's parents decided to follow Christ and gave up their pagan worship. Vanderbout and her ministry team made visits to the boy's home. With the conviction that Christ might cure, Vanderbout placed her hand on him and prayed. This boy, trusting in God's healing, put away his stick.[4] After that, he stopped using his stick, and his leg gradually straightened. By the might of God, the ulcers disappeared.

Through the ministry of Vanderbout and her team, God has saved many souls through healing encounters. There was a young child who had struggled to walk for a few years. She started to walk, thanks to a divine miracle. Through their daughter's healing, her parents found Christ, and they started going to church frequently. Such healing testimonials caused the revival to grow and increased the number of believers. The entire barrio population was typically represented among the spectators at the events. The Tuding revival shook Benguet Province, and word of this was disseminated widely to lay the groundwork for future work in the highlands.[5]

3. DEVELOPING A POSITIVE RELATIONSHIP

The tribal people are so reticent and reclusive that, after Sunday services, they shyly avoid approaching tourists who attend. I tried approaching them to communicate, but I immediately knew they were introverted. Conversations were initially challenging, but I persisted and asked several straightforward questions to keep the conversation going. They gradually spoke to me with ease as they let their hearts out. I sat with them for lunch to deepen my relationship with them. In truth, I was an introvert, too, because of my background, but I needed to come out of my shell to interact with the members of the mountain church. They are friendly and lovely individuals. They offered us a box of carrots, potatoes, and red rice as we prepared to leave after ministering to them to return home. In Christ, I felt a deep sense of sisterhood and fraternity.

Later, I was completely bedridden and immobile after suffering a severe leg injury. I was unable to conduct regular classes while attending church. The mountain people were made aware of what had occurred. It was quite a way from the mountain community to my house. Walking took hours upon hours. I was surprised when some church members brought me food boxes and offered prayers for me. My heart was indeed affected, and I could feel their love for the Lord.

The churches in the mountain are dispersed; thus, getting from one to the next requires walking for 3-5 hours or more. We once hiked for eight hours. By the time we arrived, our feet hurt, and we were pretty hungry. The group members massaged our feet while boiling some water with ginger. While receiving a massage, we were so relaxed that our fatigue almost vanished. They were kind to us, and we felt it deeply. Another experience involved making an unusual local coffee with ingredients like ginger, peanut powder, etc. The coffee has a unique flavor. Usually, we slept in the church. There are numerous holes in the church building's wall through which wind can enter. We were shivering even though we had sleeping bags. The group members became aware and they packed blankets to cover our bodies. Once more, they showed genuine concern for us.

I want to tell you a remarkable story about a Christian family. We got the opportunity to travel to Baguio, the Philippines, while we were living in England. The family members came to see us with a bag of potatoes because they knew we were in Baguio. They wanted to demonstrate their affection to us despite knowing that we couldn't carry it to England. These beautiful acts of kindness so moved me. I owe God so much for allowing my husband and me to develop such amazing friendships with the members of the mountain church.

4. HOLISTIC MISSION

A significant component of our mission is the choice to make it a holistic mission. Even missionaries engaged in traditional missions like evangelism and church planting must engage in holistic tasks that prioritize meeting people's needs. I want to present a few outstanding cases of holistic missions in connection with what we have done. American missionary Lillian Trasher was heavily involved in an orphanage mission in Egypt. She began an orphanage in 1915 with a small number of kids. By 1916, it had 50 children. It got bigger and bigger, and the structures kept growing. Even the Egyptian government acknowledged her commitment to community service and gave her an award. Over 50 years, she cared for more than 20,000 orphans and widows at an orphanage in Assiout, Egypt. On December 17, 1961, she died. She was known as "Mama Lillian" or "Mother of the Nile" by her Egyptian people.[6]

Lazarus Project, which cares for street children in Zambia, and HIV/AIDS intervention and care there are two further examples. In 1992, Senior Pastor Joshua Banda of the Northmead Assembly of God Church in Lusaka, Zambia, started counseling people with HIV/AIDS and their families. The ministry of this church successfully treated these patients.[7]

In 1954, Mark Buntain and his wife Huldah began missionary work in Calcutta, India. The Buntains quickly learned that many street children in Calcutta had no real names and were referred to as "the one with measles" or "the kid with smallpox." Some perished from malnutrition, while others succumbed to bacterial and viral infections. They weren't eating enough, and therefore, their bodies weren't strong enough to fight. These dead often have bewildered expressions as adults investigate what happened while holding a handkerchief to their nose and mouth. The Buntains launched a feeding ministry after encountering countless individuals who regularly went without or who had little to eat. The numbers were initially modest, but they kept increasing and are still doing so now. The Calcutta Street Feeding Program provides food for many people, including schoolchildren. Within a radius of 45 minutes around Calcutta, the food is transported to several locations. Although the city has developed in many ways due to the effect of technology, the situation of the impoverished seems to have gotten worse because so many people from other cities are moving here in search of jobs and somewhere to live. Since thousands of families rely on these daily meals while living on the streets, the feeding lines are still growing, and it is estimated that one million kids are homeless. Every day, it is the only meal that 25,000 pupils will receive all day.[8]

Our overall mission scope is less expensive than what is shown above. Families live in substandard housing because the mountains have no facilities, water, electricity, or sewage systems. Even though we were drenched in perspiration from climbing the mountain, there was no water for a shower. The water was obtained from a large valley. After discovering a bucket of water in the kitchen, I once had a humiliating encounter. I spent a lot of time hiking, which made me really hot. I took a shower without asking as soon as I noticed the water. Later, I understood that the bucket of water was meant for the entire crowd. I felt terrible for my team colleagues. My husband and I chose to install a water system to have the essential water after learning about and experiencing that. Without question, water is a crucial component of human life. Both drinking water and water that can be used for other purposes are necessities for the populace. For reasons of health, we also install toilet systems. The establishment of this system is essential since it has a significant impact on people's health.

5. COUNSELING

In the Philippines, we found that the churchgoers in the mountain had their own difficulties and issues in life. A female congregation member committed her life to serving God and the church. She came to me one day and shared her entire life. She claimed that her husband constantly caused her and her family problems. First, the family barely had enough money to survive because the husband didn't have work. Second, he consumed alcohol virtually daily. He even took out a loan to buy alcohol. Third, he never went to church because he led such a wretched existence. He frequently voiced his disapproval of her attending a church. Additionally, he had issues with his children, who disrespected their father. The husband's terrible life caused her heartbreak and agony. They constantly quarreled and battled because of their divergent viewpoints. She wanted to leave her house for a better life. She told me all of this. We sincerely prayed together after learning about her issues. We pleaded with the Lord. We routinely gathered and prayed nonstop.

She revealed some unexpected news to me after praying for many months. She claimed that her husband had gradually altered. He mentioned his wish to find employment and his anxiety about the youngsters' schooling in the future. And compared to earlier days, he drank far less. He even expressed a desire to visit a church. It was a miracle. I leaped with delight at the news since it was so thrilling. Without a doubt, the Lord heard our petition. We continued to pray for him and lift him in prayer until he gave himself entirely to the

Lord and consistently made it to church. He was actually behind her, assisting her. The family ended up being content and joyful and did an excellent job serving God.

6. VITAMIN A PROJECT

We decided to create a Vitamin A Project after giving it some thought. The mountain inhabitants need more nourishment because there is a paucity of nutrient-dense food, particularly vegetables. Many people had vitamin A deficiencies due to their diet, which led to blindness and eye issues. It started to overwhelm us. We established the Vitamin A Project and contacted numerous Korean and American churches to request Vitamin A. We were pleased to receive cartons of Vitamin A from multiple churches, but there still wasn't enough to provide each member with a bottle. Nevertheless, we were able to find a solution: we invited the congregation to line up after the service and placed a pill in each person's mouth. There was a long line. A report claims that a few pills a year will keep individuals from going blind. Having many of the members taking vitamin A made us extremely happy.

One exciting experience we had involved an elderly woman who stayed with us after taking her vitamin A, rather than going home. "You may now return to your house," I said. "You've taken vitamin A, and the evening service is over. There is nothing we can do. Return home and take a nap." She gave a pretty intriguing response. "I'd like to take more vitamin A," she remarked, "so that my eyes will get brighter and I can even see an angel." I was crying with laughter as I realized how pure and untarnished her heart was, remaining true to God's purity.

7. MEETING NPA IN THE MOUNTAIN

I recall another occasion when we hiked for around eight hours to get from one spot to another. We were strolling with thirst. We found a quiet resting place and collected the valley's flowing water.

On the opposite side, we discovered a small group of soldiers sitting. When we found they were members of the communist NPA (New People's Army), we realized they weren't just soldiers. After we relaxed and talked with them briefly, they rose behind us as we departed the area to continue on toward our destination. We were asking God for protection nonstop because we were so terrified. Wonsuk unexpectedly inquired about their direction as they rounded the corner. They responded by giving their destination. Wonsuk introduced himself, his name, and his mission among the tribal people. One man, upon hearing his last name, remarked, "Oh, I heard your name when we visited houses in the mountain village. A few family members mentioned your name. The Ma's helped us build a church and finish it," they claimed. We were able to share our hearts To them through such informal conversation. It naturally reduced stress and allowed us for relaxed conversation.

8. EXOTIC FOODS

I always have lovely food memories, especially when eating different foods in exotic ways. They provided excellent food when we visited deep mountain churches because they assumed we were starving. They killed a local chicken and made a delicious soup with it. Additionally, they prepared vegetables with salt, pepper, and a small amount of minced garlic. The only issue was that they did not use utensils, such as spoons, plates, or bowls. The food was placed on banana leaves and in coconut shells. What a challenge it was, scooping the chicken soup! I had to use my fingers, which required such a deft approach. I had never scooped soup with my fingers, so I dripped a lot when I started. However, laughing all the time, I kept trying until I was successful. I vividly remember it and it is a permanent memory.

Balut is one of the Philippines' unique foods. It is a partially developed chicken or duck egg that is cooked in the shell and often eaten as street food in South China and Southeast Asian countries. It seemed so strange to me when I first saw it, but I picked up eating skills from a Filipino acquaintance. Some missionaries claimed that they typically switched off the light so they could not see inside the creature's shell. However, I dared to use my eyes to see. I witnessed all the creatures' parts, including their eyes, hair, feathers, legs, and wings, gradually bursting the shells. After that, I sipped juice and nibbled on my food. For me, the flavor wasn't at all good. When my older son, who was born and raised in the Philippines and spoke the language fluently, visited the nation as an undergraduate student, he went straight for the balut and devoured it. He has been ministering as a missionary in the Philippines for over 20 years. It was a reasonably typical food for me and not particularly unique.

CONCLUDING REMARK

As I write this reflective account, my heart is overflowing with joy and gratitude to my Lord, who gave me and my husband Wonsuk the strength to see it through. I have recalled some of my fantastic experiences with the tribe members, who we talked to for hours, laughed with, and prayed with. We give God all the glory and adoration.

----

1 Julie C. Ma and Wonsuk Ma, *Mission in the Spirit: Towards a Pentecostal/Charismatic Missiology* (Oxford: Regnum Books, 2010), 131.

2 Inez Sturgeon, *Give Me the Mountain* (Oakland, CA: Hunter Advertising Co. 1960), 95.

3 Elva Vanderbout, "Report on Trip to the Alsados," *The Missionary Challenge*, (Springfield, MO. April, 1954a), 3.

4 Vanderbout, "A Work of Mercy in the Philippines," *Foreign Field Report*, (Springfield MO. July, 1954b), 3.

5 Vanderbout, "A Work of Mercy in the Philippines," *Foreign Field Report*, 3.

6 Janet & Geoff Benge, Lillian Trasher: *The Greatest Wonder in Egypt* (Seattle, WA: YWAM Pub. 2004), 93-94.

7 Joshua Banda, "Engaging with the Community, the Fight against AIDS," in Brian Woolnough (ed.), Good News from Africa: Community Transformation through the Church (Oxford: Regnum Book International, 2013), 41.

8 Huldah Buntain, *Fifty Years in Calcutta*, www.cbn.com/700club/guests/bios/huldah_buntain_101504.aspx . See also Julie C. Ma, "Touching Lives of People Through the Holistic Mission Work of the Buntains in Calcutta, India," *International Bulletin of Mission Research* 40, no. 1 (January 2016): 72.

THE POST-PANDEMIC MISSIONARY: CALLING, QUALITIES AND ROLES IN THE 21ST CENTURY NEW NORMAL WORLD

Jim Whelchel

It is an honor to share a few thoughts and (I hope) insights about the future of missionaries as part of this tribute to Doug Nichols and his wife Margaret. It is my hope that this modest contribution will benefit the continuing missionary endeavor and will challenge and prod those who follow in their footsteps to continue to impact the world for Jesus in the coming generation.

SETTING THE STAGE

There have been many shifts in the missions landscape since missionaries like Doug Nichols (and myself) first went to serve in the Philippines. Trends like reaching UPG's and UUPG's, Church Planting Movements (or Disciple-Making Movements), orality, from everywhere to everywhere (and the growing shift of missions as a whole to the Global South), digital evangelism, the focus on reaching cities, business as missions—all of these (and others) have emerged as drivers of missions over the past several decades. It can be expected that they will continue to do so.

However, over the past several years, we endured one of the most significant global disruptions of the past seven decades. Many would agree that not since World War II has there been a single event that affected the entire world to the extent that COVID-19 did. And, like World War II, I believe it will affect our pursuit of God's mission for the world for years to come. What are some ways that the future of missions will look different as a result?

COVID brought a heightened fear and uncertainty about life, health, and the future across the globe; it fueled a paradoxical rise in dependency on and distrust of all forms of authority; it revealed the underlying weakness of world economies, and our dependence on supply chains and certain crucial resources; it helped spawn cultures of control and surveillance made possible through technologies ostensibly developed to monitor health but now deployed to crack down on religious and civil liberties; and it contributed to the fracturing of societies through the application of social media algorithms that amplified our differences as those who were locked down became even more dependent on online connections for social interaction.

Taken another way, it can be seen that the pandemic fueled and deepened global trends that were already present. For instance, the culture both in Europe and the United States was seen for years as growing more secular. Yet, after COVID, some estimate that the number of regular church-goers in the United States decreased by 30%. Some predict that the United States will be as secular as Western Europe within this generation. COVID seems to have accelerated the existing trend exponentially.

All of these have had an impact on our ability to make Christ known in places where few are believers. And as with any major disruption, there are both opportunities and losses. But the reality is that our world is not going back to its pre-COVID form, and it behooves us as people committed to the expansion of the Kingdom of God and the fulfillment of the Great Commission to respond accordingly. To best understand the type of missionaries we need for the future, it is important to understand where missions is heading. With the above as a background, what are some trends we might expect missionaries to focus on?

KEY POST-PANDEMIC TRENDS

1. ONLINE MINISTRY IS REAL MINISTRY.

If COVID taught us anything, it is that online ministry is now essential. It is not second-class ministry, something we do until we return to "real" ministry (meaning face-to-face). Although some people are still pining for the day that everything will go back to face-to-face, that ship has sailed. We must adapt to the reality that ministry is and will continue to be hybrid.

We have learned that ministry can be done effectively online. In our church (Christ's Commission Fellowship in the Philippines), we were relatively well prepared for utilizing social media and the internet to continue connecting with our church members, and reaching out to others who were looking for spiritual feeding. We already were streaming services, so our pivot to digital wasn't as difficult as for others.

Yet we did more than pivot. We saw the challenges of the pandemic as an opportunity to reach people who were scared, lonely and looking for emotional and spiritual help to survive. So at the height of the pandemic we launched an online outreach process called GoViral.

Many of our members have relatives and family members scattered around the world in the "Filipino diaspora." Many of them were not yet followers of Christ. We realized that, like most people around the world, they were experiencing feelings of isolation, fear and uncertainty. So, through GoViral we encouraged our members to reach out to, show concern for, pray for, and begin small groups among their family members and loved ones scattered abroad so they could learn about Jesus and how He can give hope and meaning to their lives.

The result was amazing. Thousands of new groups were formed and tens of thousands of people heard the life-giving message of Jesus--all online.

The pandemic changed the perception that online ministry is less real, personal, or meaningful than face-to-face ministry. We have countless testimonies of people whose lives were changed by Christ through online GoViral groups. Yet, until the end of the pandemic, and in some cases until now, they never met face to face. For missions, this is an amazing opportunity. We need to keep learning and growing our capacity to utilize the digital space to reach people for Christ and make disciples online. When COVID struck, it showed how crucial it is to pivot quickly in light of the rapid changes around us. Future missionaries, like successful leaders in almost all future endeavors, will need the capacity to adjust and adapt, and to meet needs in creative ways at pace.

2. THE MISSION FIELD IS ALREADY CONNECTED THROUGH MEDIA.

Related to Trend #1 is the reality that many of the most difficult mission fields on earth are now accessible through media--satellite TV, broadcast TV, the internet, social media, and the digital space in general.

Broadcast media. One of the most astounding developments in missions over the past decade has been the explosive growth of Christianity in Iran. Some estimate that there are millions from Iran who have come to Christ from the majority religion over the past decade. The multiplication of new believers meeting in house churches has been fueled by a number of factors. But amazingly one of the key drivers has been satellite TV.

How has this happened? Many Iranians are disaffected from the faith of their fathers. They have seen the failure of the hardline government to produce the ideal society they promised. In many cases they see the failure as directly linked to the intrinsic defects of the religion the government is built on. They are open to the gospel like never before. Online and satellite preachers now are directly pointing out the superiority of the gospel of Christ compared to its religious competitor.

Programming that has made an impact in the region has been varied. Some content creators have focused on forceful evangelistic and apologetics approaches to proclaim the gospel. Others seek to present the gospel positively, yet in a less polemic way. They have presented wholesome Christian programming that counters the perception that the decadence of Hollywood and Western media accurately reflects what Christianity endorses.

Perhaps even more powerfully, these media channels produce stories and testimonies of people who have left their former faith, even some who were among the most radical adherents of their former religion. These stories are recorded, reenacted and broadcast through television and online. Like testimonies throughout Christian history, these stories have power to challenge and inspire people to consider how knowing Jesus can be relevant for them as well.

Supplementing these attempts to bring the gospel through satellite programing has been intentional training for people who have come to faith in Christ, and are led by the Lord to begin house churches to help people continue to grow in faith. Systematic biblical material on discipleship, church planting and other facets of Christian life, taught in the vernacular by Arabic or Farsi-speaking church leaders, is impacting thousands, perhaps millions, of people who are coming to know Christ in previously unreached areas. The result has been tens of thousands of house churches springing up where believers are learning to love and serve Jesus.

A similar work of God seems to be emerging in other parts of Africa, Southeast Asia and the Middle East–particularly in places which were previously the most hostile to the gospel. It is difficult for restrictive governments to entirely eliminate access to satellite

TV and regional commercial broadcasts. While Internet access to Christian programming may often be blocked, satellite broadcasts are not.

It may seem strange to include archaic technology like broadcast and satellite media in a list of trends for the future of missions. But in my view, the potential for impacting people in restricted access countries, especially in the Muslim world, is immense and still largely untapped. The Internet. According to the World in Data, as of 2023 approximately two thirds of the world's population is connected online. Since many children and older adults are not counted in the data, it is possible that the real number is over 80%. This includes people from some of the least reached areas of the world. Global Media Outreach, a network of ministries using social media to reach people in difficult-to-reach places, hosts a map on their website that shows places where people are connecting to hear the gospel in real time. For a map nerd like me, it is exciting to see the pins light up on the map. The pins indicate where people are connecting with gospel content, making commitments to Christ, and signing up for online discipleship. But most fascinating is how people are connecting in places like Saudi, or Sudan, or Libya where it is unlikely that a missionary could ever live.

Most efforts to reach out with the gospel using media face a common challenge: how to build meaningful relationships with those who connect to online content. It is difficult to create communities where they can learn about Christ and grow in their relationship with Him. Yet one of the positive gains from our pandemic experience is the realization that faith-communities do not need to meet face to face to be real.

In some areas of the world, meeting face to face with strangers who purport to be believers can be dangerous. Meeting online with the protection of pseudonyms, firewalls and VPNs can mitigate the risks and allow people to find real communities where they can grow in relative security.

A number of organizations are now training and commissioning a completely new kind of missionary: online missionaries. I met a woman in her early 70's who is decidedly not techie, but is making disciples around the world from the comfort of her kitchen table. She volunteered to work with Power to Change, Cru's ministry in Canada, where she follows up inquiries from their social media posts. They have a carefully planned and executed process of bringing a person to faith in Christ, to be discipled, and ultimately become an online missionary. Many other ministries are doing the same.

In CCF we have our own online discipleship ministry called Skypleship (yes dated, but still kind of catchy!), which engages people who want to be discipled but are far from our existing satellites. It is safe to say that more than half of our International Satellites were either initiated or helped along by people who began their discipleship journey through Skypleship groups.

Online engagement and satellite TV create opportunities for people previously unreachable by the gospel. Future missionaries may be content creators for broadcast TV, digital disciplers or run vlogs aimed at specific people groups who need to know Christ. The growth of media also provides opportunities for people to be missionaries to reach out to others across the globe from anywhere in the world.

3. DISPLACED PEOPLE

The number of displaced people around the world is at an all-time high and is continuing to rise. According to the United Nations High Commission on Refugees (UNHCR), by the end of 2022 there were over 108 million people forcibly displaced either internally or externally. That was 19 million higher than 2021, which held the previous record. And most of the conflicts are in places and among people who are most in need of the gospel.

How does this relate to missions? Several years ago we in CCF were led by the Lord to begin working in refugee camps in a Northeast African country where nearly half a million refugees had fled. The camps helped refugees fleeing government attacks against a local insurgency that had resulted in several hundred thousand people being killed. The war had been going on for nearly 20 years.

By the time we entered the picture, many Christian NGO's were already spearheading efforts to meet the needs of those who were displaced. They were providing water, food, educational programs and what little medical care was available in the camps. UNHCR had delegated most of the administration of the camps to these Christian NGO's.

This truly impacted the residents. Previously many were hostile to Christianity. Leaders of the majority religious group do continue to pressure people to reject Christianity. Nevertheless, there is an acknowledgement by many in the camps, even among the religious leaders, that Christianity is contributing positively to the welfare of the residents.

About a year after we began our engagement, we heard of a man we will call Abdu, whose children were attending a makeshift school led by Christians. Although Abdu was opposed to Christianity, he was happy that at least there was education for his kids. Since there was no alternative, he permitted them to attend. Later, after they heard the gospel, his children told him that they wanted to become Christians. Abdu's surprising response was that it was their choice. He recognized that Christianity had been a positive influence in their lives, so if they wanted to follow Christ, he would allow it. But, he forcefully added, he himself would never become a Christian.

Less than two years later, however, we were surprised to learned that Abdu had decided to become a follower of Christ after all! Through the displacement, the change in his children's lives, and the vital role of Christians meeting the needs of the refugee community, the Lord created an openness to the gospel that resulted in his whole family following Jesus.

Refugee camps can also be strategic places for outreach. In those camps there are representatives of over 90 tribes, many of which are listed in the Joshua project as UUPG's. As we trained people to reach out, they were able to reach many previously unreached groups. Later our trainees boldly returned to some of the places they had fled, and planted churches among other UUPGs. In the refugee camps the UUPGs became accessible in ways previously unimaginable.

The impact of serving displaced people is greater than the immediate relief of their suffering. It can change the responsiveness of people to the gospel as they see tangible manifestations of Christ's love through His people. And it opens doors to reaching previously difficult to reach people. As a dear friend, Pastor Jimmy Seibert, says, we should run toward pain, not away from it. That is usually where God is working.

4. IMMIGRATION PATTERNS.

Immigration has brought people from every corner of the earth to countries with strong Christian communities. These communities are uniquely positioned to reach the unreached without leaving their own country or culture.

While this is an exciting opportunity, there are very real obstacles. First, most immigrants have little contact with the majority culture. They tend to congregate with their own people, and often recreate pockets of their homeland in the midst of the new culture. It is often not easy to cross these new cultural barriers even if people live in close proximity.

Second, many people are suspicious of immigrants, especially those from religious and cultural backgrounds that are seen as threats. Rather than seeing the presence of people from such cultures as an opportunity to fulfill our role in the Great Commission, short-sighted believers see only the potential negative aspects of immigration.

Even in the Philippines there is resistance to reaching out to immigrants. Some estimate there are between 500,000 and 1,000,000 people from Mainland China working or living here. This should be a wonderful mission field for local Christians, especially since there is a large Christian Filipino-Chinese population that should be ready to reach them.

Sadly, many Filipino-Chinese do not appreciate the presence of the new immigrants. The new immigrants are (often rightly) accused of abusing immigration laws to bring in tax-free shipments of goods. These are then sold at rock bottom prices, undercutting local Filipino businesses. Others are members of gambling syndicates – so-called POGOs (Philippine Online Gaming Operators)–who run online gambling sites from the Philippines to avoid Chinese government restrictions. This has increased gang wars, kidnapping, and the criminality that often accompanies organized gambling operations.

When Christian churches have sought to mobilize Christians to reach these immigrants, they have met with apathy or even animosity. Until now, few Christians are actively reaching out to them. These challenges are common in many places where immigrants have gone. Many Christian communities are ambivalent or even hostile to the presence of immigrants who are often viewed as unwelcome intruders into the host society.

A third reason why it is difficult to reach immigrants is that there is a lack of training on how to reach out to others cross-culturally. Few churches or mission organizations have programs specifically designed to help believers reach out among immigrants.

Fortunately there are ministries reaching out among immigrant populations. Global Gates is specifically focused on reaching UPGs and UUPGs that can be reached through gateway cities in North America. Organizations like International Students Incorporated, Bridges, and Epic (both part of Cru), and others working with international students can be instruments of crossing cultural barriers to reach people locally. Other ministries directly assist in the relocation of immigrants arriving in the US and other countries.

Future missionaries will need to cast vision for local believers to reach immigrants for Christ, and provide training on how to do so. Mobilization of believers for mission, starting with the mission field at our doorstep, is crucial.

5. SOCIAL NEEDS AND MENTAL HEALTH

Throughout the history of missions, Christians have sought to engage social and economic issues as they have spread the gospel. They have rightly seen the connection between loving and serving the marginalized, and the mandate to bring the gospel of Christ to all people. And, as the story above illustrates, Christians who are the hands and feet of Christ also open doors for the gospel of Christ. This has often been manifested in social and educational programs such as disaster relief, literacy programs, medical care, community development and advocacy on behalf of marginalized communities, etc. This focus can be seen in the work of such organizations as World Vision, Compassion International, Samaritan's Purse and others working globally. But perhaps equally important has been the less visible work of local churches and smaller-scale initiatives at the local level that have "cared for the least of these" in their quest to make Christ known.

In addition to these typical areas of need, however, the pandemic brought to light another often neglected area of human need that requires a similar commitment to bring the love of Christ to people. That is to care for those suffering from mental health concerns. The COVID lockdowns revealed the vulnerability of people in times of great uncertainty. Suicide rates have skyrocketed. And even post-COVID, we have seen huge increases in mental health concerns. As Christians, we should be the ones to bring hope to people who are increasingly hopeless.

Unfortunately, within the church there is still disagreement about how best to respond. Some see mental health issues as not "real"–that is, with greater strength of character, willpower, or right thinking, people should be able to simply overcome their mental health issues. Others see every mental health issue as a medical or psychological condition, often to be attended to through medication and therapy. Many churches seem to see no middle ground.

If we are to respond meaningfully, we need to equip people to make healthier disciples. That includes helping people live not only as "spiritual" Christians, but as people who are healthy in all areas of life – spiritually, emotionally, socially, mentally, and physically. For those whose mental health issues are more severe and are legitimately diagnosed as medical conditions, we need more Christian counselors and psychologists who can balance a biblical understanding of wellness with resources in professional mental health care.

For future missionaries, we need a generation of people trained in helping people develop holistically and who have both the compassion and tools to minister to people who are increasingly struggling with mental health in an uncertain world.

6. YOUTHFUL PASSION TO IMPACT THE WORLD

Young people want to make a difference in their world. This has been true for generations, and it is as true today as ever before. For me, that reality gives me hope that the work of God in the world will continue and expand! This generation sees missions somewhat differently than my generation. Missions used to be about Christians going to people in distant places to preach about Christ to those who didn't know Him. Hopefully that would result in planting churches or beginning ministries that would help believers grow in their faith.

That certainly is an aspect of missions today. But I find two important trends that are significantly different--and in my opinion better--than the missions of my youth. The first trend is that there is no longer an unbiblical distinction between preaching the gospel and seeking to transform society.

During the generations before I went out as a missionary, there was a heated debate between theological conservatives (known then as "fundamentalists") and theological liberals. Liberals were essentially theistic humanists who rejected the Bible's accounts of miracles and the supernatural intervention of God in His world. They eschewed a literal view of the Bible as unenlightened or passÈ. Conservatives countered by reasserting the inerrancy and authority of the Bible, and defending the reality of God's personal intervention in history. It was an important battle, and today we see the fruit: the continued growth of the church, where God's Word is the foundation and source of a vibrant global movement.

But while in theory the fight was about theology, in practice liberals and conservatives were identified by their external behavior. If they sought primarily to improve society through programs aimed to address social ills, people were pegged as liberal. That was the "social gospel." If the primary exercise of their faith was seen in preaching the gospel so people would be saved through personal faith in Christ, then those people were pegged as conservative (or fundamentalist).

Conservative missionaries of that generation were suspicious of programs aimed primarily at addressing poverty or dealing with social issues. They also feared being identified as liberal for pursuing such programs. To uphold their conservative convictions, they focused primarily on the spiritual condition of people, hoping to bring as many as possible to faith in Christ. Full stop.

In retrospect, it is clear that this distinction between the gospel as personal, eternal salvation vs. the gospel as a transforming force in society would have been foreign to Jesus. But it took a while for Evangelical Christians in general, and missionaries in particular, to get over the false dichotomy that was rooted in a deep and heated theological debate.

Of course, people like Doug Nichols and organizations like Action International, Compassion International, and many others, did not succumb to the unbiblical dichotomy between "gospel ministry" and care for the needs of people. But I believe many missionaries of my generation still felt uneasy when the gospel started getting too connected with "good works" and compassionate ministry.

I mention this bit of missionary history because, praise God, the present generation has no recollection of those previous theological battles! In fact, this generation of potential missionaries would question a person's commitment to the Lord if they did not feel genuine compassion for the marginalized, did not see the connection between caring for the creation and being a kingdom citizen, or simply cared about saving people for eternity without seeing the world transformed in the process. They are holistic ministry natives.

Indeed, it is not only Christian young people who want to change the world. There are millions of young people, pretty much the whole of global youth culture, who share that desire. Many of these have limited Christian or religious background, but they are passionate about making a difference in their world. And they are willing to work with anyone—including Christians—who are doing things that will make a positive impact. This in itself is not new. Young people of every generation have had a youthful idealism that drives them to seek a better world. But what I feel is unique today is the window this gives young Christian missionaries to dispel negative caricatures of Christianity by rolling up our sleeves together with non-religious idealists so they can see what real Christian love and compassion looks like.

I believe this trend–involving pre-believers in activities and programs that actively seek the welfare of society without first committing to follow Christ–is an inversion of the way ministry has been done in the past. But it can be a powerful way to challenge the assumptions of those who have never seen the love of Christ in action. It can be a way to witness for Christ to people and society, simultaneously working to effect change and transformation, and also touch the hearts of those who join us in pursuing those ends.

In short, I believe the coming generation of missionaries will be in a better position than mine to live out a biblical, holistic understanding of the love of God and the salvation He offers His world. In doing so, they will not only show the very best of what it means to be a follower of Christ, but lead many people to a personal relationship with Him when they see in Christians a quality of love and concern that the world cannot offer.

CONCLUSION

So what do these trends tell us about the calling, qualities and roles of post-pandemic 21st -century missionaries? Let me just share a few thoughts.

Calling.

The calling of 21st -century missionaries isn't necessarily different than at other times in history. All of those who are called to serve God as missionaries, especially across cultures, must be motivated by the love of God and His desire to bring salvation and wholeness to every person, especially those far from Him. This has always been and I believe always will be at the core of our calling as missionaries.

To fulfill that calling, our future missionaries must have a deep walk with God and a commitment to His Word, be empowered by the Holy Spirit, and be mentored and discipled by others more mature then themselves. They are called to serve more than lead, to humbly work alongside fellow believers (especially from the host culture) to help them fulfill their calling to make disciples and impact the world for Christ. They don't need to be perfect, but they must be authentic in their journey with Jesus. They are called to live in sacrificial obedience to Him.

QUALITIES.

While the call remains similar, I do believe that some of the qualities needed to fulfill that calling have changed. In the past it has been the missionary who goes to the field to lead the charge. Today the missionary's posture must be to serve. There are of course some places where pioneer work will require an apostolic leader from another culture to lead the way. But those situations are getting rarer. More often, the missionary must be a valued team member and servant who empowers others to accomplish God's purposes.

The pandemic emphasized the need for future missionaries to be flexible and adaptable, holding loosely their own agendas and subordinating them to the needs of the team. Missionaries must be learners, willing to help those they work with to navigate challenges together and find effective ways to further the kingdom in the midst of rapid change. Roles. With those qualities, I believe that there is an unlimited variety of roles that future missionaries can fill in order to accomplish God's missionary purposes. I have mentioned some of those: online discipler, content creator, media specialist, apologist-vlogger, counselor, holistic program implementor among displaced people at home or abroad, mobilizer of not-yet believers who share a passion for changing the world, or home-based missionary who reaches out to immigrants or exchange students living near them. But there are many, many more.

The pandemic changed many things, and we continue to see those changes fleshed out. But the primary role of future missionaries remains the role that Jesus called His disciples to: to make disciples who make disciples who will impact the world for Jesus. So while much has changed, much also remains the same.

MISSIONARIES AND PRAYER SUPPORT: WE NEED TO TALK

Katherine Lorance

After two years of being on the field, the young missionary couple looked forward to spending time at their home sending church. They arrived well before the Sunday morning worship service to have time to chat with more people. It was heartwarming to see familiar faces and encouraging to spot a few unfamiliar ones too. One of the church leaders noticed the couple and walked over with a grin. He gave hearty handshakes as he asked, "How's Japan?"

The couple glanced at each other briefly. Which of them was going to explain that they had not been in Japan? Did this man have a moment of confusion or was he neglecting to follow their updates?

While preparing to be sent forth by mission agencies or denominations, missionaries dutifully work to gain prayer commitments from churches, small groups, and individuals. The common requirement for missionaries to raise prayer support reflects an understanding and belief that prayer is important in missions. Sadly, though, many missionaries post updates and send out prayer letters not knowing who will pray in response or even read them. Although missionaries communicating digitally can now see how many have engaged with an update, it can still be unclear how much prayer is happening.

By embracing the conversational nature of prayer, missionaries and their prayer supporters can journey together in growing in prayer, and thus experience vibrant and fruitful partnerships. This article will apply a framework for understanding prayer as a relationship-based conversation to missionary prayer support efforts and provide practical suggestions for the resulting key principles of engaging Scripture, praying with others, and listening.

CONVERSING WITH OUR FATHER

First of all, the Trinity is already in a conversation before we engage with God in prayer. As Hebrews 7:25 states, Jesus "always lives to make intercession for [those who draw near to God through him]." In Romans 8:27, we read, "The Spirit intercedes for the saints according to the will of God." In other words, Jesus and the Holy Spirit are talking with the Father about us.

When Jesus taught on how to pray and thereby join the divine conversation, He said, "Pray then like this: 'Our Father in heaven'" (Matthew 6:9a). Addressing the King of the universe as "Father" indicates the relationship we have with Him and the kinds of conversations He wants. Missionaries and their prayer supporters, like all saints, may be tempted to elevate "doing" over "being" and to view prayer primarily as a means to fruitfulness. If we attempt to completely outsource prayer efforts, if we pray for the work but not for the workers, if we think that our praying in a certain way will prompt God to give the outcome we desire, then we turn prayer into a transaction and treat the Living One like a miracle machine. Instead, our Father wants to talk with us so that we think, act, and talk more like Him.

Using the term "Father" also reminds us that we are children learning to communicate. Like babies and toddlers, we observe, we imitate others, we make attempts to talk or gesture, and we adapt from mistakes. Just as loving parents neither scold nor withhold from toddlers for incorrect grammar or pronunciation, so our Father is patient and understanding with our prayers. Friends and family members of missionaries who doubt their ability to pray effectively can be encouraged that their willingness to grow in prayer will be met by God's faithfulness to help.

The Lord being "our" Father reminds us that we pray and learn to pray within a community, however big or small, whether formally or informally. A young child cannot learn to effectively express herself to others on her own; her caregivers, siblings, friends, and teachers all contribute to her communication abilities and styles. We can grow in prayer by learning from God Himself, saints in history, and saints still on earth, by taking classes or workshops, by hearing others pray, and by praying with others. Missionaries with tenuous connections to churches, small groups, or other individuals receiving their prayer updates can suggest shared activities focused on growing in prayer and develop friendships in the process.

THE BIBLE AS PRAYER TEXTBOOK

Those interested in conversing more with the Triune God about more subjects can get to know Him better through reading, studying, and meditating on Scripture. As Jesus said, "If you abide in me, and my words abide in you, ask whatever you wish, and it will be done for you" (John 15:7). For missionaries and their supporters, reflecting on God's character and past actions informs and inspires prayers for current situations. Examining how Jesus prayed with great variety--alone, with others or for others, and at different times of day in different places with different physical stances–can encourage missionaries to try different methods of inviting others into prayer. Prayer supporters can explore different prayer styles, formats, and postures. For example, as Zephaniah 3:17 says, the Lord "will rejoice over you with singing," some prayer supporters might prefer praying by singing over the missionaries.

The recorded prayers within the Bible help us grow in prayer. Caregivers repeat a set of simple words (like "ma" and "da" in English) over and over; babies begin producing these words and over time use them with greater accuracy. Similarly, God has given us a set of prayers that we can repeat and imitate to learn the "language" of prayer. In the Scriptures we read the poetic prayers of Psalms, prayers of prophets, written prayers in letters, and prayers within narratives of various individuals, including Jesus. In some church traditions, the entirety of Psalms is read or sung on a weekly or monthly basis; someone reading a psalm daily will gradually internalize the language and attitudes of prayer for a wide variety of circumstances. Prayer supporters who are unsure how to pray for their missionaries can turn to the psalms or prayers in the epistles. People who feel uneasy about voicing prayers in a group setting can read aloud or slightly adapt Scriptural prayers. When sharing updates, missionaries can cite key verses and reference Bible stories or people to help express their circumstances or their hopes.

DISCUSSION PARTNERS

Using the prayers of Biblical figures points to how praying with others in general can help us grow in prayer. Children improve their communication skills by interacting with their elders, just as we gain insight into prayer when we pray with others. Like discussions between friends, praying with others can broaden perspectives and lead to new, richer ideas. Just as external processors find clarity by verbalizing their thoughts to others, some people find it easier to pray with others than alone. Most importantly, Jesus expected us to pray with others; He promised, "Again I say to you, if two of you agree on earth about anything they ask, it will be done for them by my Father in heaven. For where two or three are gathered in my name, there am I among them" (Matthew 18:19-20).

Sara, a field worker who had been serving in East Asia for many years, had individual supporters scattered across multiple continents. One supporter suggested that perhaps some of Sara's supporters could pray together regularly. Sara asked her longtime friend Mariam to be her prayer champion. A handful of supporters on Mariam's continent were willing to pray together once a week for about an hour. During conference calls over the phone or messaging apps, Mariam would give a brief update from Sara, the group would invite the Lord to lead the time of prayer, they would take multiple turns praying a couple minutes each at a time, and then they would end by praying briefly for divine protection over the group. One week, Mariam reported Sara's frustration in feeling she was going back and forth over the same spot, like someone rowing with an exercise machine instead of on water. When Mariam began praying, she thanked the Lord for His sovereignty as He weaves our stories into His story. Another group member noted that weaving also involves moving back and forth through the same area but produces something tangible. Mariam was then able to encourage Sara with a new perspective on her situation.

Like Sara, missionaries can encourage their prayer supporters to gather to pray, whether by phone, online, or in person. Praying with others for the same person or team can move people beyond "God bless [name]" or praying only by reading the prayer request. Praying with others allows for God to be glorified by the group when they see specific answers. It also brings to the forefront what God is doing within the missionary--how Christ is being formed in their friend– which is an important part of God's work. Churches supporting specific missionaries can encourage small groups or Sunday classes to adopt a different missionary each month/quarter/year; during each gathering, several people can voice brief prayers for the missionary or one of the stated needs. Churches can also offer to provide prayer champions like Mariam to organize times of prayer for any of the missionary's supporters. One missionary team has twelve core prayer supporters who are arranged into six praying pairs, one pair for each day of the week except for a Sabbath.

Because of Jesus's promises in Matthew 18:19-20, we can celebrate and encourage having "two or three" pray together. Just as two friends can have an intimate conversation more easily than a large group can, prayer pairs, triplets, and other small prayer groups can nimbly delve deep with the Lord. In addition, some prayer supporters may be unable to commit to a weekly time of prayer but would be willing to be "on call" for prayer needs. A group of single women in leadership met at a conference and stayed in contact afterwards through a messaging app. A pattern emerged that as soon as someone shared a prayer need, anyone who was available would call to pray with her. Whether there were several women available or only one, they had confidence based on Jesus's promises.

A LISTENING POSTURE

Like other conversations, prayer involves both talking and listening. Adopting a listening posture before the Lord is our humble recognition of who God is. After all, the so-called gods of the world are unable to speak, "but the LORD is in his holy temple; let all the earth keep silence before him" (see Habakkuk 2:18-20). Moreover, to adopt a listening posture is to follow the example of the persons of the Godhead. Jesus said of the Spirit that "He will not speak on his own authority, but whatever he hears he will speak" (see John 16:13). Jesus said to the Father, "I have given them the words that you gave me" (see John 17:8). If Father, Son, and Spirit are listening to each other, how much more should we! By intentionally listening in prayer, we pursue clarity and agreement with God.

Listening can take many forms within individual and group prayer times. Inviting the Lord to guide our prayers before or while praying for a missionary is a simple way to demonstrate our posture before Him. Having moments of silence or listening to quiet worship music can give space for the Holy Spirit to impress a Scripture passage, an image, a word, or a song. When considering a prayer request or the missionary's situation, some people are reminded of specific words, stories, or persons in the Bible while others hear a Scripture reference. For group prayer times, note that some people appreciate preparing in advance for listening activities. It is beneficial to include time for each person in the group to share and then, if desired, for all to discuss how the different pieces that were shared might fit together.

Listening can take additional forms outside traditional times of prayer. One simple way is to observe how the Lord has led in prayer. Prayer supporters can offer short summaries or highlights of their prayers. They can also write out or record audio/video prayers, which the missionary or other supporters can then pray along with. One group prays together by sharing recordings of their individual prayers with the group, which helps them agree in prayer asynchronously but also helps them stay accountable. Sometimes individuals or groups praying separately about the same topic discover that the Lord has led them all to the same Scripture, image, or theme.

Another simple way for missionaries and their prayer supporters to listen and observe more is to intentionally follow up on prayer requests. When we pray, we should expect God to answer and so we should also look for the answer. Some prayer supporters grow weary when missionaries do not follow up with prayer requests. By regularly giving updates to previous requests, missionaries invite prayer supporters to come alongside to rejoice, lament, or press in. Prayer supporters who consistently ask what has happened with specific situations can help busy missionaries remember to pause and acknowledge answers. However God has responded, missionaries will be encouraged to know that others share their burden. Prayer supporters from their vantage point can sometimes perceive possible answers more easily than missionaries who can be caught in daily minutiae.

A final suggestion for including listening in praying for missionaries is to prayer walk. "Praying on-site with insight," as Steve Hawthorne and Graham Kendrick defined prayer walking in their seminal book on the subject, spurs us to pay attention to the people and places around them and to seek God's perspective. Virtual prayer walks, while engaging fewer senses, can be more accessible and sometimes more secure than in-person prayer walks. One example of a virtual prayer walk is a live video call between the missionaries as they walk and their supporters praying elsewhere. This kind of virtual prayer walk can be done even in restricted access nations with appropriate precautions, such as a separate briefing about the area and/or a pre-recorded video of the location. Virtual prayer walks can also be conducted using a mapping app to "visit" different locations. Either missionaries can handpick strategic addresses and explain their significance or prayer supporters can explore the area on their own as the Lord leads. Examples of virtual prayer walks which are less dependent on the internet include using travel guides, local newspaper clippings or missionaries' photos of the area.

JOURNEYING TOGETHER

When it comes to prayer, whether you feel that you are like a baby making those first words or like a social butterfly livening up a party, there is room to grow. What might it look like for a missionary team and their prayer supporters to grow together in prayer? Adam had been ministering among Afghans in the States for many years. When Adam's team made commitments to grow in prayer, Adam joined other missionaries in a prayer strategy training cohort that met once a month. After the first training session, Adam's team assessed their prayer patterns as individuals and as a team. As Adam continued sharing the training he was receiving, Adam's team's prayer patterns slowly began to include focused prayer walks and weekly fasting. They also started inviting their supporters to regular prayer video calls and occasional 24-hour prayer events, where they modeled what they had been learning about prayer. Adam said, "We would add a prayer strategy that seemed extraordinary at the time, and we'd keep doing it until it seemed ordinary. Then we'd add another one." A little over a year into the team's journey in growing in prayer, the US government withdrew its forces from Afghanistan and a fresh wave of Afghans began resettling in Adam's area and many other places in the States. The Lord had been preparing Adam's team and their prayer supporters for a new season of opportunities.

The term "missionary" has been used extensively in this chapter without being defined. Because of the increasing movement of people from everywhere to everywhere, the concept of being a "missionary" is rapidly changing. Throughout the West and in urban centers globally, individuals and families from tribes who have never heard of Jesus before, including many from nations who are currently hostile to the Church, have been brought near to Christ-followers. They go to the same schools, live in the same neighborhoods, wait for the same buses, shop at the same markets, and connect to the same apps. Many brothers and sisters from the Global South carry Christ with them as they intentionally go forth, without formal religious appointments, to restricted access nations to advance God's Kingdom as medical professionals, teachers, construction workers, nannies, and so on. Prayer support teams are most common for those who have been formally appointed as missionaries by some sending organization. Jesus said, "The harvest is plentiful, but the laborers are few" (Luke 10:2a). As agency-appointed missionaries and their prayer supporters pursue growing in prayer together, might God use these Kingdom-oriented conversations and relationships to prepare more laborers to be sent forth in more diverse ways? Might these laborers in turn invite others to join them in the divine conversation?

Although much has been written on prayer, the best way to grow in prayer is to actually pray. Let's pray: *Our Father, thank You for inviting us into this conversation with You. Thank You for stirring our hearts so that we want to grow in prayer. We welcome Your Spirit to work within us and among us. Give us wisdom and creativity so that all missionaries can serve in their appointed fields knowing that others are walking alongside them in prayer. What is the next step on this journey? Speak, Lord, for Your servants are listening...*

Names and details of people mentioned in anecdotes have been changed for security reasons.
All scripture quotations are from English Standard Version, 2016.
Fellowship of Prayer Strategists have a prayer strategy training program based on Discovery Bible Study sets. See prayerstrategists.net
*Parts of this chapter have been published previously in the following (used by permission): Lorance, Katherine "Missionaries and Prayer Support: We Need to Talk" Evangelical Missions Quarterly 59, no. 1 (2023): 37–41.

CONCLUSION

Sadiri Joy Tira

Indeed, the Nicholses' "Feet are Beautiful" because they responded to the prophetic challenge: "And who will go?" "Here [we] are; send [us]." Isaiah 6:8-13).

Doug and Margaret arrived in the Philippines in 1970, two years before martial law was declared by then President Ferdinand Marcos, Sr. It was during the '70s when there were strong negative feelings against American colonialism. Also, missionaries were suspected of supporting the Communist movement. In 1971, Filipino theologian Rev. Bishop Emerito Nacpil boldly called on the missionaries to leave the country! In his speech to the gathering of church leaders with the National Council of Churches, he declared " The missionary is a symbol of Western imperialism. Hence, the present structure of missions is dead, to be eulogized and buried. Missionaries in Asia can go home. " (To read Nacpil's speech, see Gerald Anderson's article on the website Religion Online).

It is interesting to note that 50 years ago, many missionaries submitted to the voice of Bishop Nacpil, and several organizations and agencies entirely withdrew from the Philippines. Some Evangelical denominations withdrew their personnel claiming that the Philippines was already reached after 100 years of missions work.

The Nicholses were not scared to enter a new mission field at the height of political turmoil in a poverty-stricken and chaotic country. They defied Nacpil's challenge and did not join the exodus of Kingdom Workers. Instead of leaving, they remained in the

Philippines, supporting the indigenous mountain people, caring for the orphans, gathering the hungry urban street-kids, and providing meals for them. They regularly visited jails to share the good news of salvation, forgiveness of sins, and hope in Jesus to the criminals and inmates. They also supported poor pastors by providing them training, preaching, and Bible study tool boxes (e.g., books, commentaries and study Bibles). Only eternity will reveal how many are now recorded in the heavenly Book of Life because Doug and Margaret remained in the Philippines to help fulfill the Great Commission and build the Kingdom.

In our increasingly 21st century globalized world, a hybrid, pluralistic, but borderless world in the technological age, is there a place for missionaries, or is their task already finished? The task of nurturing and multiplying disciples and of planting churches remains the same--the field is still ripe for harvest!

This book is full of case studies and proven missions strategies. It is a renewed call, not just for the Philippine Church, but for the Global Church to pray for world evangelization and to consistently uphold Kingdom Workers in prayer.

The Apostle Paul declared: "Therefore, my dear brothers and sisters, stand firm. Let nothing move you. Always give yourselves fully to the work of the Lord, because you know that your labor in the Lord is not in vain" (I Corinthians 15:58, NIV).

The Nichols steadfastness faithfulness and courage is to be emulated by future and younger missionaries.

CONTRIBUTORS OF BEAUTIFUL FEET

Donna Castillo-Tan *is a published author ("Brave and Beautiful: Serving God with Courage and Grace in Marriage and Ministry." CSM 2018) and a contributing writer for The Evangelicals Today (PCEC) and Global Proclamation Commission for Pastoral Trainers (GProCommission.org). She is a trained counselor, pastoral trainer, professional editor, and resource speaker for conferences and retreats on the topics of marriage, family life and parenting, Biblical womanhood, and spirituality. She and her husband, Jason, are missionaries with GlobalGrace Fellowship (TX, USA), with their mission base in the Philippines.*

Jeff Haanen *is the founder of Denver Institute for Faith & Work, an educational organization that creates content and experiences around topics related to faith, work, the economy, and modern culture.. He has written An Uncommon Guide to Retirement: Finding God's Purpose for the Next Season of Life and Working from the Inside Out, as well as numerous articles for major publications. He lives with his wife and four daughters in Denver, Colorado.*

Patrick Johnstone *is the founder and Author Emeritus of Operation World. His other books include The Future of the Global Church and The Church is Bigger Than You Think. Patrick was brought up in England, served in Southern African and aboard the OM Ships, and has worked for many decades in the UK with WEC International. He and his wife Robyn currently live in Derby, England.*

David S. Lim, Ph.D., *Dr. David S. Lim is the Executive Board Chairman of Lausanne Philippines Partnership, which has "Cooperatives as Mission" as its flagship program, and an Executive Council member of Asia Lausanne Committee of World Evangelization. He serves as the President of the Asian School for Development and Cross-cultural Studies (ASDECS), which provides graduate degree and certificate training programs for community transformation. He is also the President of China Ministries International-Phil., the Vice-President of Asian Society of Missiology, an Executive Committee member of Asian Society of Frontier Missions, and a Steering Group member of SEANET, the global network to bless the Buddhist World. He earned his Th.M. (New Testament) from Asian Center for Theological Studies in Seoul, Korea, and his Ph.D. Theology (New Testament) from Fuller Theological Seminary. He co-edited the compendium of Asian Society of Missiology's conference: Christian Mission in Religious Pluralistic Society.*

Katherine Lorance *Katherine serves in prayer leadership roles for the Lausanne Movement, Ethne Prayer Team and Endiro Coffee. She previously coordinated prayer for Global Diaspora Network. She lives near Chicago with her husband Cody and their three children. Katherine has a BA in English and French Literature from Stanford University.*

Julie C. Ma, Ph.D., *is a Professor of Missiology and Intercultural Studies at Oral Roberts University, Tulsa, OK. Previously served as a Korean missionary in the Philippines (1981-2006) and as a Research Tutor of Missiology at Oxford Centre for Mission Studies, Oxford, UK. Publications include When the Spirit Meets the Spirits: Pentecostal Ministry Among the Kankana-ey Tribe in the Philippines (Peter Lang, 2000). and Mission Possible: Biblical Strategies in Reaching the Lost (Oxford: Regnum Books, 2005 for 1st edition; 2016 for the 2nd edition), and numerous articles published in different Journals.*

Jason Mandryk *was born, grew up, and studied in Canada before moving to the UK to join the Operation World team. For over 20 years, he has served through multiple editions and publications of this ministry, as researcher, editor, author, and co-director. He and his wife Becky are currently based in Seoul, South Korea.*

Martin Otto, M.Th. *is based in Hamburg, Germany. He is Married with his wife Monika. They have 2 children and 4 grandchildren. He is the Founder of an international Seafarer's Ministry in 1987 and the Church on the Ocean seminar in Manila, 1998. He is the author of 6 books: Faith at Sea; Seafarers: a Forgotten People; Church on the Ocean; Help! How can I Overcome Temptation? ; The Seafarer's Mind; How to be a Successful Seafarer*

Nativity Petallar, PhD *is a Professor of Christian Education, Associate Dean of PhD Studies, and Program Director of Holistic Child Development at Asia-Pacific Nazarene Theological Seminary (APNTS). Recently, she co-edited with Rosalind Lim-Tan and Lucy Hefford the book, God's Heart for Children: Practical Theology from Global Perspectives. She is a Board Member of Shechem Children's Home and serves as a member of the Lausanne Steering Committee for Children at Risk.*

Narry F. Santos, PhD *is Associate Professor of Practical Ministry and Intercultural Leadership at the seminary of Tyndale University and Vice President of the Evangelical Missiological Society Canada. He has served as part-time Senior Pastor of Greenhills Christian Fellowship (GCF) York (in Vaughan) and GCF Peel (in Mississauga) since 2017, after having planted Saddleback South Manila (now Saddleback Santa Rosa) for three years. Before Saddleback Church, he ministered at GCF in different pastoral responsibilities for 20 years, including helping plant six churches in Canada and four*

in the Philippines. He holds a PhD in New Testament (Dallas Theological Seminary) and another in Philippine Studies (University of the Philippines).

Mark Edward Sudhir, DICS (candidate) ThM, *is the lead pastor of Fil-Indian Fellowship and Emmanuel Masihi Punjabi Fellowship. He serves as a missionary and church planter among the Hindu and Sikh diaspora, discipling and raising indigenous disciple makers from HBB and SBB, serving also as executive member of LSWG and GDN Philippines. In addition, he is a facilitator of International Sindhi Partnership Consultation and a resource person for diaspora ministry, and a Christian musician.*

Jason Richard Tan, PhD, *is the President of the Great Commission Missionary Training Center (GCMTC) in Antipolo City, Philippines. He serves as a ministry coach and mentor for pastoral leaders, church planters, and pastoral trainers. He is also the program director of the Ph.D. in Intercultural Studies at the Asia Graduate School of Theology (AGST-Philippines). His global ministry includes the GProCommission for Trainers of Pastors, serving as a ministry strategist and as a course developer for RREACH Courses. He is also the author of several published works, including Teach the Church to Pray (2020), Ama Namin: The Lord's Prayer in Philippine Life and Spirituality (2023), and Teach the Church to Make Disciples (2023).*

Sadiri Joy Tira, DMiss, DMin, *Diaspora Missiology Specialist at Jaffray Centre for Global Initiatives, Ambrose University (Calgary, Alberta, Canada. Dr. Tira was the Founding Chairman of the Global Diaspora Network (2010-2015 and served as Senior Associate/ Catalyst for Diasporas (2007-2019) of the Lausanne Movement. He is currently on staff of the PALM Ministry Association. [He studied Missiology and Theology from Canadian Theological Seminary, Taylor Seminary, Reformed Theological Seminary, and Western Seminary.*

Dr. Juliet Lee Uytanlet, PhD *finished her PhD Intercultural Studies at Asbury Theological Seminary in 2014. She served as The Lausanne Movement Catalyst for Diasporas from 2016–2018. She is the author of The Hybrid Tsinoys: Challenges of Hybridity and Homogeneity as Sociocultural Constructs among the Chinese in the Philippines (2016, Wipf and Stock, American Society of Missiology Monograph Series #25). She teaches at Asian Theological Seminary in Quezon City.*

Juno Wang, D.I. S *Juno Wang is a Chinese diaspora in the U.S. from Taiwan. She served at a Chinese mission organization under the leadership of the late Dr. Thomas Wang for almost 18 years before pursuing her seminary intercultural training. Juno has been involved in the multi-ethnic community outreach in the heart of the Silicon Valley since 2009. She is a practitioner, researcher, and trainer for glocal missions.*

Jim Whelchel, Phd *is an Elder, Area Pastor and Missions Director of Christ's Commission Fellowship, overseeing CCF's ministries outside of the Philippines. He has served with CCC/ CRU and was a professor and administrator of the International Graduate School of Leadership in Asia (Manila Campus)*

www.ingramcontent.com/pod-product-compliance
Lightning Source LLC
LaVergne TN
LVHW020057090426
835510LV00040B/2024